Welcome to My Breakdown

NOVELS BY BENILDE LITTLE

Good Hair

The Itch

Acting Out

Who Does She Think She Is?

Welcome to My Breakdown

A MEMOIR

BENILDE LITTLE

ATRIA BOOKS

New York   London   Toronto   Sydney   New Delhi

ATRIA BOOKS

An Imprint of Simon & Schuster, Inc.
1230 Avenue of the Americas
New York, NY 10020

First Atria Books hardcover edition April 2015

ATRIA B O O K S and colophon are trademarks of Simon & Schuster, Inc.

For information about special discounts for bulk purchases,
please contact Simon & Schuster Special Sales at 1-866-506-1949
or business@simonandschuster.com.

The Simon & Schuster Speakers Bureau can bring authors to your live event. For more information or to book an event, contact the Simon & Schuster Speakers Bureau at 1-866-248-3049 or visit our website at www.simonspeakers.com.

Interior design by Kyoko Watanabe

Manufactured in the United States of America

10 9 8 7 6 5 4 3 2 1

Library of Congress Cataloging-in-Publication Data
Little, Benilde.
 Welcome to my breakdown : a memoir / Benilde Little.
   pages cm
 Summary: "A chronicle of clinical depression from a bestselling novelist"—Provided by publisher.
 1. Little, Benilde—Mental health. 2. Novelists—United States—Biography.
3. Women novelists, American—Biography. 4. Depressed persons—United States—Biography. I. Title.
 PS3562.I78276Z46 2015
 813'.54—dc23
 [B]   2015001624

ISBN 978-1-4767-5195-5
ISBN 978-1-4767-5197-9 (ebook)

"An effortless life is a meaningless life."

—HA JIN

Welcome to My Breakdown

Prologue

Mom holding me up in our backyard, 1958.

MY MOTHER was gone. I never thought I would survive her death.

I was, in so many ways, her creation. She literally spoke me into being. When she was pregnant with me, she told everyone she was having a girl, and they believed her. This was 1958, when she was in her thirties, and no one had even heard of amniocentesis. Her friends at her job at St. Michael's Medical Center decorated the nurses' lounge in pink, and all the baby presents were pink: the jumpers, booties, coats, and hats. "I told that doctor, 'If it's a boy, don't even bring him to me,'" she used to tell me. She had already birthed three sons and was ready to welcome her daughter.

After I arrived, she went to work designing her girl. I would have everything she thought her cherished daughter should have. I took piano and ballet lessons, and wore well-made white shirts with Peter Pan collars and wool plaid jumpers and skirts. I even wore a camel hair coat to my elementary school, which was right across the street from our house, close enough for my mother to watch over me. I was an introspective child, quick to cry, more at ease with my books and dolls than with the rough-and-tumble of the playground. As tough and no-nonsense as my mother could be, she had breathed into me not just life but also the gift of sensitivity. I felt everything too deeply. The gift would become my burden.

My brother Marc, me, and Mom at
Easter in Weequahic Park.

For the two years before my mother died, I had been in a midlife malaise made worse by the arrival of menopause and the unrelenting routine of ferrying school-age children while caring for my aging parents. When my mother stopped breathing, I fell deep into a cavern of grief. I missed her with an ache that bore into every cell of my body. I couldn't get out of bed, other than to wake my daughter up for eighth grade, drive my son, a second grader, to school, and slug through walking Charlie, my constant companion in the form of a bichon-poodle mix. My entire body hurt, yet I was numb. When my family came home in the evening, I'd move from my bed to the sectional in the basement and watch TV. It didn't matter what was on. I simply wanted the noise.

I had expected to feel grief for the first several months, but then seven months passed, eight, a year, and I still couldn't lift myself out of the pervasive sadness. I didn't know what to do. When I climbed into bed at night, this feeling, this "nausea of the soul," as the writer David Foster Wallace described it, clung to me along with my pajamas and woke up in the night before I did. It greeted me as I opened my eyes at two, three, four in the morning, and I would turn to look at my husband, Cliff, lying on the pillow next to mine.

Feeling me stir, Cliff would open his eyes.

"You're going to have to put me away," I would tell him every morning and every night. "I can't keep going like this."

Cliff had lost his father to cancer only two months before my mom died, and he was still wrestling with his own grief, but he pushed it away to try and help me deal with mine.

"You just miss her," he said, trying to soothe me. "It'll pass."

But it didn't.

I made an appointment with a therapist provided by the hospice that had helped care for my mother during her final days. This couldn't be normal grief, I told the grad student sitting in for the psychologist, who'd had an emergency and didn't show. The student was empathetic but ineffectual. I was so swamped by sorrow at that point, it's possible no one could have reached me. I remembered how Cliff had cried when we got the news about his dad; how he had comforted his mom and helped plan a beautiful memorial service and then eventually went back to work. He was sad, for sure; he had worshipped his dad, but he had remained himself as he dealt with everything, even maintaining his outrageous sense of humor.

I, on the other hand, was most definitely not myself.

Whenever I talked about my needing to be institutionalized, Cliff would respond with his trademark wit. "You'll be like Diana Ross in *Lady Sings the Blues*, with dark sunglasses on in a white bathrobe and a towel around your head," he joked.

He could always make me laugh, but this time, nothing. The Mack truck–sized depression refused to move. I had become emotionally unglued. I had officially fallen apart. But what I've learned on this journey through clinical depression is that my breakdown was actually about me learning how to own my sensitivity and love myself in all of my vulnerability, all my privilege and confusion and loss. This is the story of my mother and the life she dreamed for me. It's also the story of the dank joylessness I fell into after she died, and how one breath at a time I am finding my way through.

1

Tenderhearted

Mom and me at Easter on my block,
across the street from my house.

MOM DIED in the middle of the night in her bedroom downstairs in my house. She was eighty-four and had been in hospice care. The night she died, our dog Charlie came up to our room barking and barking at one thirty in the morning. I was bleary-eyed and didn't want to budge. But his barking was adamant, so I got up and turned on the light, thinking he might be hurt. I picked him up, ran my hand through his fur, held him up, and looked under his body. There was no sign of anything amiss, so I went back to sleep, and eventually he stopped barking.

At 6 a.m. I went to check on Mom. I'd had a feeling of dread the moment I'd opened my eyes, and I was afraid to go and see.

I had asked Cliff to go with me.

"What's that?" he said groggily.

"I think Mom is gone. I need you to come with me downstairs."

"Okay, just let me go to the bathroom."

He took longer than I could wait. I was simultaneously afraid and compelled to go and see my mother. I rushed down the stairs to the room we'd outfitted for her after her heart got so weak she'd moved in with us six weeks earlier. As I entered the room, I saw that she was turned onto her right side in the hospital bed I'd rented for her, the exact position that she'd been in when I'd tucked her in the night before. I went over and touched her shoulder; it felt hard. I leaned over to look at her face. It was frozen, with her mouth wide open. Her expression was a frown, not peaceful, which led me to think that she'd fought off death. As sick as she was and as much as she'd been praying to Jesus to take her, she'd still tried to resist at the end.

Cliff had come downstairs after me and was watching from the doorway. He saw my shoulders jerking and my head moving toward the inside of my hands, and he came to me, turned me around, and held me. I was surprised at that moment that I hadn't completely fallen apart. I was crying, but not the deep, guttural, primal sobs that would come moments later.

When a hospice patient dies, the protocol is that you are to call the hospice people immediately. I called my dad first. I couldn't have done it any other way. My mom had come to stay with us only temporarily, above my father's objections that he could take care of her. But after my mother's last stint in the hospital following a fall, we realized my father needed a break. When I called to tell him she was gone, he didn't speak for a moment and then quietly said, "I'll be there in a little while."

He came dressed in a suit and tie. It was March 24, 2009, a chilly spring morning, and he was wearing his trench overcoat and a Borsalino hat, the kind men of a certain age still wear. He came in and we hugged as we always do. He went into the room where Mom lay and looked at her. When he leaned over to kiss her on her open mouth and said, "Good-bye, sweetheart," I lost it. I went into the dining room and opened my mouth in a scream. At first nothing came out. I remember holding my mouth open, saliva coating the corners, running down my chin and onto my neck before a sound came that I hope never to hear again.

When I called hospice around 7 a.m., our regular nurse, Joe, wasn't on duty.

"We'll send Sister Angela," they said.

I thought, *Catholic?*

"She's a nun."

My mother wasn't Catholic, but I was too weak to protest.

Sister Angela was White, with wind-burned skin. She arrived dressed in jeans and purple polar fleece, and she greeted me with a warm, Southern Black church hug. She called the funeral home and then went into my mom's room to attend to her and write down the approximate time and cause of death. I didn't know the time, but I told her about Charlie's insistent early morning barking. "The dogs always know," she said. She put in Mom's dentures, closed her mouth, removed her diaper, and washed her up. Cliff and I were sitting in the living room. Our son, Ford, then eight years old, was still asleep, but Baldwin, who was fourteen, was up and moving around upstairs. It was nearing time for her to leave for school. We ushered her out the door without telling her that Grandma had died. I'm not sure why I made that decision then—perhaps my grief was so much I couldn't yet bear hers—but I would make the same one today. Baldwin and my mother had been very close. The Grandma she'd known was the one who had come three days a week to babysit her for the first two years of her life, the one who believed the sun rose and set in Baldwin's eyes, who sewed outfits for her Barbies, who always brought her and Ford her famous applesauce or apple pie when she came to visit. But during my mother's illness, Baldwin became wary of her. She wouldn't go into her room unless I was there; she hated to see her grandmother so reduced. I can only think that it was all too much for her.

Ford, on the other hand, only remembered his Grandma as old and frail. He wasn't afraid and would go into her room by himself every morning. He'd say "Mornin', Grandma," and every night,

Mom beaming at Baldwin, July 1996.

8

Ford and Mom on her birthday; his is three days later.

"Night, Grandma." Whenever my mother saw him, she'd smile and say, "Hey, good-lookin'." She always called him that.

For years before this final break in my world, I'd been only showing up in pieces. I had my mommy friends, with whom I'd talk only about our kids, and I'd put away my ambitious writer self. With my writer friends, it was easier to show up more fully, but when I stopped writing, I felt as if I no longer had anything to contribute. My gym friends were on the light side; I showed up not as a writer or a mother, just as someone who worked out alongside them and maybe went for coffee afterward. I functioned by being propped up and medicated by materialism and escapism—dopamine bursts coming from shopping; intense cardio to ease the sadness; and vodka or wine to keep me from feeling too much. I wanted to be numb.

I'd been holding myself back, taking only shallow breaths. My surroundings were shiny, impressive—the house, the car, the country club that I'd never wanted to join and hardly ever went to. I had turned into someone I couldn't figure out, a bored, lonely suburban wife and mother whose writing career had inexplicably stalled. I had no role models for this life, no road maps to follow. Where were the creative, sensitive women who were making a living while married and raising kids in the suburbs and who were also Black and proud? I felt lost. I *was* lost.

When I'd had my mom, I could talk to her about these things. She knew me better than anyone did, and to the end, she saw me whole. And even though my life, as it had become, was as foreign to her as eating meat on Friday, she understood me and knew the core of me was the same. And as long as she held that vision of me, I could shelter in that reflection and hold the idea of myself as whole, too. Now that she was gone, the vision had shattered. I felt as if all that was left of me was Clara's broken daughter, searching for home.

It didn't help that I knew my mother would want me to be tougher than this. I had grown up hearing stories about Clara and her six sisters, mostly about what hell-raisers they were, especially my aunt Eva and aunt Thelma. Legend had it that Aunt Eva, upon overhearing a woman on a Jersey Shore boardwalk call her a slut, jumped on that woman, beating her so ferociously that several men were required to pull her off. Then there was the time Aunt Thelma chased one of her brothers-in-law down the street, threatening to kick his ass in retaliation for his shooting her sister. My uncle was still holding the gun, but he knew to run from Aunt Thelma.

Another afternoon, Aunt Eva and my mother were in my aunt's new car with my dad at the wheel, on the way home from a Brooklyn Dodgers game. When their car was tapped from behind, Aunt Eva and my mother jumped out, ready to beat down the man trying to apologize that his car had "simply rolled." My kindhearted father, knowing what his wife and her sister were capable of, had to talk them out of hurting the man. After some coaxing, the sisters relented and got back in the car. My aunt was many months pregnant at the time.

My head was filled with stories like these, tales I overheard as the petticoated child who was always hanging on to her mother's skirt tail. I loved being with my mother, and she loved being with her sisters. In addition to the seven girls, there were four boys. All the girls were proud of being tough, mean, take-no-mess women. They thrilled (and scared) me because they were pretty and pressed, and they could drink and play cards with abandon.

But it was clear to me, even at five years old, that I was not like these women. I was more like my father. I enjoyed retreating into the comfort of my own bedroom, where I could spend hours creating fantasies. Alone there, I didn't have to worry about hiding my tears when my feelings were hurt, or maybe when I was just touched by a kindness, like my friend Louie's letting me have his turn jumping rope. My aunts tolerated me, but not silently. They let me know that "all that cryin' and carryin' on" just was not nor-

Aunt Thelma; cousin Eddie, holding my
brother Larry; and Mom, circa 1943.

mal. "She spoiled," they'd say to my mother as I sobbed quietly over some ache or other. As the aunts held court around the kitchen table, instructing their sister Clara on how to toughen me up, my mother would simply hold me, pat my back, and pretend I wasn't crying. Every night when I said my prayers, I would beg God to take away my tears. I was so ashamed of myself.

In a culture where Black women are expected to be tough, hands on hips, wielding words like knives, I had often wondered where I fit in. Much later I began to understand that my aunts' unsentimental toughness was merely a posture, adopted for their survival. The story of my mother's family is the story of many Black families in the early part of the last century. They came from a share-cropping background in Little Mountain, South Carolina, and Summit, Georgia. My grandmother's first husband was killed in a well accident when she was pregnant with her second child, a boy born "slow" whom we knew as Hap. Some speculated that Hap's intellectual challenges had been caused by trauma in the womb. My grandmother was pretty and light-skinned, and I only say that because it was what attracted her second husband, my coal-colored grandfather, as well as a lot of other male attention, which made Grandpa Charlie violent. "My father was mean, just the meanest thing you'd ever seen in your life," my mother used to say. "He used to tell us if someone hits you, you make sure you kill 'em."

My grandmother had eleven children with him, and when he died, she moved the eight younger ones north, joining the older children, who had jobs by then. The move was supposed to make life easier, but things didn't quite go that way. Early pregnancies, bad marriages, and limited opportunity made my aunts bitter, forcing them to rely on no one but themselves. So they worked extra jobs to send us to a better life, took care of grandchildren long after their best child-rearing days, and watched their own dreams slip away like dandelion dust as their insides hardened to stone.

Some of their daughters would grow up to have better lives, but things still weren't easy. As Black women, we weren't likely to have much of a financial cushion should we fall down. Most of us were still a couple of paychecks away from poverty, so we had to be as competent, resilient, clear eyed, and strong as our mothers were. But did we also have to be as tough as old leather, as sharp-tongued and mean as my aunts had always insisted I should be?

Not long before my mother got sick, I asked her about my grandmother, who died before I was born. She told me that despite her hardships, my grandmother had been a tender woman. "Mama had that mean husband," she said, "but you know what she would do? On Sunday mornings, she'd let it all out in church." My mother's voice trailed off, and I pictured my grandmother standing up in her A.M.E. Church, arms outstretched, knowing someone or something would be there to lift her up, that there was always a place where her pain and suffering would be understood. That, I realized, is why my grandmother always knew she would survive. She knew that when it came right down to it, a strong Black woman could also be tender. Now, reeling in the aftermath of my mother's death, I clung to that idea for dear life.

2

My Mother, the Insurgent

MY MOTHER was tall, five feet seven inches, and broad shouldered. She was a size 12 for most of her life but rail thin in her teens and twenties and would revert to that frame as an elder. In some old pictures, she looked Olive Oyl thin, and her hairstyle was like Princess Leia's—those two spiral buns on either side of her ears.

She was passionate and intense and idiosyncratic. She read the newspaper at night in bed and watched *Eyewitness News* at five o'clock every day. She had opinions, she didn't care if they were unpopular, and everybody in the neighborhood knew not to waste her time with "fool talk," which was her estimation of small talk. If someone, friend or acquaintance, burdened her with too much, she had no problem saying, "I ain't got time for this fool talk!" And *boom*, she'd hang up the phone. I remember more than once witnessing her ending a phone call this way and saying to her, "How do you have any friends?" She'd look at me and her grin would turn into a cackle. "Mabel know I'm busy," she'd say.

My mother was purposeful. President of the block club and the PTA and a Boy Scout den mother, she worked full time at night, 11 p.m. until 7 a.m. at Saint Michael's hospital in Newark as a pediatric nurse's aide. She worked that job for thirty-two long years—thirty-two years of nights. And she cleaned our two-family frame house like Pac-Man. She was an impeccable housekeeper and had set days when she cleaned certain rooms in particular ways. She'd do the floors and wash the towels (always with Tide) on Mondays, drying everything on the clothesline that hung from the second-floor back hall window because doing so made them smell fresh. On Tuesdays she did the bathroom and the kitchen floors, scrubbing with a brush soaked with Mr. Clean and water, on her knees. Every week she would clean the creases in the lampshades, do the ironing, which included her bras and my father's boxer shorts, and clean out the refrigerator, wiping it out with a little ammonia mixed in a bucket of water. She'd defrost the freezer every other week and take the stove apart about that often as well. She was a flash of activity—cleaning, cleaning, cleaning. It wasn't until I was a woman with a family of my own that I finally realized that, for my mother, who grew up with the notion that a clean house made one superior, cleaning was also her therapy. It was how she'd work out all that anxiety that was always in her. She wasn't judgmental, except about other people's housekeeping abilities. "You know, she got a nasty house," said in a conspiratorial whisper, was the worst thing she could say about someone. To her, an unclean house was a major character flaw.

I never saw my mother relax or just lie down on our brown floral slipcovered couch, or soak in the tub, or go for a walk. The only time she would come close to kicking back was when her sister Thelma came for a late-afternoon visit, and even then, while they were having a cold one—always Schaeffer—my mom was iron-

coupons, or balancing her checkbook to the nickel.

..elma was my favorite of my mother's six sisters. (I ..ve no memory of Aunt Eva, who died when I was very young.) Thelma was the only sister who was childless and was one of the few people who could tell my mother off, and whom my mom would actually listen to. They were that close. Aunt Thelma was as tough as a workingman, yet always dressed in pretty clothes, royal blue chiffon, powder makeup from her compact, and red lipstick. When Mom wasn't in her mint-green work uniform, she dressed in classic clothes like pressed cotton shirtwaist dresses, skirts, and turtlenecks, but at home, my mother always wore a housedress—a shapeless, cotton *shmatte* that snapped up the front and had patch pockets. These were popular in the '50s and '60s, but my mom wore them her entire life. It was usually the only thing she'd ever ask for on her birthday or at Christmas. It became really hard to find such things by the '90s.

On my mom's nights off, Thursday and sometimes Friday, we'd have family Pokeno night. Aunt Thelma had introduced Mom to Pokeno. We'd have little Dixie cups filled with pennies and boards similar to bingo cards, and Mom would bake a Tree Tavern frozen pizza, topped with olive oil. These are some of my all-time favorite childhood memories. She was relaxed, and she and my dad and everybody got along. It was the only time that I can remember my brothers Marc and Duane, Mom, Daddy, and me playing something together. Aunt Thelma and Miss Bertha, who lived in our downstairs apartment, were also included.

Miss Bertha was a childhood friend of my mother and her sisters. She was divorced from a prominent man in Newark who had left her for another woman. In those days, divorce was still scandalous—but not for my mother and her sisters, each of whom had had at least two marriages. One had had three. Before she met my father, my own mother had been married to another man. She'd become pregnant at sixteen and had wed the father of my oldest brother, Larry. She had divorced that first husband not too long after the baby was born and moved home to her mother's house. It seemed to me that the Eleazer sisters would cut a husband loose with as much thought as they gave to changing their stockings. Miss Bertha, on the other hand, had been devastated by her divorce, and my mother and sisters despised her ex-husband for it. The sadness that surrounded her was discernible even to me at ten years old. My mom always included Miss Bertha in whatever we did, and often I would go down to her apartment, equally bleach-clean as ours, to just sit with her. We'd watch TV and eat ice cream. She was really thin, had ice-blue eyes, light skin, and a deep baritone voice that would sometimes tremble because of some unknown (to me) health issue that made her frail. She looked a lot like a mixed gray-haired Lauren Bacall. She was very kind to me, always. While my mom had lots of friends, there were a few women who were "family." Miss Bertha was family.

When Aunt Thelma died of a stroke in her midfifties, it was the first time I'd seen my mother cry. My aunt was having coffee after church when it happened and died a few days later. At the funeral, as the family viewed the body, I became hysterical, dropping to my knees when I saw her in the coffin. I hated that the lady ushers dressed in white picked me up and took me off to the ladies' room to fan me and put water on my face. Even at fourteen, I viscerally understood that this was an appropriate response to losing someone you loved. Why sweep the person away? Let the tears and all of it come. It was the first time I'd lost someone close to me, and also, knowing how much pain my mother was in was killing me. My mother was the strongest person I knew, and back then I thought strong people didn't cry.

Mom and our dog Rinny outside
of our house in Newark.

Clara Little was a renegade without ever using the word. When Mom was in elementary school in Elizabeth, New Jersey, around 1935, her class used to sing a song called "Old Black Joe." This was a common song in those days of legalized Jim Crow apartheid.

Gone are the days when my heart was young and gay,
Gone are my friends from the cotton fields away,
Gone from the earth to a better land I know,
I hear their gentle voices calling, "Old Black Joe."

One day, my mother decided the song was demeaning and she wasn't going to sing it anymore. She got her hands slapped with a ruler, but once she'd decided she was never going to sing the song again, she took the ruler every time.

Her insurgency continued in her lifelong commitment to the

PTA. It was her heart's work. She was serious about improving educational opportunity for inner-city kids. She didn't believe in referring to these kids as "underprivileged." "Ain't nothing under-privileged about them," she'd say. "It's the damn big shots who don't want to spend the money on kids and the mamas who don't vote." She remained active in the PTA long after her own children had graduated from high school. She was eventually elected president of the Essex County chapter, which included twenty-two towns. She often said, "All children are my children." And she spent a good part of her life fighting for people who didn't know how to fight for themselves. She knew in her bones that it was just morally wrong that wealthy towns should have better public schools than poorer ones. The PTA was so much a part of our lives that before I was old enough to go to kindergarten, I used to answer the phone, "Are you a member of the PTA?"

If one of her PTA cronies called and it was one of her two nights off, well, she could be on the phone for an hour discussing who wasn't carrying their weight, what teacher had to go, what other school districts in the county got that Newark didn't, and the strategy sessions to demand change. She'd help run campaigns for local council people and would regularly raise hell at city council and school board meetings. Former Newark mayor Sharpe James, who in 2008 was convicted of fraud, had a close relationship with my mother for decades before becoming mayor. He wrote a letter from jail that was read at her funeral. She had mentored him when he began his career as a block club president, then ward leader, then councilman representing our South Ward neighborhood.

After the 1968 riots in Newark, Detroit, and Cleveland, Black people decided it was time for them to be in charge of the cities where they were the majority. After the riots ("rebellion" is what certain Newarkers call them) there was an exodus from Newark of 100,000 people, most of whom were White. The city's population went from 400,000 to 300,000 almost overnight. A group of kingmakers, Amiri Baraka among them, convened to decide which Black man (I doubt a woman was ever actually considered) would be the first Black mayor of Newark. They chose an Alabama-born-and-raised civil engineer named Ken Gibson, but while there was much excitement around his candidacy, my mother didn't support him. I'm sure many people were surprised at her decision. "Aren't you a race woman?" they'd ask, knowing how dedicated she was to the betterment of Black people. But she was not confused about being an advocate for her people and choosing someone whose sole qualifications, in her opinion, were that he was Black and college educated. She was a practical, strategic person, one who'd turned down many officials who'd tried to get her either to run for the South Ward city council or to be appointed to the school board. She wasn't interested in power for power's sake, but she knew it was vital to have the ear of those in power. But just as she didn't like "fool talk" from her friends, she eschewed it from politicians as well.

By 1974, Gibson had alienated some of his supporters in his efforts to keep White businesses from leaving the city. One of those who lost faith in him was Amiri Baraka, who called him a "neo-colonialist." He said that Gibson was for the profit of "huge corporations that run in and around and through and out of Newark paying little or no taxes," while the residents were ignored. It was true that corporate and state interests had major influence in the city. Unemployment soon reached 50 percent. Mom resisted gloating.

I once asked her why she hadn't supported Ken Gibson. "I was my own woman, had my own mind, and I just didn't think Gibson was the one," she told me. "Never was impressed by him. Matter of fact, thought he was kinda dim. I ain't care that he was some

Mom (*third from the right*)
and her PTA cronies.

engineer. I ain't ever felt like I had to prove nothin' to Black folks," she went on. "I was born in the South when it was rough, where we could only take a few baths a week, where we slept on mattresses stuffed with straw. Shoot, you talk about uncomfortable."

When Alice Walker's *The Color Purple* was published, I read it in one night and all the while I couldn't stop thinking about my mother. I bought her a copy, and she also inhaled it. Many writers and activists said the book told an unflattering and untrue story of Black men, and they launched a major attack on Alice Walker, saying she hated Black men. When the movie came out, there were lots of protests, some of them televised.

I took my mom to see the movie and afterward we had lunch. "I don't know what them folks on TV was talkin' about," she told me. "I knew plenty men like Mister down South, okay. Alice Walker ain't made nothin' up. There were plenty of men just like him down South. Just mean as hell."

Mom told me years after this conversation that she'd been raped in the fields in Georgia by an older man, a Mister. I was left speechless and pained by her revelation, yet she showed little to no affect in the telling. She said it just as a fact of being a vulnerable Black girl, as if she had no choice but to survive. She'd been twelve.

3

My Neighborhood

My brother Duane and me after watching a
parade with our dad in downtown Newark.

HUNTERDON STREET, where I grew up, runs almost the
length of Newark, crossing roughly three of its five wards. Newark was a city of neighborhoods. Our block was a self-contained
island, filled with characters.

My porch was often the gathering spot where we'd hang. That

was when kids used to have long afternoons free after school, after homework was finished and before we were called inside for dinner, before Mandarin and soccer practice three times a week became de rigueur. In addition to playing jacks and jumping French rope, our favorite form of amusement was Mr. Webb coming home from his construction job every Friday drunk as "Coota" Brown. Louie, my next-door neighbor and first best friend, would stand on a banister, holding on to a pillar, which allowed him to see all the way to the corner of our block.

"Here he come!"

Monday through Thursday Mr. Webb would walk past us, construction boots dusty from the day's work, lunch pail in hand, sober as a Mormon, back straight as a pole, head erect, gaze directly forward. He would never speak, even if we said hello. But on Fridays, we'd see him weaving up the block from one end of the sidewalk to the other. He'd stumble and stop in front of us on the porch, alcohol fumes strong enough for us to get a contact high. He'd look at us and start to wave his finger, as if he knew something that we didn't.

"I know you," he'd say, pointing at me. "You Missa Liddle's daughter."

He'd stand, swaying like a sapling in the wind, smiling like a toothless baby as he peered at us.

"I know you, too," he'd say to Louie. "You Missa Goosby boy."

After appraising the other kids on the porch, he'd be on his way, weaving down to the end of the block, where he and his wife lived. They were the only childless couple on the block. We'd hold our composure until he was gone, and then we'd fall out laughing, holding onto our sides. It cracked us up every time.

One of our neighbors, Miss Jackie, was a lesbian. We didn't know that word at the time, but even as children we saw clearly that

Daddy and Mom with Mom's lifelong friend
Ruth Brooks and her husband, Jesse.

Miss Jackie was different from the other women on our street. She lived alone in the first-floor apartment of the three-family house that she owned. She mostly dressed in her khaki or navy-blue work uniform, the kind men wore, and she carried a lunch pail to work, like Mr. Webb. She had dark chocolate skin and a gold tooth in the front of her mouth. Her short hair was relaxed and slicked down to her head, and sometimes she'd wear a do-rag knotted in the front of her forehead, like a man with a process. She smiled a lot and was always kind to us children. Miss Jackie was also a grandmother. Her grandkids lived down South somewhere but would come up every summer and stay with her. The girls, three of them, became part of our group during those visits.

"How you doin', baby?" Miss Jackie would say enthusiastically whenever I'd see her. She lived next door to Direen, part of our posse, whose porch we hung out on when we got older and moved from hanging out on mine. Louie, who was gay and way more mature than the rest of us, introduced us to the slur "bull dagger." Sometimes when Miss Jackie would walk past and out of earshot, Louie would spell "b-u-l-l-" and add with a dramatic flair, "dagger." We all started saying it too, but just like when Louie would speak pig Latin or when he would say he was "paper bag tan," I had no idea what he was talking about. Miss Jackie was as much a part of the neighborhood as anybody. I never heard any of the grown-ups talk badly about her or mention anything different about her. She was a part of the Block Association, which meant she was a good neighbor, often sweeping the front of her house and the houses nearby. We knew Miss Jackie was "mannish," and that was just a fact, as was Louie being chubby and a "sissy" and me being a crybaby. Miss Jackie had a funny kind of walk, fast and slightly hunched over to one side—a pimp walk—and her voice was kind of raspy, like too many cigarettes and too much whiskey, although I never saw her appear anything close to drunk. Back then everybody smoked, and she often had a cigarette dangling from the side of her lips, the ash long and miraculously hanging on.

Upstairs at Miss Jackie's house in the second-floor apartment lived the Harris* family. Mr. Richard,* his wife, Miss Rita,* and their three daughters were our closest family friends. Miss Rita, like my mother, was a nurse's aide. Mr. Richard was square. He didn't smoke or drink; he drove a square car, a Dodge Dart; and he liked to take pictures with his square camera. I was right in the middle of the Harrises' younger daughters, Pamela* and Sadie.* I always preferred Pamela; I loved her. We'd go to the beach together during the summer holidays. It was one of those rare situations where the moms and dads and kids were all friends with one another. In most ways, our households were identical.

---

* Asterisked names have been changed.

There were three differences, though: the Harrises always took a family photograph and sent it as their Christmas card; they didn't own their house; and they used to get the Sears catalog. I used to love to go over to their house and leaf through every single page of that Sears catalog.

I vividly remember the day I came home early from kindergarten and found my mom crying because President Kennedy had been killed. Two years later when I came home and found almost the same scenario, I was scared to death. I went to Mom and put my arms around her. I asked her what happened and she mumbled something I couldn't understand. She repeated herself, and then again, and finally I understood what she was trying to say: Miss Rita had died. Mom told me that Miss Rita had died of a heart attack. Not until I was an adult did Mom reveal that Miss Rita had actually bled to death after having an abortion. It was 1965 and abortion was still illegal. Miss Rita had apparently had an affair and gotten pregnant. Mr. Richard had known that the baby wasn't his and had told her to get rid of it. She did, and had come home after, lain down, and bled to death. Her daughter Sadie, who was still in kindergarten, had found her mother dead in bed, the sheets soaked with her blood.

Many years later, I was on a spring break from college, watching TV in our den with my dad when we heard a loud boom. We looked at each other, and Daddy told me to stay put. He headed out of the house, down the street to where the sound had come from. It had been a gunshot from Mr. Richard's gun. He'd shot himself in the head. The adults figured Mr. Richard could no longer live with the guilt he'd carried all those years for making his wife have the abortion. After his death, the girls scattered. The eldest moved to Arizona with her football player husband; Pamela died of something drug-related; and last I knew, Sadie was living in Atlanta.

Miss Margaret was another one of our neighbors. She and Mr.

Dave, her husband, lived in a three-family house across the street from us. She was one of my mother's close friends, like family. She was also one of the few stay-at-home moms on the block. Mr. Dave drove a Cadillac, had a gold tooth in place of one of his front teeth, a process, and was so black he looked blue. Sometimes I'd see him in his silk do-rag, and I couldn't understand why Miss Margaret, who was pretty, with light-brown hair down to her shoulders, would be with him. He looked like a scary creature, except he was really charming and nice. Mr. Dave also worked a lot. I have no idea what he did, but like most men in the neighborhood, it was something with his hands and seemed to involve multiple shifts.

I was crazy about Miss Margaret. She was kind and spoke in a soft Kentucky-tinged voice. She had three sons; I think only one was biologically Mr. Dave's. Maybe that's why she liked having me around—all those sons. On the afternoons that I'd hang out at her apartment, she would make me tuna fish sandwiches and cut off the crusts. I've yet to taste tuna better than hers. We'd watch TV, the hours free and unencumbered, until Mr. Dave came home, always grinning and nice to me, but I'd be disappointed because I knew that my time with Miss Margaret was over. She'd have to serve him his dinner, which she'd cooked earlier in the day, and would sit with him to listen to him talk. My mother liked to tell me with a laugh that I used to ask Miss Margaret, "Does he have to come here?" We were a tribe of women, and all of us, young and old, understood that when a man entered, the coven was over; our ties to one another were put away until the men were gone again. Until next time.

But perhaps my favorite person on the block was Louie. He and I became best friends when his family moved next door to our house when he was five and I was four. Louie lived with his mom, Miss Earlene, another woman I adored and who adored me back.

There was his dad, Mr. Louie Goolsby, a college football star, who walked with a limp because of a sports injury. He was the head of one of the Boys Clubs in Newark. Louie's younger brother, Brian, was the Dennis the Menace of the block. His parents were much younger than mine.

Louie and I spent all our time "playing dolls." First, baby dolls, then, later, we moved on to Barbies. Because Louie was a boy, whenever we played house, I'd tell him that he was the dad. He'd say no, that he was a mommy too, and he would put my brother's plastic typewriter cover over his head as a wig. I loved Louie. I didn't care what he put on his head, his face, or his body—in high school he started dressing full-on as a woman: dress, heels, makeup. He was smart and quick and hilarious. He knew pig Latin before anybody and tried to teach me so we could talk in front of grown-ups and they wouldn't have a clue what we were saying. I couldn't get the hang of it. He did everything well: jumped French and double Dutch, played jacks, kickball, hopscotch. What he wouldn't do was play baseball or basketball or any ball with the boys in the neighborhood, even when they taunted him.

Sometimes when I was at their apartment, Miss Earlene would sit me in front of her mirror and redo my hair. She would brush it up in a top ponytail, and then she'd put my hair around a mesh doughnut to make a bun. Smoothing out my hair by running her hand in upward motions, she'd tell me how pretty I was. When her sister, Shirley, was visiting, which was often, she'd chime in, "Gonna be a knockout." I'd smile, although I had no idea what that meant. I only knew that Shirley, who was single and childless and looked like Ronnie Spector, was beyond glamorous. Like Miss Earlene, she was cream-colored and tall, but she was thinner, wore dramatic black cat-eye makeup, and dressed in extravagant outfits like Pucci-printed jumpsuits.

By the time we were in middle school, when it was apparent and mostly accepted that Louie was gay, some boys would call him "sissy, sissy fag." Louie always had a comeback. I saw his skin grow tougher, thicker. Louie was big for his age, tall and full. When he was about thirteen, he'd go around the corner to the packaged goods store to buy beer. He was that grown-up-looking, and he was fearless. Most of the time, he'd come back with the beer. We'd shake it up and splash it, but Louie would drink his.

Louie and his mother were close. He called her by her first name and had the same body type and walk. She was tall and full and would walk with her back straight and her head high. They were both slew-footed. My mom used to lovingly refer to her as that "big yella woman." Miss Earlene came home from work every day usually wearing stretch pants and some kind of fitted top. She'd wave as she passed us kids gathered on my porch. Sometimes Louie would have to go inside with her, and sometimes she'd stop and talk to us and let him stay.

I never knew how Miss Earlene felt about Louie being gay—she certainly seemed to love him unconditionally—but we all knew how Miss Earlene felt about her other son's behaviors. Everybody on the block knew that Brian was always up to trouble. He'd throw a soda bottle from their third-story window to hear it crash on the pavement. My mom would come outside, hands on her hips, and call for Brian to come outside. She'd grab him by his shirt or jacket and ring his body around a few times, yelling at him that he knew better and that someone could get hurt. Later, when she'd tell his mother, Miss Earlene would thank her.

While I never heard him say anything, I think Louie felt his dad's disapproval. All the rest of us certainly did, once Louie started wearing women's clothes. We were in high school at that point, and Louie hung out with a group of gay guys who dressed up and wore makeup. When he was in drag, he wouldn't speak to me; he'd act as if I were a stranger. It remains a painful memory.

When I tell people I grew up in Newark, the response is sometimes "Oh, the hood." I hate that, because it's reductive, and in my mind I didn't grow up in the hood, at least not the kind that most people imagine. There were no muggings, shootings (Mr. Richard's suicide notwithstanding), or robberies, if you don't count the purse-snatching I once witnessed as my mother and I were leaving the A&P on Bergen Street. A boy snatched a woman's purse and took off. My mother, recognizing him as one of her former Boy Scouts, yelled after him, "Kevin, you bedda put that down, stop it!"

The next thing I knew, she'd thrown her brown leather satchel onto the pavement and taken off after him. She must have chased him two blocks before giving up when he'd gotten too far away. As she came back toward me, huffing, I was so embarrassed I wanted to pry up a piece of the asphalt and crawl underneath. *Why,* I thought, *did I have to get the crazy mother?*

Now it's one of my treasured memories of her.

My childhood holds many embarrassing Clara moments that I now smile and feel proud about, like seeing her pushing a long-handled broom down the middle of our block, furiously mumbling to herself because the street cleaner had missed our street that day. Before she'd set out with her broom to do their job, she would call the sanitation department and cuss out the person in charge, along with the unfortunate soul who'd had the bad luck to have answered the phone. After a few of those calls, the street cleaner didn't miss our block again.

When I think about where I grew up, and who made the difference between Hunterdon Street being just another stereotyped ghetto block or something better, it was my mother. Clara's will, presence, and expectations gave children, hers and the neighborhood's, a sense of deportment. She made sure everyone kept up their property, even the renters, and if they needed help, she and my dad were there to show them how to trim hedges and keep the front litter-free. I can only imagine what new people thought when my mother would show up at their door with a welcome and marching orders. She didn't allow us or other kids to eat anything other than ice cream from the Good Humor truck outside. She created the image of a small town, where she was the sheriff.

When the large oaks and maples on our street later started dying and being cut down, it changed the look of the block. My mother went out and made planters, cutting plastic garbage bins in half and filling them with dirt and petunias. When people started abandoning their properties and the city tore those buildings down, my dad created full lot-sized urban gardens. Prompted by my mother, he grew everything from collards to corn—perfectly tilled, neat rows of vegetables. A few years before my mother died, the courtyard of our elementary school was named after her.

4

Sister Soldier

I'D COME home from middle school and was standing in the back doorway dressed in my starched white shirt with the Peter Pan collar and a wool plaid jumper. I was looking at my mother on her knees, scrubbing the floor, pushing and pulling that scrub brush across the brown and yellow linoleum as if it had done something to her. She pushed strands of sweat-soaked hair back from her forehead and looked up at me, her expression *What now?*

I was standing, chest puffing in and out, trying unsuccessfully to hold in the tears.

"The girls don't like me," I blubbered. "I don't understand why."

She went back to scrubbing. She'd heard this all before.

"They say that I'm a White girl. They say I think I'm better than them."

Now, I was crying and snot was running.

Mom looked back up with an appraising, no-empathy look.

"They're just jealous."

"Jealous of what?"

I couldn't imagine anyone envying my corny clothes, the double-breasted wool coat that I'd had to wear every year when everybody else had a plastic "wet-look" coat from Lerner's.

"Why are they jealous?" I pleaded.

Mom wouldn't answer me but would just repeat herself.

"They just are."

In addition to the taunts, I lived with constant bullying. Notes were left on my desk: "You and me outside," "I'ma kick your ass on Friday." Girls I didn't even know would come up to me at lunch and say they wanted to fight me after school. Even as I write this, fortysomething years later, I still feel a twinge in my body, a fight-or-flight response. To this day, I don't want to be around people who have harsh, bossy personalities. I will overact with them and become overly harsh myself, a place I don't like to be.

Mom used to tell me to ignore their words, but "If one of 'em hits you, pick up a brick and hit 'em in the head."

Eventually someone's taunts did turn to hitting—JoAnn Burwell. We were in Mr. Wilson's sixth grade decorating the classroom for spring. She was at the back corkboard, putting up the paper tulips and robins and watering cans, and I was sitting toward the front of the class, cutting the construction-paper shapes. I was facing the front of the class, and she came up from behind me and punched me on the back of my head. JoAnn ran back to the corkboard, laughing and covering her mouth. I walked up to her, punched her in the face as hard as I could, and the fight began. We were punching and scratching. I threw her against the chalkboard, on top of desks—she was surprisingly light—while I was punching her. She was pulling at my blouse, trying unsuccessfully to grab me.

When Mr. Wilson came back, he found the class surrounding us and chanting, *Fight, fight.* He bore through the crowd, separating us and holding each of us by the shirt as he ushered us to the principal's office. I was still breathing hard, my heart was racing, but I remember the look on the faces of the two secretaries when they saw us: my shirt askew, ponytail half undone, and JoAnn's bloody nose, jacked-up hair, and scratches all over her face. The secretaries both knew my mother. They didn't try to hide their horrified looks. They called our parents.

My family lived directly across the street from my elementary school, so my mother appeared in what seemed like seconds.

"What happened?" she said, as soon as she entered the small office where the secretaries sat outside the principal's office.

I was sitting in a hard wooden chair, breathing slightly less hard, but my heart was still jumping out of my chest. JoAnn was sitting across from me, staring me down. I wanted to cry but couldn't let her see that. I had, after all, beaten her ass.

The principal came out and greeted my mother; since she was the PTA president, they were on a first-name basis. She must have been so embarrassed, but I knew she was secretly proud of me for finally standing up to a bully.

My mother took my hand and quickly dragged me out of there. She probably knew I was about to cry—I cried all the time—and she didn't want any of them to see me. I'd been telling her about JoAnn bothering me. It had been going on for months. She used to tell me that once I fought back one of them, they'd all leave me alone.

We got outside onto the limestone steps.

"I did it, Mommy. I did it."

I'd fought back. I was excited because I thought, now, finally they would all just leave me alone, just as she had said they would.

For the first time in my life, she was wrong.

The girls kept coming after me.

It's never a good idea to pick a fight with someone who is afraid. I had superhuman strength that was fueled by fear, which is why I never lost a fight—except maybe with Sheila, who was on top of me in a field next to Miss Jackie's house one lazy summer afternoon. We were punching each other, but she was straddling me, getting more in, before someone came and pulled her off. In addition to JoAnn Burwell, I'd had two other fights. One in high school with a girl with whom I'd never had any contact or consciously laid eyes on. I was at the glass door of my best friend Carolyn's class, mouthing to her to meet me after class. This girl, Kim was her name I would later learn, came out of the classroom and told me to get away from the door. I said I didn't know her and she needed to stay out of it. She pushed me hard; I told her not to do it again. She did, and I said she was acting like a nigger; in those days of high Black political awareness, this was a serious insult. She pushed me a third time and while I was terrified and didn't want to fight, I threw a George Foreman country haymaker, hitting her hard enough to knock her into the lockers that lined the walls. I punched her again and grabbed her and slammed her against the lockers. I then bit her on her cheek as hard as I could.

Security came and broke up the fight, and we were taken to the principal's office. My dad's first cousin Benny was the vice principal. Benny used to babysit me when I was a toddler and he was a college student. I was ashamed when I saw his face; I also needed him to know that I didn't have a choice. Well, I guess I could've let Kim push me until she got tired, but even then, the way the street worked, she would've continued to come for me. As it was, when a family friend drove Carolyn and me to my house from school that day, Kim and her friend were there waiting for me. She had been to the hospital to get a tetanus shot and had a large gauze bandage on her face and still wanted to fight some more. We decided not to get out the car and drove the few blocks to Carolyn's house, where we waited a while. I did go home eventually, and as I was telling my parents what had happened, the bell rang. My dad went to the door and it was Kim and her girlfriend wanting me to come outside so we could fight some more. I stood at the top of the stairs, my heart clomping in my chest. I heard my father say to her in his calm, soft way, "Why don't you just go home. Look at you, got your face all messed up. It's enough already."

They left then, and after that there was no more from Kim. I think my mother might've gone to talk to her mother, but the details are sketchy.

What I do remember vividly is that twenty-eight years later, I was entering Unity Church one Sunday morning. I had on clogs, a fur jacket and a polyester maternity top, although I'd recently given birth to Ford. There were a few members standing at the entrance, greeting people. A woman said, "Hi, Benilde." I thought it was strange because I didn't attend church often enough for anyone to know my name. Then she said she wanted to talk to me after service. I said okay, though I had no idea who the woman was. I sat in my seat searching my mind for who she might be. I have an exceptional memory for faces, but I kept drawing a blank.

When she came up to me after the program, she said, "Do you remember me?"

I looked into her eyes and suddenly it all came back.

"Yes, I remember," I said.

Before I could say anything else, Kim said, "I just wanted to say that I'm sorry. I'm so sorry. I was young and dumb."

I was astounded. I half expected Oprah to come from behind a curtain.

"Do you forgive me?" she said.

I looked at her. Her sincerity was evident, and I said, "Of course."

She was tall, a good two or three inches taller than my five foot six. She asked if we could hug and I said yes. We both had tears on our cheeks. At that moment, I told myself that her apology was for all of the girls who had ever bullied me, who had made so much of my childhood a waking nightmare.

My mother decided I should have piano lessons. To say she made me take them isn't an overstatement. She found a teacher, Mrs. Ryan, an elegant woman who lived across from Weequahic Park and looked a little like Diahann Carroll. Mom saved up and bought a piano, a carved upright, from Griffith Pianos on Broad Street in downtown Newark. After a few years with Mrs. Ryan, whom I adored, she had some kind of nervous breakdown, and my mom found another teacher, a woman who couldn't pronounce my name and decided it was "Bernice." My new teacher, Mrs. Thomas, was stout, wore a lopsided wig, and had a raspy voice like Moms Mabley. She could play that piano. After every lesson, when my mom or dad would pick me up, Mrs. Thomas would report, "Bernice needs to practice more." My mother would say, "Benilde," and Mrs. Thomas would pronounce a version of Benilde, but by next week I was Bernice again. I was too shy to correct her.

We had piano recitals once a year and before each one, my mother would tell me to tell Mrs. Thomas my name. We'd get certificates, and every one of mine says, "Bernice Little." I hated to practice, and it was made even worse by the neighborhood kids who'd stand outside my house listening through the window and shouting at me to play boogie-woogie. They'd laugh at me for having to take lessons, for having to do something so "corny." I would put in the effort when a recital was coming up, but every time, I would be so petrified when I was onstage that my fingers would literally shake side to side and hit the adjoining keys. It would be a mess. I'd be sweating with embarrassment, fighting back tears, and there would be my parents, sitting in the audience beaming, my mother's head held high.

After my part, I'd slink off the stage and join the rest of the students in a pew, and my mother would come to the end, whisper my name, and hand me a box. One time it was a bracelet, another time a charm, one time a gold chain with one pearl on it. I cry to this day when I think about the look on her face. She was proud of me. Even though I messed up, it was as if I'd been the star student. She never said a word about the mistakes, just gave me a trinket and patted me on the back and said, "All I ever wanted was a girl."

While my mother and I were deeply in love with each other, I was in many ways her opposite. I was dreamy and fearful. She was down-to-earth and fearless. In the 1960s and '70s Newark was a hothouse of political action—especially post the 1967 rebellion, which happened when I was nine. There was Amiri Baraka's New Ark, a group who lived together, took African names, rejected Christianity, and built their own way of life. There were Garveyites, Father Divine followers, and the Nation of Islam. The Nation was the most visible one when I was teenager. There were two mosques—a main one in the middle of postriot blighted South Orange Avenue and a satellite in my neighborhood on the residential Lehigh Avenue. The Nation owned a chain of restaurants called Steak-N-Take and ran a K–12 school. There were brothers, spit-shine clean, fine, polite, and confident, selling the newspaper *Muhammad Speaks* on every other corner. These "soldiers" were also recruiters of lost and founds, the term they used for folks who weren't Muslims. On the heels of one of the country's worst heroin epidemics, it wasn't unusual to see someone go from a heroin-using, body-selling, no-count to an upstanding citizen—a soldier or a sister—in a matter of months.

These brothers would ride around on Wednesday and Friday nights, and on Sundays, when the meetings were held, they would literally pick people up off the streets and drive them to the mosque to hear the teachings of their leader, the Honorable Elijah Muhammad. The Nation was as much about community "nation building" as it was about religion. The teaching was that Christianity had been forced upon Black people by slave masters, that it had been the White master's religion, not the original religion of Africans, and that it was part of what continued to enslave Black people. The Nation was about self-reliance and self-respect. Members rejected ideas that many Black people had been carrying since slavery, that the White man's ice was colder, that he was inherently superior. This was the main reason the group wanted segregation from Whites, or "devils," as they were called. They jettisoned last names because they were slave names given by the Whites who had owned them. Members were given an "X" to replace the true last name, which we as a captured and enslaved people didn't know.

I began going to the mosque in my neighborhood because, like a lot of other people, someone I knew who was a member, Akbar Muhammad, aka Thurman Perry, invited me to come. My friends Carolyn Craft, Shirley Snell, Linda Judd, and I went at first for entertainment, bored teenagers looking for something to make fun of. And we did. We knew better than to do so while we were at the Temple, but as soon as we ran down a steep flight of stairs and were out the door, we'd fall into laughter mimicking their greeting, *As-salaam alaikum, my sister.*

I'm not sure why I ended up returning. Perhaps it had to do with the fact that I'd been somewhat politicized by my brothers Marc and Duane, who talked at the dinner table about the books they kept in our house like *Black Skin, White Masks* by Frantz Fanon, *Soul on Ice* by Black Panther cofounder Eldridge Cleaver, and *Black Rage* by William Grier and Price Cobbs, two Black psychiatrists. I got the part about embracing one's Blackness and not believing that we were in any way inferior. I was also influenced by what was in the air in Newark during that time—it was all about Black Pride. Both my brothers were away at college when I started going to the mosque, but Duane had joined the Nation earlier in the '70s while he was a student at Stevens Institute of Technology, while Marc used to go to basement meetings of Amiri Baraka's group in the mid-'60s. I started attending mosque regularly at the beginning of my junior year in high school, 1975, sometimes with Carolyn, my best friend, and sometimes alone. I liked that the members were so nice to me and to one another; I liked the feeling of community and of being cosseted; it was also a respite from being bullied. I decided to become a member. I had just turned seventeen.

Often, when girls joined the mosque, there was a man involved, and in time, there was for me, too. I'd met him at the Steak-N-Take in my neighborhood, where I'd go to buy a fish sandwich once a week. Becoming a member of the mosque was a simple process of writing three letters, copying a xeroxed sheet exactly. Every potential member copied the letters sent. I never asked what they meant. I vaguely recall they said something like "Elijah Muhammad is the messenger from the God Allah," or some such declaration of faith. After you received three separate responses from the headquarters in Chicago, you were granted your "X." You were official. Because of my unusual name, I was Benilde X; someone with a common name, like James, could be CX; my brother Duane was 4X. I later took the name Rashida.

The man I became involved with was ten years my senior and married. At first the interaction at the Steak-N-Take was respectful. It slowly became slightly flirtatious, although I knew he was married. All brothers, if they were out of high school, were. I didn't know he was so much older than me, and I now don't remember how we went from slight flirting to him asking me out—a strictly forbidden thing, even if he had been single. The rules said dates had to be approved and chaperoned. But we fell into an intense, passionate relationship that lasted a year. After a few months we were talking about him leaving his wife and marrying me. I was applying to colleges but decided to stop. I'd decided that I would not go, that I wouldn't do anything other than be his wife and have a gaggle of kids. He did leave his wife. For a couple of weeks he moved in with his mother, a woman who so mourned the passing of her husband, his father, that she kept his shoes lined up on his side of the bed. I got to know his mother and liked her; she seemed to like me. I even spent a Thanksgiving with them.

I graduated from high school and began working full-time at Bamberger's in downtown Newark. We were happily going along, together every day. I was completely ignorant of the pain I was helping to cause his young wife, whom he'd been with since high school and who had borne him two children. All of a sudden, one day I didn't hear from him; that turned into two days, then three. I panicked. I had that sick feeling in my stomach that something had gone very wrong. I called and called. Remember—I was eighteen. When I didn't hear from him, I decided to drive to his house to see if his car was in front. It was. I parked. I sat, stunned and crying, going out of my mind with grief and betrayal and who knows what else. Part of me thought, *Drive away and forget him*, but the emotional creature that I was overwhelmed any good sense. I got out of my car, walked up the stairs, and rang the doorbell. He answered the door wearing a shirt, pants, and socks.

"Rashida, what are you doing here?"

He spoke to me as if I were a naughty child.

I cried, "What are *you* doing here?"

He closed the door behind him. He continued talking to me in calm tones, pleading with me to stop crying and to get in my car and go home, promising to call me later.

His wife came from behind him, snatching open the door and screaming curses at me, windmill-swinging her arms. I started swinging too, and we were soon punching each other in a whirlwind, down the steps and onto the East Orange sidewalk, both of us screaming and cursing and pulling at hair. He managed to get between us and push us apart—both of us, breathing hard, glaring at one another, him talking, and neither of us hearing what he was saying. Eventually he convinced his wife to go inside and walked me to my car and sent me home.

A few days later, he picked me up from my job at Bamberger's and we drove to a quiet spot on Renner Avenue, near Weequahic Park, where he turned off the engine of his maroon Buick Regency. He told me that he had gone back home. He wouldn't be leaving his wife after all.

I broke out in a rash that covered my neck and back. That was my first breakdown. But it was also the breakthrough that officially began the end of my childhood.

5

Divine Intervention

I MOVED to Jacksonville, Florida. Mom figured that I needed to be removed from my environment, and she asked my brother Marc to allow me to live with him. The whole thing with the Nation and the married man was simply too much; she seriously needed to rein me in. She'd somehow maneuvered the relocation so that I thought moving to Jacksonville was my idea. My brother was twenty-four, a famous radio disc jockey there, and lots of women considered him a catch. He let me stay with him in his one-bedroom apartment because my mother asked him. He gave me his room, complete with water bed, and a lot of freedom. He even got me a job at a record store.

I loved almost everything about my job—my coworkers, playing records for customers, giving them recommendations, and even unpacking the albums. The thing I didn't like was that I was making minimum wage. I quickly learned about budgeting and the reality of wanting things that were way out of reach, like the yellow Ralph Lauren cardigan sweater that sold for eighty dollars—my entire paycheck. I realized that I needed to figure out a career and get myself into college. After a year of living with my brother, he suggested I apply to Howard University in Washington, DC, because it had a good communications department. I planned to study journalism. It was too late to apply for that year, so I decided to go home and do my first year's core subjects at Kean College (now University) in Union, New Jersey. It was a short drive from our house, and I attended full-time and went back to working part-time at Bamberger's.

To say that Howard changed my life would be understating the lasting impact those years had on me. When I enrolled there, I didn't know anything about the school's legacy or about HBCUs (Historically Black Colleges and Universities). I didn't go there because it was a Black school; I went because my brother said it had a good communications school, which had been founded by pioneer

Glenn, holding his and Monique's daughter, Glynn; Monique; me; and Cliff after the book party they hosted for me in Brooklyn, 1996.

journalist Tony Brown. When I opened the acceptance letter from Howard, Mom and I were together on the front porch. She stood watching me, waiting. When I read the word "congratulations," I looked at her and said, "I got in," and we both starting jumping up and down. The truth is, she'd have been happy wherever I went, as long as I went. I knew how badly she had wanted to go to college.

Two months before I was to begin at Howard, I realized I hadn't gotten a room assignment. I called the school and was told that there was no record on file of me requesting housing. I'm not sure what happened to my request for housing, if I'd even filed one. I had done the entire application process on my own—not that unusual in those days, but unheard of in today's college admissions frenzy. I remember holding the tan Trimline receiver in my hand, my mind racing. What was I going to do? How would I go to school in Washington, DC, without a place to live? I was on my way to a new life, my new beginning at my new school; I'd had a clear plan. I hung up the phone with no idea what came next. My mom, who was in the kitchen, took a look at me and asked, "What's the matter?"

"They don't have my housing application. There's no dorm room for me, and it's too late now. All the dorms are full."

Mom wiped her wet hands on the apron tied in front of her cotton housedress; she had been cleaning the stove, which for her meant disassembling it in order to clean it part by part. Flummoxed for about a second, she said something like, "We'll figure it out." We both knew I wasn't going to let this fairly large obstacle stop me, but I'm sure I had a mini-breakdown, since that's generally my default reaction to things that don't go as I'd like. I gave myself a day to wallow. While I still didn't know how I was going to fix this, I just knew I was going to enroll at Howard come fall.

It was all in divine order when I ran into one of my high school classmates, Zara, at Bamberger's days later. We hadn't seen each other since our high school graduation two years before. She was the kind of self-defined girl who wore cool glasses and had a hip haircut. I'd admired her from afar, but we'd never hung out together. Her group consisted of some girls I'd gone to elementary school with, including my former best friend Robin, whom I had dropped in order to hang out with the popular girls, most of whom were cheerleaders. In retrospect, Robin had always been way cooler because she was comfortable being herself. I had been faking it because I wanted so badly to belong. I've never gotten over feeling horribly guilty for leaving Robin. We had had a deep connection in elementary school, all the way through eighth grade. Eventually I apologized to her at our thirtieth high school reunion.

I don't remember where Zara was going to college, but I told her that I was on my way to Howard but didn't have a room. "Oh, wow," she said. "My cousin Crystal is a senior at Howard and she and her roommate, Leslie, another girl from Newark, have a three-bedroom apartment, and they're looking for a third roommate."

My body began to vibrate.

"Yeah, their other roommate isn't going back to school."

How could it be this perfect?

Zara wrote down her cousin's phone number and I gave her mine. As soon as I got home, I called Crystal. We talked a little while on the phone, and she told me about Leslie, whose mother knew mine. Crystal lived not far from me in Newark, in the South Ward, and told me I could come and pick up the key. As a transfer student, I would be starting school before her.

Back then parents taking their kids to college hadn't yet become an event. I was nineteen, and that idea wasn't even entertained. My friend Joni and our older and more worldly friend Winnie offered to drive with me to school in the brand-new Chevette that my dad had bought for me. What should have been a four-hour drive ended up being double that. We got to DC without a problem, but getting around the city and finding Tacoma Park, Maryland, proved as confusing as my first semester at school. DC is designed in a circle, with all the streets named from "A" to "Z," starting with one syllable, going to two, then three. We didn't know that and must have spent hours going in circles. When we finally found the Park Ritchie apartment building, it was way past nightfall. And it was August, which in DC is beyond hot and sticky.

As we were schlepping my stuffed yellow suitcases, my fake floor plant, and garage sale mirror from the car, a handsome, bearded, happy-faced brother was trying to exit the building.

"Hey, let me get the door for you," he said.

He took the plant, a suitcase, and held the door for us.

I could hear a twang that was different from the garbled "R"s we'd already become tired of after stopping a thousand times asking for directions.

We thanked him over and over. He looked at us with kindness and in his amused baritone said, "Hi, I'm Danny Meachum," as he stuck out his hand.

Thirty-plus years later, he is still my closest male friend.

Our stories differ here. He remembers that we basically handed him boxes and suitcases and insisted that he help us, ignoring that he was wearing a suit and was on his way out. The suit part is undoubtedly true because Danny always wore a suit or a jacket. He lived in the building with two roommates who, like him, were students at Howard Law. He helped me that night and his roommates and mine spent the remaining year in DC sharing food, fun, and sorrows. Danny and I, born the same year, two days apart, forged a bond. While we were the same age, his parents had started him in school early, and I'd taken a year off before starting college, which is why he was in law school, while I was a sophomore. He'd grown up an only child in rural North Carolina and is a combination of nice, small-town boy and barrister baller. He would become a successful lawyer in Atlanta, with A-list celebs as clients and friends.

Danny is still one of the few people I laugh hardest with and with whom I have some of the most fun. Danny I and will go years without seeing each other and maybe even without speaking on the phone, but we always can pick back up. A few years ago when Cliff, the children, and I went to Georgia for our niece's college graduation, we stayed with Danny. My children, who didn't remember meeting him before, began calling him Uncle Danny without either of us suggesting it. "Danny is the coolest person ever," my daughter Baldwin said after she rode in his convertible Aston Martin when we all went out to dinner. Years later, on the morning of my mom's funeral, I got dressed and walked downstairs, and standing in my living room was Danny. I didn't even know that Cliff had called him. I will never forget that for as long as I live.

Howard proved to be as confusing initially as the city itself. I'd thought being in school with Black people would be familiar, not taking into account that one in four students is from another country, and that the Black American students were from cities and towns across the nation, even from places like Wyoming and North Dakota. The most confusing group turned out to be the people from closer to home—DC folks, Virginians, and the folks from places that had a class and color stratification thing going on that I didn't know anything about. I wasn't aware of such distinctions when I was growing up. Where I came from, you were simply Black. I now see that the distinctions were there, even in Newark; I was just oblivious to them. It was there when girls picked on me in school, for example. My mom tried to explain that they were "just jealous," but I couldn't imagine anyone being jealous of the corny, oxblood-colored Buster Brown oxfords or the velvet-collared coat she made me wear. Belatedly, I understood that we'd had slightly more than many postriot Black Newark households in the way of material things—GM provided my dad a good salary—and we were an intact family. My mom's salary pushed us another rung or two up the socioeconomic ladder, allowing for Marc's braces, Duane's science camps, two weeks every summer on the Jersey Shore, and all the other "cultural necessities" my mother deemed important, such as piano and dance lessons and theater tickets.

But when I got to Howard, any notion that we were "comfortable" went out the window. Many kids there were from families who were third- and fourth-generation college educated; their fathers were federal and state supreme court judges, surgeons, and boldface-name entrepreneurs. There were also the activist kids (some who came from those same types of backgrounds), the art kids, and the Greeks (usually Southerners who were legacies).

The second student I met when I got to Howard was a girl I'll call Linda. She was a transfer student from Boston College, and we met sweating it out waiting on the registration line. The building my roommates and I lived in had a pool, and I was planning to go home to get in it as soon as the process was over. Linda was outgoing and comical. She talked as if we had known each other forever, and she invited herself over. We began hanging out from that point till we graduated three years later. It took me a semester to get my bearings, and Linda, who was a native Washingtonian, served as my guide to local mores. She knew who was who in high-income DC zip codes, whose daddy was a doctor, and who lived on the Gold Coast, even though she lived in the more modest section of Northeast. I had no idea that Black people like this existed, and I was fascinated. Linda took me to parties where almost everyone looked biracial. Few natty dreads and kufis in these crowds, and some of the houses had indoor pools. It took me a while to notice that most of the girls and a fair number of the guys had light bone or beige or golden skin with straight or curly hair. They were considered the beautiful ones. I'd come from a place where beauty was more democratic. To Linda, my experience was just as foreign.

The third friend I made was Monique Greenwood. We were both journalism majors and had a lot of the same classes. One day as we were leaving one class on our way to the next, we noticed we were both huffing uphill, heading toward main campus, or the "Yard." Monique was a deep fashion diva who would wear yellow pumps with purple tights and a black and white striped miniskirt. She was also from "the District," but unlike Linda, whose mother was a teacher, Monique was from working-class folk who lived not far from campus. She also was very light-skinned but oblivious to the world that Linda had been presenting to me. My friendship with Monique was formed based on our common major and ambition. She wanted to be a fashion journalist, and I wanted to cover hard news. Thirty-five years later, she is still one of my closest friends; her husband, Glenn, is my daughter's godfather and my husband's best friend.

Monique and I became close with another classmate, Lynne Scott (later Jackson), another driven student, who convinced us to run on her ticket for president of the School of Communications student government. I would become vice president, Monique secretary, and we drafted a male student from Radio, TV and Film, Wendell Williamson, to be treasurer. We won, and that began my career as a student leader. We went on to run the college newspaper, *The Hilltop,* with Lynne as editor in chief, me as campus news editor, and Monique in charge of the supplement, "Extensions," which covered, among other things, fashion. *The Hilltop* was then headquartered in an old house on Bryant Street, near the all-girls dorm, Bethune Hall. All of us editors were at the *Hilltop* house every day, and I loved every minute. It felt as if we were part of a TV version of college life. In addition to assigning and editing stories, I also had a column called What's the Deal? that answered student questions about issues on campus, usually related to the poorly run administration.

Some people say that Black schools don't teach students how to deal in the real world. I no longer debate them. I've come to understand that unless they've been there, most people just don't get it. Going to school with people who look like you, race becomes ancillary, and that is freedom. Freedom allows people to be who they are. Freedom allowed me to become who I am as a person, not just as a Black person or as a woman. It also helped me to be someone who is comfortable in her skin and with all kinds of people, Black, White, and other. I got to see, to recognize, to live the overarching truth that under the skin, all people really are the same.

While I was serious about my work as a student journalist, I also had serious college fun. Partying was usually Linda's domain. She had a boyfriend who was also from DC and who was a law school classmate of Danny's, so most of the parties I went to were with law, medical, and dental students; hence most of the guys I dated were in one of those schools. One of them was Steve. I met Steve at the annual welcome-back-to-school party on the lawn of the law school. He was wearing a Brown T-shirt. He had squinty eyes, honey-colored skin, and very loose, dark curls. Linda didn't know who he was, but she knew how to find out. She was intrepid that way. I had no idea what Brown was, but she did and knew that one of her boyfriend's law school classmates, Donna, had also gone there. She gave me Steve's dossier—from New Orleans, a medical student. She sent him over to me to introduce himself, and we dated off and on for two years.

When I graduated on a hot, muggy day in May in Washington, DC, my mother was in the audience beaming in the white suit she'd made on her Singer sewing machine. In all the pictures, at the center, she is there, surrounded by Daddy; Marc and his then-wife, Judy, who was pregnant with my nephew Matthew; Duane and his girlfriend Willa; my nephew Kamal, who was three years old and dressed in a red blazer and bow tie; and me. I'd seen Mom that happy only a handful of times in my life. I should have handed my diploma over to her, but I didn't understand then what I know now, that it was her force of will that had pushed me to this point. She had a belief that I could do something great, a vision that I hadn't even imagined for myself until Howard. Instinctively and with the same bull-like drive, I would one day do the same with my own children, pushing them not just for the sake of it, but from a knowing that they possessed something unique in themselves that they couldn't yet see.

One of my mother's big beliefs was in exposure. She felt in her

(*Clockwise, from left*) Tony Simmons, me, Monique Greenwood, Stephanie Harris, and Glenn Pogue.

bones that Black people could overcome any obstacle by getting out of their familiar worlds. She used to take us to plays, which we liked, and museums, which we didn't. When she'd drag us through yet another museum, I'd ask her why we had to do this, and she'd say, "Culture." Why'd I have to take piano and ballet lessons? Her answer: "Culture." I didn't know what that meant, and I'm not sure that she did, either.

In addition to our summer day trips to Lake Hopatcong and two weeks at the Jersey Shore, our family took road trips. The farthest was to Montreal in 1967 for the World's Fair. Mom also set an example for us by reading widely. I remember her laughing out loud at *Portnoy's Complaint* by Philip Roth, who was not only a Newark native but from our neighborhood. She also read James Baldwin and Jacqueline Susann, and subscribed to *Life* magazine. I would lie on the floor looking at the pictures in *Life,* entertaining myself for hours, even before I could read. My future as a journalist was already calling me.

Mom and me, circa 1985.

After Howard, I was accepted to a very prestigious graduate school in journalism. I'm not sure my mother realized that it was a very big deal, although I'm sure she researched it afterward. The first and second quarters went well, but in the third one I had a tough time. It was the broadcast sequence of the yearlong journalism program, and each day we'd go out with a team of three, rotating as the on-camera talent, the cameraperson, and the sound person. We would then have to edit our tapes and present them in class so that the teacher and our fellow students could critique us. Every time it was my turn to show my piece, my tape would make a *pop*-like sound and stop midway. I couldn't figure out what the problem was, and no professor ever offered an explanation. The tape kept snapping each time I tried to present my story and I was completely at a loss as to why. This went on for the entire quarter. At the very end, during our final documentary project, I finally figured out that the problem had to do with tracking. I needed to run blank tape first, before laying down the sound and picture.

I couldn't believe the solution was such a simple thing. Why had no one bothered to mention it? I completed my final project, a ten-minute documentary on gun control, in the middle of the night. There were only two editing machines, and we had to fight to get to the sign-up sheet first in order to secure a decent time slot. It was the first time I'd ever suspected that I had been treated differently because of my race. I didn't even know how to talk about how I felt. I was confused and lonely even though I had a small group of friends who were all the misfits in the otherwise White-bread land of Protestants: two other Blacks, two Jews, one of whom was a gay man, and an irreverent closeted gay WASP from Edina, Minnesota. I had never before had to wonder if my teachers' unwillingness to help me was racism. Until then my world had been nurturing and mostly Black, so I had no experience with this feeling. The two teachers who taught video and radio broadcasting were high school graduates. The broadcast class counted for two grades and I got Cs. According to the school's grading system, that was one too many. I flunked out with only one more quarter to go.

I remember the sick feeling I had when I met with the two instructors in a small, airless office. I forced myself to hold on, not to let them see me cry. I couldn't help feeling that these two journeymen in the news business were gleeful at my failure. Both of them used to tell us proudly how they hadn't even attended college. One had been a news anchor in Jacksonville, Florida, and had worked with my brother Marc, who was by then a sports anchor. Smugly, he told me to think of my flunking out as "$17,000 worth of therapy," the amount I'd spent on tuition, room, and board.

I left quickly, ashamed, walking away from the tiny, hot office, down the stairs and outside the building to a phone booth. I dialed home. I was crying hard, screaming in fact, when my mother answered the phone. I had dropped to my knees in the tiny booth. Mom was trying to hear me, to understand what I was saying, but I was sobbing too much. She told me later she was scared out of her mind. She thought something had happened to me, that I'd been raped or had had my life threatened.

When I could finally speak and told her what had happened, she was relieved and even a little angry.

"That's all?" she said. "That ain't no big deal. Come home. Just come home."

I think I felt as bad about failing as I did about having to tell my mother. I didn't want to disappoint her. We'd been on such a high. I had finally given her the kind of success she could be proud of. I'd made up for my fresh-girl phase from high school, where I cut class, smoked weed, shoplifted. My shoplifting days during my sophomore year of high school ended when I got caught leaving Valley

Fair with Marvin Gaye's *What's Going On* album tucked under my shirt. Instead of pressing charges, the store detective called my mother. She came and got me, and when we got home she made me get on my knees and beg God to forgive me.

I'd come out of my rebellion, and better than most had expected.

When I was in college, I recall overhearing Mom brag about my work on the college newspaper on the phone with her girlfriends, the same ones she'd previously fretted to about me. It used to thrill me inside. I hadn't known how much I wanted my mother's approval, although I always knew I had her love. I'd feel it in the way she kissed me on both cheeks and then rubbed in the lipstick stain on the mornings I'd greet her downstairs at the front door after her night shift at the hospital. Still dressed in her mint-green uniform, support hose, and white nurse's shoes, she smelled of coffee and cigarettes and Avon lipstick. I always loved the way she looked in her uniform, so competent. "Now you have rouge," she'd say as she rubbed the lipstick stain with a circular motion into my cheek. Then she'd safety-pin an ironed handkerchief onto my skirt before I left for school across the street.

I was remembering all this as I exited the phone booth that day. As my sobbing abated and I dried my tears, I thought: *This time, it's my mother who is waiting.* I understood then that no matter what happened, whatever I did or didn't do, as long as Clara was alive, there would always be someone waiting to welcome me home.

6

Labor Day Weekend 1991

Cliff and me after coming home from
our St. Bart's honeymoon, 1992.

I MET Cliff at the end of summer on a beach in Sag Harbor, a community on the tip of Long Island, New York. Sag Harbor is part of a cluster of tony beach towns jointly referred to as the Hamptons. There was a time when Sag Harbor stood apart—a little like Quogue, Water Mill, and Sagaponack—as the un-Hamptons or the quiet Hamptons. Now it's as crowded and as loudly entitled as the rest. The Hamptons are like Manhattan without the poor people, I once heard someone say.

There is a Black enclave in Sag Harbor, where three strips of mostly modest houses converge onto a small, private bay. This area was established in the first part of the 1900s, but there were Blacks working as whalers in Sag Harbor as early as 1800. All the Black people pretty much know one another, if not directly then distanced by only one degree of separation. The majority of the natives, meaning the original summer people, came from the city—Harlem, Queens, and Brooklyn—and were doctors, teachers, municipal workers, and business owners.

That summer, I had rented an attached cottage from my friend and *Essence* magazine colleague Audrey Edwards, who owned a house in Nineveh. I loved the beach. I could sit on the sand all day, even in dreary weather and read, think, or just stare at the water. When you live in the city, summer turns the cement and crowds into an unbearable crush of steam and bodies. For me, it was crucial to get away and see the sky and be with ocean, grass, and trees.

At the beginning of my rental, Memorial Day weekend, I'd gotten clear enough to write a "Dear John" letter to my then boyfriend, let's call him Bruce, ending our three-year on-again, off-again relationship. I'd finally run out of stamina.

A few weeks into the summer, I had to leave my beach paradise for a week to travel on assignment for *Essence,* where I worked as a senior editor. I'd come to *Essence* from *People* magazine, which is a part of the behemoth publishing company Time Inc. It was the kind of company where benefits were plentiful and work was cushy and people stayed for a lifetime, but when I was offered a job at *Essence,* then only a single magazine—before the music festivals, multiple award shows, and long before Time Inc. owned it—I decided to take it. I would have much more responsibility there than I would have had if I'd stayed at *People*. At *Essence* I was involved in choosing cover subjects and responsible for all the artists featured in the magazine: singers, actors, authors, dancers, painters, and filmmakers. For five years at *People*, my attempts to move up were met with, "Just wait." A lot of people thought I was crazy to leave Time Inc. for *Essence*. I didn't agree then and I don't now, although I do wish I'd taken advantage of Time Inc.'s stock options. But I hadn't met Cliff yet and didn't know the difference between a stock and a sock.

My assignment that July would take me to Southern France to do a piece on the brilliant dancer and choreographer Bill T. Jones. Bill wasn't yet as famous as he would later become, at least not with a Black audience, and his people wanted that to change. I leapt at the chance to go, and when I finally met him, I was happy I did. Bill is a combination of grand and grounded. His diction is somewhat majestic but he never tried to distance himself from his migrant farming background. He owned all of himself and I remember feeling like I wanted to be able to do that; I fell under his spell. In those years, smoking was still allowed on planes. I was on Air France, seated in the last row before the smoking section, and I complained. To make amends, the flight attendants kept bringing me wine; even cheap wine from France tastes good. They kept bringing and I kept drinking, even though I wasn't much of a drinker then. At some point I looked at my travel itinerary and realized that Bill wasn't performing for three days after the dance festival began. I didn't have to be in Montpellier for three days, which meant I could get off in Paris and spend the time there. With the encouragement of the wine and my seatmate, Flame (yes, that was her name), who was from San Francisco and who was going to

Paris to spend three weeks with an American expat she'd met once in a deli in Manhattan, I made a plan.

I had the name of an inexpensive hotel where Mikki Taylor, the *Essence* beauty editor, had once stayed. Flame's would-be lover met us at the gate and called the hotel for me, asking in French if there was a vacancy. I booked the room right then and there, they put me on a bus, we waved good-bye, and I was off on my adventure. It happened to be July Fourth, three days before my birthday. The detour was a glorious, spontaneous mini-vacation for me. It was my thirty-third birthday, and I celebrated it by doing one of things I most loved—wandering around a city, this one of light and love and all things chic, and where, at least then, Black Americans were still beloved.

The hotel was small and mostly clean. A brown man, probably Algerian (unloved by the French), greeted me in French. I pulled out my translation book; he smiled warmly and spoke to me in lovely accented English. The transaction was quick, too fast for butterflies to take hold. But the elevator was tiny, with an old-timey gate that you had to tug open and closed, and for some reason that gave me pause. *What the hell am I doing?* I thought, but my other voice said, *Let go, lâche.*

I opened the door to a tiny space with just enough room for a twin bed, a small dresser painted light green, and a nightstand. There was, however, the requisite French floor-to-ceiling window with the wrought-iron fence across a tiny terrace. It overlooked a deserted yet charming avenue. I was giddy with excitement and, although I was sleepy from the flight, I couldn't shut my mind off enough to rest on the lumpy twin bed. I went into the hall to find the communal bathroom to wash up. I changed my clothes, conscious of trying to achieve that casual yet sophisticated look that the non-French have a hard time emulating. I might have failed, but

I left my hotel to walk outside. I didn't know where I was going. After I'd wandered till my feet were starting to blister, I sat down at one of the million outdoor cafés and had dinner and a glass of white wine. It was nine o'clock and still light out, the sky a magnificent beryl, a color I'd never seen before and haven't seen since. I breathed it all in until the jet lag and wine kicked in, forcing me to limp on my blistered feet back to my hotel. I was afraid that I wouldn't be able to find it, but I did. Once upstairs, I immediately collapsed in my bed.

The next two days were more of the same. I did get myself to the Louvre and managed to bypass the throngs viewing the *Mona Lisa*, which I'd seen before on a stopover en route to Egypt six years earlier. I walked the parks; I went to shopping areas; and I took the Métro to the edge of Paris to a famous flea market, Porte de Clignancourt, where I bought a sleeveless beige jacket that had an off-center zipper. I wore that thing until it fell apart. I took myself to a light lunch and to dinner on my birthday, my last night there. I sat outside, and a group of Parisians and Americans at the neighboring table started a conversation. When I told them it was my birthday, they ordered champagne, and we drank and talked until it got dark. I thanked them and walked back to my hotel feeling like Holly Hunter in *Living Out Loud,* a movie about a spunky medical school dropout who rediscovers her free formidable self after her divorce.

I had to leave early the next day to catch the train to Montpellier. I didn't know about the weekend sardine-like train-station traffic, and while I don't think the French have a monopoly on rudeness, if I'd had only that experience I would have said that they absolutely were. But everyone I encountered before that had been nice to me, perhaps because I always greeted them with respect, a smile, and my very limited French—my knowledge of the language consisted mostly of "hello," "good-bye," "thank you," "see you later." I'd always believed that when traveling abroad, it was important to acknowledge that you are a guest in someone else's country. Something else occurred to me about why the French like Black people: Could it be that we inherently understand that you treat people the way you want to be treated? Entitlement doesn't get you anywhere, especially there. What I also observed at the train station was that the pushing and shoving wasn't reserved for foreigners; they treated each other the same way. Although the French do suffer from tourist fatigue—can you blame them?—even with the mass exodus at the station, the no-frills hotel, and my blistered feet, I was euphoric.

Montpellier was quiet, with beautiful cobblestone streets and wisteria-covered buildings. But virtually no one spoke English in the countryside. While my stay was lovely, it wasn't Paris.

I went back to work the following week and announced that I wanted to move to Paris. It was impractical and completely out of character for me. And while I knew deep down I probably wouldn't pursue this dream, people around me could sense that I had been transformed. No one saw it more clearly than my boss, Susan L. Taylor, the legendary editor in chief of *Essence.* Susan was a force, and to me she had always been loving, kind, and encouraging. I don't know what she saw in me, but we bonded from my first day working at the magazine. Susan, who constantly traveled the country speaking, increasing the *Essence* readership, had taken it upon herself to find my Mr. Right. She had never approved of Bruce and had sent me on several blind dates that she'd arranged. When I went into her office, post-Paris, and told her that I'd found my spiritual home, she looked at me and said, "Now, you're going to meet him."

And I did.

It was Labor Day weekend. I had gone to the beach alone. I'd planned to meet my friend from *People,* Lee, who was supposed to hang out with me for the day. She'd been renting across the bay on Shelter Island. Those were the days before cell phones, and the cottage didn't have a landline, so she couldn't reach me to let me know she couldn't make it. After waiting for a few hours, I grabbed my chair and a book and trudged through the sand on my own. I was wearing white Lycra bike shorts, an oversized Howard sweatshirt, a droopy khaki hat and sunglasses, and I was looking for a spot to flop when I saw Leslie,* an account executive at *Essence,* who was sitting with two guys. She waved me over. Cliff told me much later that he'd told her not to, because I was alone, and he thought that I must've been a loser.

Leslie was dating one of the guys; he was handsome and bearded, wearing a blue T-shirt with "Yale" in letters that were eighteen inches high. The other guy was cute, shirtless, and wearing swim trucks and Ray-Ban sunglasses. He sat with his face turned upward, getting a tan. I took one look and thought "Morehouse Kappa." I'm not sure why I narrowed Cliff down to that demographic—maybe it was the utter assurance, the successful humble brag that often marks graduates from the all-male historically Black college. Cliff emanated that kind of confidence. I sat down on their blanket as Leslie introduced me. Yale T-shirt seemed engaged; Sun Boy barely acknowledged me. After we discussed the office, books we were reading, and *New Yorker* articles, the conversation inevitably moved to the dating scene. We were in our thirties and had been at it for a while and were tired. I wanted to get married.

"It's really hard to meet a guy who is well rounded and who reads more than the business pages or the sports section," Leslie said.

"Yeah, it's like the difference between someone who reads the book and someone who just reads the Book Review," I added.

At this point, Sun Boy, aka Cliff, turned toward us and recited:

Two roads diverged in a yellow wood,
And sorry I could not travel both
And be one traveler, long I stood
And looked down one as far as I could
To where it bent in the undergrowth.

It was the first stanza of Robert Frost's poem "The Road Not Taken," and when he was finished, he turned his attention back to sunning himself. I had to admit I was surprised and impressed. I'd figured he was strictly a Sports section reader. Now I was intrigued, but I had the impression that the feeling wasn't mutual. Leslie and I kept gabbing away, and at some point I mentioned that I'd graduated from high school in 1976.

Cliff turned to look at me and said, "Take off your sunglasses."

I removed my sunglasses.

I looked him in the eyes, pushed my feet deep into the sand, and inhaled.

"Okay, thanks," he said, and continued tanning.

More than twenty years later, I still don't know why I responded to his request by removing my sunglasses. Normally, I would have made a sarcastic comment or offered some kind of who-do-you-think-you-are attitude. Later he told me that before he saw me without sunglasses, he'd thought that I was much older. When I took off the glasses and he realized we were the same age, Cliff gradually joined Yale T-shirt, Leslie, and me in our conversation. We were talking about the foreign film *La Femme Nikita*, which was playing in town and which we all wanted to see.

We ended up going to dinner first. It was not a double date. It was more like high school, when you're with your friend, and she's with her boyfriend, and her boyfriend's friend is with him. By default, you become a couple. We walked into the restaurant, an old-style, nondescript seafood joint that had become gentrified when Sag Harbor became like the other Hamptons. Cliff walked in like he owned it. He greeted the maître d' as if he knew him and talked to everybody who worked there the same way. I knew that I liked him—he was funny and easy to be around—but I wasn't sure if he was a little too much, with all his glad-handing.

One thing we agree on completely is that if we'd met in New York City, we wouldn't have gotten together. In Sag Harbor, our guard was down; we didn't have on our Manhattan faces, the default defensive posture of *I'm so cool, successful, happening that I can't be bothered.* In the city, you get pummeled with the three questions: *Where did you grow up? Where did you go to school? What do you do?* But in Sag Harbor we went to eat because we were hungry. The place had no provenance. We never asked the three questions. We didn't "flex."

After the movie, Cliff drove me home and came into the cottage for a drink. He had cranberry juice. We sat on stools at the kitchen counter. "Be right back," he said, in the middle of our conversation. He went into the bathroom and fixed the toilet, which had been running all summer. I made a mental note and was impressed, for real.

I was leaving the next day and he offered to give me a ride back to the city. He said he'd be there at eleven the next morning and at eleven he was.

I had half a summer's worth of stuff, including my big, fat comforter, at the cottage. How I thought I was going to get all that stuff home on the train I don't know. I was so grateful to Cliff for offering me a ride back to Manhattan. When he showed up the next morning, he found several pieces of luggage and a few huge garbage bags to take to the dump. He made fun of me but didn't seem fazed. He good-naturedly loaded it all up into his Hyundai.

At this point all I knew was his name, he was from Mount Vernon, New York, and he lived in Bloomfield, New Jersey. It had been a relief not to know more, although the more he talked on the ride home, the more curious I became. He could've been a plumber (although I didn't really think that, his fixing the toilet withstanding), a teacher, a bartender, a lawyer; nothing would've surprised me about him. I couldn't place an occupation on him. On the way home, we stopped at a McDonald's. We sat in the window and shared French fries. Being with him was easy and sweet. While he was a little cocky, he was also very considerate. He was familiar, like the boys I'd grown up with whose mothers, like his, had also been teachers. He was also a riot, like my old *People* magazine friends Alan Carter and James McBride, who could make me laugh until I cried and wet myself.

When we got to my apartment three hours later, Cliff insisted on carrying my things upstairs. I let him. Once inside, I couldn't offer him anything to drink, because there was nothing in my kitchen. Before I left him in my apartment to head to the Red Apple supermarket down the street, he pulled me toward him where he was stretched out on the couch and we had our first kiss. It was soft and gentle, considerate and generous. I dissected his kiss while I was in the aisles at the supermarket. When I got back we talked more, and kissed a little more before he left to meet his family for dinner at Sylvia's in Harlem to celebrate his brother Raymond's birthday. Cliff invited me, but I said no, thinking it was too much, too fast. I didn't tell him that; I just thanked him. Later, he told me that he'd invited me knowing I'd decline.

Back at work after the weekend, Cliff sent flowers to me at the office. The card said, "Share the fantasy." As I was reading it, Leslie walked by my cubicle. I'd told her the flowers were from Cliff.

"He's a good guy," she said. "He comes from a good family."

I thought the "good family" comment strange, like it was code for something I should've understood but didn't.

He called me the next day and the next day and the day after that. He'd call me from phone booths, home, work, often in between appointments. Never asking me out. After two weeks of these phone calls, I said, "So are you gonna ask me out or what?" He said he was trying to decide and revealed that he had commitments to go to destination weddings with two different women. He was trying to figure out how he could put me on the calendar in January. It was now September.

I said, now or never.

He said okay, and we started dating.

7

Yin and Yang

CLIFF WENT to Maryland with one of the women in October and to Arizona with the other around Thanksgiving. Both times, he called me while he was away. By the time he came back from Arizona in November, I knew that I really liked him, but after a few heartbreaks I was determined to do this one right—whatever that meant. The way we got to know each other was mellow; we did the standard courtship dance, dinner, movies, drinks, and the theater. But what made me fall for him were the little things: For our first date, he brought me a copy of the children's book *Clifford the Big Red Dog.* We took walks in parts of Central Park where I'd never been. He took me to the Belvedere Castle; we'd go for drives in Westchester County; and he showed me the woods where he'd played as a child and the airfield where he flew Cessna 172 planes in the Civil Air Patrol as a teenager. The biggest difference from other boyfriends, though, was that he always did what he said he was going to do. He'd always show up on time, and he was generous. I was constantly waiting for the other shoe to drop, for him to disappoint me, to one day just not call, to not show up, as had happened with a few guys in the past.

He introduced me to people who had known him for years: guy friends he'd had since second grade, his very quirky extended family: Aunt Miriam, Uncle Gene, and his cousin Em Sue (Emily Susan). I loved them immediately. They reminded me of the Leary family in the Anne Tyler novel *The Accidental Tourist*. To this day they're still among my favorite extended family. In Sag Harbor I had met Mrs. Day, who had been his family's neighbor in Mount Vernon for his entire life. I met his parents—he clearly got his sense of humor from his mother, who is eerily similar to George Costanza's mother from *Seinfeld*. I introduced him to all my close friends but decided he wouldn't meet my parents until we were seriously serious. He said, "What does that mean?"

I said, "Engaged."

He said, "Well, do you want to get married?"

We were lying in my bed. I remember that had I on my white terry-cloth bathrobe, but I don't remember what I said. I do remember feeling a strange mix of giddy and calm. A month or two later, he made the official ask at our favorite restaurant, Lola, with a two-carat emerald-cut diamond ring dropped in my coffee.

Cliff had moved from the city to a one-bedroom in Bloomfield, New Jersey, to enter the retail stockbroker-in-training program for Shearson Lehman Brothers. When I met him, it had been two years since he'd gotten his license and he'd just finished two years of cold-calling to build a client base. He survived on whatever tiny commissions he'd earned, living on very little money. The Will Smith movie *The Pursuit of Happyness*, based on the true-life story of Chris Gardner, is an accurate portrayal of what it's like to become a broker.

Prior to this, he'd been pushed out of a comfortable salaried job at the treasurer's office at Shearson in the city. That turned out to be a blessing in disguise, after he realized that trying to advance on a straight corporate ladder wasn't going to work for him. His nonconformist style was more suited to being his own boss in wealth management, which also meant he gave up a salary, a guaranteed bonus, and paid vacations for an all-commission career. "I eat what I kill," he likes to say, and it's true. He has the umbrella of a company—then it was Smith Barney—and clients of his own. While that kind of uncertainty can be difficult at times, I admire him for being willing and able to do it.

When we were dating, I was living in a one-bedroom, rent-controlled apartment on the Upper West Side in Manhattan, and I'd often take the train to visit him on weekends. My *Essence* job required long days and that I go out most nights, as I needed to keep up with what was going on in entertainment. I was spent on weekends and happy to take a break from the city. He'd pick me up at Penn Station in Newark and we'd go to our pub-type place in Montclair and have drinks and eat bar food: potato skins, nachos, and mozzarella sticks. I didn't miss the nouvelle cuisine in the New York restaurants that I frequented during the week.

I didn't realize at the time that, for Cliff, our meeting was timed right for his life plan. He is methodical, he strategizes; once he had established a path in his career, could see his business growing, and had a respectable amount of savings, he was ready to settle down. He was going to buy an Audi, but he bought my ring instead. He wanted someone who had been with him on the climb, not someone who'd joined him once he'd reached the summit. He didn't want to have to question whether someone was with him for his checkbook rather than for his character. When I met him, he drove a basic Hyundai, lived in a dust-covered walk-up in a blue-collar section of Bloomfield, and had a tiny amount of disposable income. He liked that I was creative. He'd dated very nice lawyers and women with MBAs but wanted someone with more yin to his yang.

We married the following June. We moved into a luxury highrise on the New Jersey side of the Hudson, with a glorious view of the river, furnished with our matched-up furniture from our old single lives. We lived there for three years; it was where I finished my first book and sold it, and where Baldwin was conceived. Marriage proved to be a lot different from dating; living together was hard for me. I'd never lived with anyone before. Cliff had. There was no downtime. My job was constant meetings with my coeditors or with publicists pitching their clients over the phone or over lunch or dinner, then I'd go home, and my husband would want to talk some more—it was a lot. I'd been working on my novel *Good Hair* for years on the side and hadn't managed more than twenty pages and the two main characters. I had come up with the characters Alice and Jack long before I actually started writing the novel.

Alice came to me when I was at a Howard homecoming football game, as Monique and I were every year. Sitting in the bleachers, I was struck by some of the families around us. There were two and three generations of Howardites and other legacy college graduates. I knew these people were, for the most part—the *Cosby Show* and *A Different World* notwithstanding—invisible to the larger culture and to other ethnic groups.

I wanted to write about these people, upper-middle-class Blacks, and their traditions and lives.

Alice started out as me, but she wasn't me. I envisioned what I would've been like had I gone to the all-girl Catholic high school my mother wanted me to attend. What I might've become if I'd gone to a women's college, such as Wellesley or Mt. Holyoke. I needed for her details not to be completely my details, although she was also from a working-class family and her childhood was based on mine. When creating characters, in order for them to come alive, they cannot be you but separate, breathing entities. Otherwise the work is stagnant.

Jack was a third-generation Harvard grad, a descendant of free Blacks. In addition to showing his milieu, I wanted to talk about class conflicts among Black folks, which I became aware of while at Howard.

I told Cliff I wanted to quit to write full-time. I figured I could accomplish my long-planned dream and have much-needed quiet time before he came home from work. He wasn't on board with this plan and didn't understand why I couldn't write on the weekends. "Because weekends are ours, not mine," I argued, "and we just got married, and I want to spend that time with you, and we don't have any big bills, no mortgage. Now is the time."

He didn't like it, but a few months later, I quit anyway. At home, I wrote all day, every day. The only break I'd take was to run two miles and eat lunch. Cliff would come home and read what I'd written that day. It kept me honest. I didn't want to disappoint him or myself.

While I was working on the novel, I was also writing freelance magazine articles, and I wrote a chapter for my friend Linda Villarosa's book, a definitive work on Black women's health titled *Body & Soul.* The chapter I wrote included information about fertility. In doing my research, I learned that after age thirty-five, the risk of having a baby with Down syndrome went up by 25 percent. I was already thirty-five. I started pressing Cliff to agree to us getting pregnant. He wanted to wait until I finished my book. He was afraid that my dream would fade if a baby came along too soon. To this day I'm grateful to him for his insight. After eight months,

I finished the book, and after another six, my agent, Faith Childs, sold it.

I couldn't have been happier when I became pregnant with Baldwin during this period. Cliff wanted us to move immediately to the suburbs; he said that our unborn baby needed to have a backyard. I'd wanted to move back into the city, but after quitting my job, I lost my bargaining chit, which was the need to be within walking distance of or a short subway ride from work. So we pooled our money and bought our first house, a lovely, yellow four-bedroom center-hall Colonial with black shutters, on a quiet street in South Orange. Baldwin was born four months later. I was thrilled to have a daughter, and my novel *Good Hair* was going to be published the following year. We had little extra money. We had one car, a Toyota that Cliff would usually drive to work, but things were good—except for the fact that I detested living in the suburbs.

I felt as if I were the only creative person in town. I felt surrounded by women who were married to investment bankers, home full-time, and had no interest in doing anything other than being a wife and mother and carrying the latest Prada bag to the Short Hills Mall. I craved conversation about the human condition, I wanted the spontaneity of city living, and I wanted . . . something else. Then I met Belinda, who lived up the street, and she and I would take her son Marcus and Baldwin around. We'd buy them baby clothes, get ice cream, go to lunch. I met Gale Monk, who lived a few blocks west, who I could always drop in on while I was out walking and feeling dismayed at not seeing a soul on the sidewalks. She'd always have "a nice white" in the refrigerator, and that helped when I was feeling so lonely.

As I waited for my novel to be published, I was in a holding pattern. And then I met my friend Lynne Toye at a newcomers' picnic that South Orange hosted. It was held on a big field in the center green where tennis courts, a pool, and the community center converged. Cliff and I were standing in the field among lots of new homeowners. I was holding Baldwin, who was about six months, on my hip, and I was talking to someone. Lynne's husband, Vince, overheard me say that I worked three days a week from home and told Lynne, a marketing consultant who also worked three days a week from home. She came over, all cheerful smiles, bouncing her ten-month-old son on her hip.

"Hi, I'm Lynne, and this is Chester." She put her hand out to shake mine.

"And who's this?" she asked, admiring Baldwin, whose giant brown eyes were peering out, her head topped with wild curls, perched on my shoulder.

I shook her hand, told her our names. She was so bubbly and happy; I retreated, thinking again that I was stranger in a strange land. We exchanged numbers, and she said she'd think of something fun for us to do with the children.

And a few days later she called: "How about the pool?"

"Nah."

She called again: "How about the farmers' market?"

"Um, no."

"Why don't you and Baldwin come to my baby group?"

No way, I thought, but I was beginning to feel bad because she was so earnest. I said yes.

I met her at an Indian woman's house in Summit. There on the floor with their toddlers were an assortment of used-to-be's: a lawyer, an architect, an engineer. I tried plopping down with Baldwin, who wouldn't let me put her down, wrapping her legs around me like a cobra. She didn't want to be there any more than I did.

Lynne's next invitation was for a casual family dinner al fresco. I hated cooking and really couldn't, so I jumped at this invite. Cliff and I packed up Baldwin, the diaper bag, and a bottle of wine and headed five minutes away to Lynne's large Victorian. An Audi with a "Virginia" sticker emblazoned in large letters on the back window was in the driveway. A table set on the porch, complete with shabby chic tablecloth and a pitcher of homemade lemonade, was waiting for us. It was August. I was touched and charmed by this smart, welcoming, unpretentious woman and her handsome, down-to-earth husband, whom she'd met while they were studying engineering at the University of Virginia.

Lynne's persistence and belief that anything was possible restored my sanity and showed me a way to appreciate this life I'd made. She always had a plan for something to do with the babies, even if it was just playing with a watering can in a small plastic pool in the backyard. It was unusual to enter her home and not smell something baking, and she was always in a good mood. She had worked briefly on Wall Street (she also had an MBA), but after she'd had Chester, she said she couldn't imagine going back to work and leaving him for twelve hours a day. I was constantly grilling her about where she'd put all her ambition.

She said she wasn't conflicted about being a homemaker; she was happy and fulfilled; she had two adjunct teaching jobs at local colleges and was still doing the marketing consulting part time. She was so excited about my book coming out and convinced me that I needed something to do in the interim, in the year before the novel would actually be on the shelves. One day we were in her upstairs home office.

"Okay," she said, rolling her office chair to mine so that our knees were touching. "What do you want to do?"

I'd written the novel and sold it. I did what I wanted to do, and now I was in a holding mode. I didn't know what else.

She persisted, basically telling me that I couldn't just sit and wait for a whole year. I told her how much I missed being in the company of other writers, of other creative people. How much I'd loved the writing workshop I had taken in the city.

"Well then, create one."

I looked at her blankly. Yeah, *uh-huh.*

"No, really. We'll make up some flyers, put them around town, and see what happens."

Lynne literally took me by the hand, helped me type up flyers, print them out in large print, and post them on bulletin boards around town. My friend Wendy put one up in an independent bookstore in Montclair.

Seven people signed up; six women, one guy. Three of the women were lawyers, one was an editorial assistant at *Essence,* one a homemaker. Then there was Wendy, and the guy, Frank, who worked in the town library. I taught once a week in my living room, baked Duncan Hines brownies, and charged $125 for six weeks. I designed my class based on the one I'd taken with Abby Thomas, my workshop teacher in the city. After I'd quit my job at *Essence* to work full-time on my novel, Lucy, a friend from my previous job at the *Newark Star-Ledger,* had told me about Abby's workshop. I'd gone once and was hooked. Abby had gotten us to just write, giving us short exercises. We met weekly; I went for a year and made major progress on my book. I would never have done my own workshop without Lynne. My life lesson is that people are always more than we initially think. If we give it time, we may find that we all have many more facets than we initially imagined.

8

The Slippery Slope

The late E. Lynn Harris and me at a party
after the San Francisco Book festival.
(Photo by Vicki Hughes, 1996)

SOON AFTER my novel came out, I stopped running the
workshop so that I could promote the book. *Good Hair* was, in
publishing parlance, a big book, meaning big sales, tons of media

attention, a movie deal brokered by big Hollywood agents, and a fat three-book deal. The novel centered on Alice, who was simultaneously confident and insecure about who she was, and didn't fit into any of the prescribed boxes Black women are expected to fit into. The novel spent months on bestseller lists and was optioned for a movie by Natalie Cole, the Grammy Award–winning daughter of legend Nat "King" Cole. She said she had related to the story of "otherness" as a child growing up in affluent Hancock Park in Los Angeles during the '50s and '60s, when the only other people who looked like her family did housework for White families.

For three years she renewed her option for *Good Hair*, and eventually she got a deal with Regency Films, a respected Hollywood studio, which had taken the books *A Time to Kill*, *Fight Club*, and *Marley and Me* and made them into movies. Regency had also produced *Man on Fire*, *L.A. Confidential*, and *Heat*, among many others. When my novel made it to preproduction, which meant there was a script, a director, and an executive producer attached, I began to think that maybe it would actually happen. While the film didn't get made, and the option rights were returned to me, the process got more attention for the book. I was featured in the *New York Times*, *Newsweek*, *Jet*, *People*, and on and on. That kind of attention was very unusual for a first novel, particularly in the pre-social-media days, and it catapulted me to the top of the fiction food chain. My career trajectory was going exactly as I'd planned: newspaper reporter at the *Star-Ledger* in my hometown, Newark, then a move to New York to work at *People* magazine, then a coveted job as senior editor at *Essence* magazine, and now my glamorous new life as a successful author with a royalty checks arriving regularly in the mail.

For Cliff and me, after six or seven years of living on a modest but increasing income, our financial and emotional life had become more comfortable. We could take nice vacations and buy much of what we wanted without a lot of thought. Within five years, we moved to a six-bedroom, five-and-a-half-bathroom house in Montclair, New Jersey. I was living every writer's fantasy.

And yet I can't say it was a dream come true, because when I wrote my first book, all I wanted to do was get the feelings into words. I didn't think about anyone actually reading it. I remember being on the phone with the writer Jackie Woodson while I was writing at home, feeling isolated after having left my job at *Essence*, where I had a tight-knit circle of work friends. Jackie was the best friend of my *Essence* best friend, Linda. During the course of the conversation, Jackie asked me who the audience for my novel was.

"Audience?" The thought sickened my stomach. "I never envisioned people actually reading it." I know this sounds silly, but it was true. When the book was published in September 1996, friends who had suffered through the long process of writing it with me gathered round to throw me a string of book signings. Cliff asked clients, the ones with whom he was friendly, to host parties in various parts of the country. After interviewing me to test my publicity-worthiness, the head of publicity at Simon & Schuster decided to send me on a book tour, increasing the initial four cities that Cliff and I would pay for to ten.

At my kickoff party, given by Monique and Glenn in their 1860s Italianate mansion in pre-gentrified Bed-Stuy, Brooklyn, all the Simon & Schuster heavies came out, including the then publisher and trade president, Carolyn Reidy (now president and CEO). I was pulled aside by a publishing insider, who whispered, "Carolyn never goes to book parties and certainly not outside of Manhattan." That night, after Monique introduced me, I read from my novel in public for the first time. Afterward, my editor, Dominick Anfuso, got up and announced that even though the book had just been published, it had already gone into a ninth printing. He came to the party with a three-book contract the size of a small-town phone book for me to sign. After dealing with my agent, Faith, they had offered a very nice sum.

It was so much to take in; I think my way of dealing with it all was to not. I simply packed my bags, kissed Cliff and my two-year-old Baldwin, and hit the road. It was incredibly hard to be away from her because she was so young and we'd never been apart since she was born—except for a long weekend getaway to Bermuda Cliff and I took when she was eighteen months. Mom stayed with her. I had insisted that I not be booked for signings or appearances on the weekends, so I could fly home.

The tour lasted for eight weeks, with interviews, book parties, and signings piling on as I traveled the country. It was exhilarating and grueling. My brother Marc, who had run respectably for Congress in Jacksonville, Florida, said it was just like running for political office. When my second novel, *The Itch,* was published two years later, I was also on NPR, PBS, BET, and many local TV stations. Again, I didn't process that this was highly unusual, especially for a novel—any novel. I just did what had to be done to sell books.

When I came back home to South Orange, I cuddled with my Baldwin and Cliff and caught up on sleep, blissful to be in my own bed. I also spent some time with my mom and dad before it was time to hit the road again. One of the best things about being on the road was catching up with my friends from Howard who were spread out across the country and who happily hosted *Good Hair* book parties: Jocelyn Winston gave me a party in DC; Danny, who was in Philly at the time, also hosted a book signing; and Alvin Kendall did one in Atlanta in a client's nightclub. My former South Orange neighbor Cardy Jones did a beautiful ladies' brunch in her home in Naperville, Illinois; Lynne and Lori Woolridge hosted one in our town; and my mom did a big one at the main branch of the Newark Public Library, where my eighth-grade teacher, Willie Hutcherson, introduced me. And there were others: Michelle Terry in Seattle; her mom Mercedes Terry along with Bob and Joan Austin in Houston; and Joni in Los Angeles.

Someone I'd never met, Ken Reynolds, who had a connection to my publisher, also did a book signing for *The Itch* in LA. He hired beautiful young boys dressed only in loincloths to serve all the women guests, which included actresses C. C. H. Pounder, Hattie Winston, and Denise Nicholas, who did readings from the book. All this wasn't counting the parties that were thrown by friends and colleagues at home. Nina and Ted Wells hosted a party for more than a hundred people. The support was outstanding and overwhelming, and as much as I was swept up in a wave, I never really stopped and thought about all that was happening to me.

For all the glamour of the book tour, I would discover that being a published author is not for the faint of heart. I was in San Francisco for their book festival. I was on a panel with Eric Jerome Dickey, Tavis Smiley, and Christopher John Farley—all of us a first-time authors, none of us with big audiences yet, except maybe Tavis, whose talk show was new on BET. That night Marcus Books—the oldest Black bookstore in the country—held a party for us. A bunch of big-name authors were there, including E. Lynn Harris, Iyanla Vanzant, Tina McElroy Ansa, and Michael Eric Dyson. I had invited a childhood friend from Newark who now lived in Oakland. She came and ended up knowing lots of people there and having a good time. When she was leaving, we hugged and she said in my ear, "You know they're mad at you back home." No, I hadn't known that; in fact, I had no idea what she was talking about. I made her sit down and tell me exactly what she meant.

She told me that one of our two best friends from back in the day was angry at my portrayal of the main characters' neighborhood because I'd said everyone had had plastic on the furniture except us.

I called this friend as soon as I got home and asked her about what our Oakland friend had said. She denied it, saying she didn't know what our mutual friend was talking about. Okay, I said, and dropped it.

The next year my friend turned forty. We didn't talk often but always spoke on our birthdays and would usually see each other around the holidays. I called her for her birthday, asked what her plans were to celebrate, and she said her sister had given her a birthday party. My heart sank. I hadn't been invited. Now I realized that no matter what she'd told me, she and her sister really had been angry and they had cut me out. Hurt, I got off the phone.

I wrote her an angry letter in which I accused her of being a "hater." I told her I was shocked that she hadn't invited me to her birthday party, and that it must have been because she was jealous, and how could she be, after all we'd been through? She wrote me back an equally angry letter accusing me, essentially, of having not been a very good friend because I had not supported her home-based framing business.

Years passed. I softened and assumed we would make our way back to each other. I ran into her grown son, a boy I hadn't seen since he was in elementary school. He owned a restaurant and was taking orders for dinner at the salon where I was getting my hair done. He recognized me immediately. I was happy to see him. I asked about his mom. He said she was fine. I called her a few days later, left a message. No one ever called back. Shortly after, maybe a few months, my friend Wendy called me at 5 p.m. and told me that my friend's obituary had been in the paper that day. I hadn't known she was sick and didn't know until that moment that she had died.

No one had ever bothered to tell me. I would've gone to the hospital. I would have gone to the service. I would've apologized for writing such an angry letter. But it was too late. She was gone, and I was left with a bunch of would-haves.

⁂

During Baldwin's first two years, I took care of her with help from my mom, who came three days a week to babysit. I realized then, and even more so later, what a gift it was to have had her to care for Baldwin. By the time my daughter started school, I'd written two books; both had gone from hardcover to trade to mass-market paperback; and I'd done four book tours. I was able to do all this without worry because I'd had Cliff and I'd had my mother.

I delivered my second child, all nine pounds six ounces of him, via C-section on Valentine's Day 2001. At the time, I still had two more books on my contract but decided to take off the year to be with him. When Ford was three months old, I got a call from Neil Baldwin, then executive director of the National Book Awards, asking me to be a judge. I was sitting in my dressing room, nursing Ford, cradling him with one arm and holding the phone with the other. I looked down at my luminous-skinned, brown-black, shiny-haired, giant baby boy as I ignored the warning *ping* in my stomach and said yes. It was a huge honor to be asked. It would put me in the company of boldface-name writers like Colin Harrison, Mary Morris, and Susan Richards Shreve. A chance to sit with the popular kids in the cafeteria, how could I say no?

I hung up the phone and felt simultaneously thrilled and nauseated. I called my longtime agent and friend, Faith, and told her the news. She was way more excited than I was. "Of course you should do it; it's second only to being nominated," she said. I let her enthusiasm wash over me.

Three days later, the books started arriving. I would be judging in the fiction category, and I would have to read something like two hundred books. Three boxes arrived one day, three the next; I opened one. How in the hell would I get through reading them? I was nursing Ford every two hours, twelve to fourteen hours a day, and Cliff would bottle-feed him my pumped milk at night. How could I get through one book? I decided I needed to hire someone. I didn't have any child care, not even for a few hours during the day as I'd had for Baldwin. My mom was less robust, and while she wanted to help out, she couldn't do it anymore. I needed another Dawn, the great young Jamaican woman who was a live-in nanny for our family friends the Thames and babysat Baldwin after my mom. I began the interview process, but I felt like I was in the scene from the Diane Keaton movie *Baby Boom* when she's interviewing possible babysitters. The quick cuts from interviews with one more awful than the next. In the movie, a promiscuous, corn-fed teen is shown making out on the couch with a guy whom she's picked up in the park while out with the baby; another is a cold German nurse who believes that picking up a baby is coddling. I didn't feel comfortable with any of the women I'd interviewed. When I told my mom, she said, "That's cuz you don't want no nanny."

I could always count on her to tell the truth. She was seventy-six at the time, and while her spirit was still vital, she'd begun to show signs of wear on her body. This was around the time she acknowledged that in working the night shift at the hospital for thirty-two years, along with all her civic commitments, she had simply worked too hard. She would later say to me, "I worked myself to death." She kept thinking she was going to feel better and then be able to help out with Ford. I didn't expect her to, but never said so. I just wanted her advice.

But there was another truth hiding behind my concerns about finding a nanny: I didn't feel worthy to judge those books. Many writers want to be invited to the party, but do you really want to go? I wanted to be seen, but if I couldn't show up as the best of who I was as a writer, a mother, a Black woman, then I'd rather not be on the scene.

Even though Ford was a much better sleeper than Baldwin (Dracula was a better night sleeper than Baldwin was!), I was still exhausted from caring for him. I was forty-three and didn't understand then, as I know now, that having babies is a young woman's game. Sure, you can birth a baby at forty, but in ten years you're fifty with a child in elementary school. Menopause and milk money is a road I would advise avoiding.

I looked at the boxes piling up in my foyer like Tinkertoys as I maneuvered the stroller past them to take Ford for our walk. I had opened just one book.

We strolled down Park Street to Watchung Plaza. One of the things I love most about my town is that it's a walking town. We have two big centers with shops, restaurants, and movie theaters: Upper Montclair, also called Uptown, and the strip of Bloomfield Avenue known as Downtown. There are several smaller sections of restaurants and shops like the one at Watchung, where Watchung Booksellers, one of the best independent bookstores in the country, is located. With its children's area full of big comfy chairs and books and games, Watchung Booksellers was a lifesaver for me during Ford's early years. It's a place to flop and let the baby roam, so that mothers can get out of the house and browse books and have stimulating conversation with grown-ups.

Just as we got to Watchung Plaza, heading to the bookstore, I heard a rumble of thunder, and I thought, *Shit, I don't have a raincoat, no umbrella, nothing.* The rumble was louder the second time, and I wheeled the stroller into a U-turn to head back home. The closer I got to home, the darker it got, and the louder the thunder became. Two and a half blocks from home, the clouds released a flood of hard, insistent rain. Fortuitously, I did have a plastic cover that I put over the stroller to protect Ford from getting wet. I was wearing a Gap cotton T-shirt, thin Italian jeans, and Nikes. Within a few feet, I was drenched.

When we got home, I could barely get into the foyer because it was filled with the boxes of books. I looked at the mound of them just staring up at me, summoning me to open them, to read them. *All.* I just wanted to pull off my wet clothes, put on something soft and flannel, and take my baby to bed for a nice nap. I looked at my delightful smiley boy and knew these moments would be fleeting. I picked up the phone and called Neil Baldwin and told him I had to back out. I couldn't do it. I needed to be with my son.

He was gracious, although I could tell that he was annoyed. He'd have to find someone else to step in. I'd have to wait for the new person to be chosen in order to ship all the boxes to him or her. I hung up and felt pure relief.

The year went by, and we celebrated Ford's first year with a combination African naming ceremony and christening at home. We had the same minister, Phyllis Crutchfield, who had performed Baldwin's ceremony at the Unity Church. The naming ceremony consists of putting six different tastes on the child's tongue to symbolize wishes for the child. There is salt for vigor and happiness; water because it has no enemy; sugar or honey mixed with kola nut to symbolize the duality of the sweet and sour in life; palm oil as an emollient to ease life's problems; and pepper to energize speech.

We served a huge dinner for fifty to sixty friends and family, and my big boy was passed from hug to hug. The air was thick with happiness. I knew I'd made the right decision when late in the day I looked down at him holding onto my pant leg and gazing up at me with an expression of pure adoration. He'd started walking two months earlier. I'd been there for his first attempts. I saw him let go and stand for a second before falling and I saw him get up again, hold onto the coffee table, let go, stand for several seconds, grin when he realized what he was doing, and finally to take the first few steps. I was thrilled that I hadn't missed anything, even though I would later come to question some of my choices.

9

Who Do You Think You Are?

Baldwin, Ford, and me.

IN 2003, ten days after Ford turned two, my third book, *Acting Out*, was published. Then, just before he was to start kindergarten, *Who Does She Think She Is?*, my fourth novel, hit bookstores. A year later, I still hadn't begun working on anything new. I was in full-on mommy, wife, and housekeeper mode. My writer identity was slipping away like the long summer days in late September. I'd run into people in town, and after "How're the kids? Cliff? Charlie?" came the invariable question, "Are you writing?"

They'd look at me eagerly, ready to hear about the plot line, the characters.

"No," I'd say, "I'm taking time off to be with Ford."

That was now officially my plan. To be with Ford until he was in kindergarten, one year, then *poof*, I'd find a great nanny and get back to writing bestsellers.

Ford had fallen in love with Elmo, and when he turned two I decided to hire an Elmo character to come to his birthday party. In all the huge birthday celebrations we'd had for Baldwin, I'd never once considered hiring a life-sized character or any kitschy kid stuff, but I thought Ford would be tickled. On the day of the party, when the six-foot-tall Elmo arrived, Ford screamed in terror. For the entire party, all twenty-five pounds of my boy's arms and legs were wrapped around my neck and torso with every bit of strength he had. The only other person he'd allow to take him from his monkey pose was Sister, his name for Baldwin.

I should've seen the hiring of a *Sesame Street* character as a sign that I was morphing into someone who would eventually become as constricting as Ford's grip, but I didn't. I was happy. *Then*.

My book, *Acting Out,* is the story about a woman whose husband leaves her (it appears) for another woman. The story explores how the main character loses her core self, her artist self, when she gives up her career to became a full-time mother and wife. The funny thing was, I didn't see the novel as being about me at all. After all, I was still writing full-time. I hadn't yet fallen into the domestic dungeon.

I hired our first au pair, Gosia, who was from Poland, when Ford was two. She'd come to New Jersey to work for another family who, after a few weeks, had sent her back to the agency because she was "too quiet." The Montclair coordinator, Larissa, with whom I'd been in touch, mentioned Gosia and asked if I wanted to meet her. Larissa brought Gosia over, and after we'd sat and talked for an hour and the kids met her, I decided to give her a try. She turned out to be perfect: a hard worker, loving to the kids, especially to Ford, who adored her. Her easygoing, quiet way was a plus in my mind. She had only a one-year visa and after her year was over, she decided to extend it and stay on with us. All was well for a while. But a few months later, she came to me and said she needed to talk—unusual, because Gosia didn't talk much. She stood in the kitchen against the counter in front of the toaster and her body started to shake.

"What? What's the matter?" I asked, concerned that a family member was sick or that she was.

Even though she'd worked prodigiously on her English and had been successful, her accent was still very heavy. Eventually I made out that she was leaving us.

Another family in town, who undoubtedly had heard about how great she was, had poached her. Gosia explained through sobs that she didn't want to leave, but she couldn't turn down their gigantic cash offer. She was supporting her parents back in Poland, where the unemployment rate, she said, was 25 percent. I didn't even attempt to counteroffer when she told me that the family had a private jet.

After Gosia left, I had two more years of au pairs, both from Germany. They were very good, but after their time was up, I decided I wanted the kids to be cared for by someone of color and who spoke Spanish. Not that I hadn't been comfortable having European nannies. They didn't have a lot of the race baggage and I had also considered that having European Whites working for us sent an unspoken message to my kids that Black people aren't always the ones doing the caregiving.

Our next au pair was a brown Spanish speaker from Lima, Peru. She was sweet and cute, and her English was excellent. In order to be an au pair, facility with English has to be above proficient. What I didn't realize was that, because of the huge caste divide in Latin America, only the upper caste is fluent in other languages. It turned out that our girl was a princess: Her family had several homes, horses, and servants. She had never made a bed or picked up after herself. She had never operated a washing machine and didn't understand that being an au pair involved more than playing with children, that it also meant cleaning up after them, helping with homework, cooking, doing their laundry.

After two weeks, which included teaching her how to operate a dishwasher, washer, and dryer, and even how to drive (she'd had a license but had never had to use it, because her father had provided her with a car and driver). When she crashed the car into the garage, we sent her back to the agency, and they sent her back home. The timing worked out fine, since I'd recently completed my fourth contracted book and all the book tour promotions. It was time to get out of the au pair business. Instead, I hired Rose, a happy, positive, older woman whose best friend, Jean, was the longtime nanny of one of Baldwin's preschool friends. The part-time situation was great. Rose was like an Auntie Mame to my kids. She'd dance and sing songs from her home in Jamaica. She cooked like a dream, but as Ford got older and more active, Rose got older and less active. She had a hard time keeping up with him, and eventually told me that she'd have to leave but would stay on until I could find someone.

Then she called in sick, and one day turned to a week, then two. Her heart began to fail quickly. During the third week she went to the emergency room for chest pains and passed away. I didn't find out until Jean called me with the news. I'd been prepared to lose

Rose as a nanny, but not her complete presence. I silently mourned her passing and couldn't bring myself to tell Ford what had happened to her. For a while, whenever I would head up the hill to my house after my walk in Brookdale Park, I'd remember the smell of curry that would let me know Rose was at my stove, singing and taking and care of not just Ford, but all of us.

Thus began my full-time stay-at-home phase. In the beginning, I loved being able to meet Ford's school bus every day. We would walk hand in hand down our block, but by the time he was a third grader, he stopped holding my hand. I remember watching him run ahead one day, his thin, longs legs in skinny jeans, leaping over slabs of slate, and I was filled with something so tender and sweet it was a breathing cliché.

I'm an accidental housewife, I thought.

I used to have a career, first as a magazine editor and then as a bestselling novelist. Now this. But it's not permanent, I told myself, *and besides, look at how cute my son is. That smile he gives me as he gets off the bus is so bright that even the jaded bus attendant breaks into a huge grin.* I knew how lucky I was to have the freedom to be there when he got home. I decided to continue channeling Donna Reed.

I began to "do lunch," something I'd never allowed my previous writer self to do because I was losing valuable writing time. I went shopping—lots of that. I tried new recipes; I entertained. It was okay. Ford was now in first grade, and Baldwin was in the seventh. I was hearing the refrain from other stay-at-homes: "When they're in middle school, that's really when you need to be there."

While waiting at Ford's biweekly tae kwon do lesson, I became pals with a few mommies. The ones whose hair and clothes were too pulled together, I didn't bother talking to, except for my Puerto Rican girl, Vanessa, who was always turned out with the newest, most coveted designer bags and jewelry. I also became friendly with Tory, a blond former college lacrosse player. Tory had quit her job at iVillage after having two kids and moving to the burbs. After the third one was born, she said that she had to get back to work. She admitted that she was losing her mind being home all day. Her frankness hit me in the gut. A few weeks later, Tory met a woman, Jane, at a dinner party, and they decided to open a women's shoe store. Tory Janes stocked cool, comfortable shoes for moms that were not Rockports or Tevas, just hip platforms, heels, clogs, and boots. The store quickly became a success. I was happy for Tory but secretly jealous. I probably already knew at a visceral level that the domestic rapture wouldn't last.

All the same, I was still feeling good. We'd gotten a puppy for Baldwin, whom we named Charlie, and every day, I would walk

Family, 2004.

Ford and Charlie to school. I was consistently happier than I could ever recall being. I had accomplished my list: married a great partner, check; became a novelist, check; had my first child, a girl that I'd wanted with my whole being, check. Then came this lovely bonus baby boy at forty-three (without any fertility support); and for the first time in twenty years I didn't have a deadline hanging over my head. I had given myself until Ford started kindergarten. I figured after that year was over, Ford would be well settled in school and I'd find a Mabel Perkins—that would be a Black Mary Poppins—to help with the kids and the housework for twenty-five hours a week while I got back to writing bestselling novels. Right? Wrong.

No word of mouth, no agency, no nanny websites, newspaper ads, prayer (my mother's suggestion) yielded Mabel. When a nanny didn't materialize, I took that as a sign that I was to stay at home a little longer. I was enjoying it. I told myself that I should give it more time, that my son needed me; Baldwin, who was entering the morass of middle school, needed me. I would rise to the occasion. I would become an über-stay-at-home mom. I ran an after-school writing class at Baldwin's school; I was the head of the PTA T-shirt committee (of one). At my friend Patti's urging, I chaired the Montclair Art Museum gala twice, with her as my wingman; I was a group chair in Jack and Jill. I became friends with women whose lives revolved around their children, the ones who know every child her child knows; the ones who run their children's student council presidential campaigns; the ones who know the details of the elementary-school grading system; the ones who know, by Christmastime, what extracurricular activities their kids will be doing during the summer. These are the mothers who are praised by the principal and the teachers because they are at the school, helping, raising money, giving teachers Staples gift cards. Other mothers listen when they speak. They run school fundraisers like Art in the Park and Green Eggs and Ham and Fun Day. They seemed satisfied. Among them, I felt like a fraud. Baldwin couldn't have cared less that I was working at her school, while Ford wanted me there as often as the doors opened. This kind of mania of enrichment was not what I'd envisioned when I decided to step off for a minute to be with them. I wanted to show up for them, and I did, but more and more often it was at the expense of myself.

As time went on, the housewife hat became harder to wear than I'd anticipated. I tried hard to put on a good face, even though inside I had to fight daily the feeling of being nobody and nothing: a loser. I'm in no way saying that stay-at-home moms don't work hard; it's an incredible challenge raising kids and running a house. But for me, I wasn't cut out for the job.

I went to a birthday party with Ford for one of his friends from nursery school. It was held at Bradford Bath and Tennis Club. The club sat on a hill, with the main pool in the center of gorgeous, manicured rolling lawn, a pergola swathed with wisteria giving the place a Gatsbyesque feeling while providing shade for parents and toddlers in the kiddie pool. There were New York City views from the upper-level adult pool; there was also a larger family pool and a small one for babies and toddlers. The tennis courts required white attire only (no trim), and they were surrounded by white wooden benches and white planters filled with annuals. The club was just beautiful. After spending the afternoon there, I decided to join. I was going to be one of those moms who hung out at the pool all day, looking peaceful and fit.

The reality was that I never could bring myself to actually sign up for tennis lessons, although I did lug Ford in for tennis and swim lessons. But the half hour he was in the pool was almost less time than it took me to park the car and put sunblock on him. The attempt to force myself into some kind of fantasy version of myself merely cost me a lot of aggravation and self-criticism for not going there more often. I'd fooled myself into believing that if I paid a lot of money and just showed up there, I could seem normal, and then I'd become that. We probably went a total of ten times during the three years we were members—I think Cliff was there twice. I figure at the cost of the membership, it amounted to about three hundred dollars a swim. I knew a few people by name and plenty by face, some who actually talked to me. From the others I heard far too often: "Are you a member here?"

"Why don't you ever come?" the friendlier ones would ask, catching a glimpse of me on one of my rare visits.

It was a question I asked myself often, but I just said, "I don't know." The truth was too embarrassing to admit: That I would never be one of those mommies who pack up the cooler with just the right lunch and snacks and wipes and change of clothes for the kids, who smile beatifically at their charges, and chat away animatedly with other mommies, feeling hopelessly fulfilled. The one

At Ford's second birthday party with Baldwin and niece Sumayyah.

time that I did remember to pack all the right stuff, Ford, his best friend Ryan, and I were going to stay till evening for family movie night on the lawn, with popcorn provided in old-fashioned paper containers. I thought it might be the start of a lovely tradition, but that day it rained so hard that we got wet even as we tried to wait out the storm on the screened-in snack bar porch. And movie night was canceled.

10

"This Created Some Schizophrenia"

SOON AFTER moving to Montclair, I had gone to our local bookseller, Margot Sage-EL, and told her that I desperately needed to meet other women novelists who were also mothers. I had been creatively isolated when we lived in South Orange, and I didn't want to repeat that. She immediately said, "You need to meet Christina Baker Kline." Margo gave me Christina's number, I called her right away, and she came over the next day, coffee in hand and six months pregnant. We sat on my living room couch and talked for hours, like old friends. I even asked her why she was having another baby; she had two sons, the older one the same age as Baldwin. Christina didn't flinch at my bluntness. She understood that the question had been asked only in relation to her being a working writer, a novelist no less, and the difficulty involved in also being a mother. She laughed at my question, saying that she had three sisters and was used to big families. Later, I'd realize that she was the energizer organizer. She introduced me to another author/mother, Alice Elliott Dark, and we three started meeting once a week. Pamela Redmond Satran joined our group a few years later.

For six years, we'd meet at Starbucks or Bluestone Coffee Co., have breakfast—sometimes it was lunch; occasionally it would be wine in the early evenings—and we'd talk about everything having to do with writing and life. After I stopped publishing regularly in 2004, they became my only contact with my writer self, and by 2006, when my last book came out, I'd sit there, not having anything to say about what I was working on, my writing routine, or my characters, but for a while the discussions were my life support. I lunged like a bearcat at every piece of publishing gossip or discussion of their writing process that they cared to share.

When we had started our weekly gatherings, I'd published the most novels and had gotten a lot of acclaim. Alice had had her second short-story collection, *In the Gloaming,* made into a movie starring Glenn Close. But by this point, 2007, Pam, who had already published a hugely successful series of baby-name books, had added two novels, *The Man I Should Have Married* and *Younger* (just made into a TV series). Christina had published two novels, *Sweet Water* and *Desire Lines,* and two anthologies, plus a nonfiction book with her mom. Christina, who'd had her own four-year stint in the mommy hole, was up and running again with her third novel, *The Way Life Should Be.* A fourth one had already sold, and she had a teaching fellowship at Fordham.

Several years later, Christina's most recent novel, *Orphan Train,* would hold steady on the *New York Times* bestseller list for over a year, at times hitting number one. Pam went on to publish seven more books, and Alice eventually got a tenure-track writing professor gig at Rutgers.

Just as I was about to start wallowing in self-pity at being unproductive, a *New York Times* editor reached out to me through Alice and asked me to write an essay about mothering, suburban life, really anything I wanted to write about. I jumped at the chance. I decided to write about what was burning a hole in my consciousness at the time: all the permutations around deciding between public and private middle school for Baldwin. I'd considered sending her to a private middle school and then bringing her back to town for public high school. This was part of my article:

Images of the Pingry School in Martinsville, the Rolls-Royce of educational institutions, danced in our heads as my husband, Cliff, and I headed home from a meeting with the admissions director and alumni. The school was indeed impressive, but the travel time, a good hour each way, was just too much for an 11-year-old to handle every day.

Then I spoke with the parents of students at Kent Place in Summit, a bucolic all-girls' school that Baldwin refused even to consider . . . because it was all girl. (She also said that she could go there for high school—a fib. We later realized that she had no intention of going there.) Cliff had explored Newark Academy's 68-acre campus in Livingston a while ago, and I revisited it online, again weighing the pros of independent schools (smaller classes, more individualized attention and fabulous-looking facilities) and the cons (elitist attitudes of some children and more than $20,000 in tuition added to property taxes that are already enough for a private school education) . . .

I would wake Cliff in the middle of the night with all kinds of scenarios, many of them products of being a black parent in suburbia. If we sent our daughter to public school, suppose the girls were mean, suppose she had to start choosing her friends based on race and not common interests, suppose some eighth-grade boy turned her head. The same things could happen in private school, of course, plus she would be around youngsters with so much money she could end up feeling as if she were underprivileged. Suppose she felt she had to choose to sit at the black table at lunchtime or, worse, what if she was a minority of one in some of the private-school classes and felt she must wave the race flag full time.

Now I was getting to the guts of my insanity. I was tortured in the Newark public school I attended, which was practically all black; the misery began in sixth grade, and it was downhill from there. I was reliving my demons—the taunts of "Who do you think you are?" "You think you cute?" and my personal favorite, given the junior revolutionary that I was, "You think you white?" I worry that things are neither worse nor better, that they have probably, pathetically, stayed the same . . .

But as a black parent I have an extra job. Not only did I have to help Baldwin navigate her class work, always do her best and all that, but I've also got to teach her that when three black boys act out in class, it's not because they're black . . .

I have to teach my girl and my little guy, who just started kindergarten, to be proud of their heritage. I have to encourage them to immerse themselves in black history, both in and out of the classroom, so they understand why some history books talk about enslaved people as if they were born that way—without a culture and centuries-old traditions. I have to teach, as so many of my peers were taught, that no one is better than you and you aren't better than anyone. As my old pal, the director

George C. Wolfe said of his Kentucky childhood, "This created some schizophrenia."

I had also looked at Montclair Kimberley Academy without Cliff, because we'd already toured it together when Baldwin was entering pre-K. During the wrap-up with the head of the elementary school, he'd raised his hand and asked her what extras the school offers children at $18,000 a year. The principal paused, then said, "No hitting, no biting, and no spitting." Cliff was done with MKA after that.

After talking with parents whom we respected whose kids had gone through the public middle school we were slated for, Glenfield, Cliff, Baldwin, and I decided that she would get a great all-around education there. I had many feelings and opinions on the topic, most of it centering on socioeconomic background. I had to get real honest with myself about who I was and what I wanted for my daughter. I believe when the education is good, public is best. I think education should be democratic, and I think that the public process educates the whole child, and that when they go to school with a variety of kids from a variety of racial, economic, and familial backgrounds, kids become better citizens of the world. They understand that some kids have two moms or two dads or not enough money to afford a cell phone or have single parents or spend winter weekends at ski houses. Private schools are a select group of kids from families with money and/or social-status awareness. Many parents do send their kids to private school for the education, period. And if I'm completely honest, the resources are much better and, depending on the school, the education is deeper. But some parents do it simply because they want their kids to socialize with kids from more privileged backgrounds—and not with poor kids.

Glenfield was no panacea, nor was it a picnic. Baldwin did end up having all White friends, and she did get asked, "Why all your friends White?" by one or two Black girls. She answered with aplomb: "Why are you in my business?"

Her response pretty much shut that down. One day in eighth grade, while watching a film, sitting on the floor in an elective at the end of the school year, a girl said to Baldwin, "So y'all like mad rich, huh?" Rich is obviously relative, and this kind of misperception of us was real to kids who were getting free lunch. I imagined Baldwin answered that question with her version of *Girl, please*. It was an issue I knew would be raised as we made the decision to go to into public school. In a large part, Black parents who are middle- or upper-income in our area tend to send their kids to private school, so a Black kid with two parents and an above-median income could be a double minority in public school.

One thing I consciously did in order for Baldwin and some of her Black classmates to have a more natural way to get to know each other was always provide a ride. When she was playing middle school lacrosse, there was a girl, Lakisha,* on the team. She lived in the low-income apartments on the other side of town, miles away from the field. The coaches had asked her to be on the team because she was an amazing lacrosse player, but because her mother worked nights, she could never drive her daughter to and from practice. The girl would walk about five miles to get there.

The second day of practice, Baldwin asked me if I could give Lakisha a ride home. Every day, I happily drove her home, even though it was in the opposite direction of our house. The three of us would talk on the ride. She was a great girl, with a funny, outgoing personality. As a result of her getting to know Baldwin, and probably as important, her mom, Lakisha would report back to her friends at school that, "Honestly, Baldwin is cool."

In a similar way, the *New York Times* piece put me in the spotlight in my town among people who hadn't read my novels or even known that I was a writer. I had some "burb cred," and that kept me going for a time because the piece was read, discussed, and debated all over town: public school people loved it, while a few parents at the local private school hated it and vehemently disagreed with me, and let me know it. Black women from around the Northeast told me they'd sent the piece to friends across the country. Some said that they kept it posted on a bulletin board. This was the stimulation I needed, and it was cathartic.

After a while, though, I wasn't feeling fine. I started to dread the now bimonthly get-togethers with my writing women's circle. I kept telling them that I felt like a fraud being there, since I had no work to talk about, but they wanted me to come anyway; we'd become good friends. But I didn't like how I felt, like I was a housewife first and an author second, as if my work had become a hobby, not my primary occupation.

Even though they welcomed me and wanted me to stay, by the end of the year I'd stopped meeting with our group. I'd gotten tired of hearing myself complain about not writing and not being able to figure out why. I was already deep in the domestic dungeon, but I didn't actually know it.

11

I Could Sell Shoes

JANE, THE other half of Tory Janes, and I had gotten to be friendly at a step-funk-sculpt class taught by a woman who at the time was the workout goddess of Montclair. She had lost more than two hundred of her former four hundred pounds through exercise. One day, while we were waiting for her class to begin—you had to be there early to get a spot—Jane and I were talking about how well the shoe store was doing and the fact that they needed to hire more people.

"I'll work there," I said.

Jane looked at me. "You're kidding."

"No, really. I need something to do."

Jane was skeptical.

"Well, we need someone who can work around three."

She figured that would deter me.

"I can do it then."

"Don't you have to do pickup?"

"Ford goes to aftercare."

I'd put Ford in aftercare run by the Y three days a week. It was generally for kids whose parents worked full-time. Enrolling him there had been one of my many attempts to force myself back into a regular writing schedule.

"I'm serious," I said. "I need a job. I need to do something."

"Okay, email me the hours you're available."

After sweating it out in Angel's class, I sat in the lobby of the sports club, downing water and talking with Joy Kay, a Jack and Jill cohort. We complained about how hard mothering was, the constant monitoring of homework, driving to sports and tutoring, all of it. We agreed it wore us down, that it could sometimes be soul depleting. I then shared with her that I'd decided to work at Jane's shoe store.

"What?"

I thought she hadn't heard me. I repeated my plan.

"You can't work in a shoe store. You're a writer. Why aren't you writing?"

"My brain is spent," I whined. "I just don't have the focus anymore. I'm perimenopausal. I'm renovating the basement and picking out all these paint colors and carpet and tile. It's all a distraction."

"If I can write grant proposals, you can get your work done," Joy said. "Once the renovations are over, you can get back to it. Take your laptop to Starbucks, or even better, to Panera, like everybody else."

Joy and I walked out of the sports club with my trainer Lisa and gym pal Sarah. Lisa pointed out that working in the shoe store would really be working.

"You're gonna have to do what they tell you to do and deal with customers, and not all of 'em are gonna be nice or considerate."

I hadn't played out the details of the actual work. I'd just pictured myself putting on makeup and clothes that weren't yoga pants.

"It's not going to be like now, where you go there and just hang out."

Lisa was right and so was Joy. I was going to have to show up at a certain time and deal with all the things one has to do when one has a minimum-wage job. I hadn't had one of those decades. I'd even forgotten what it was like to have a boss. I'd worked in magazines and newspapers, where one doesn't really punch a clock but you still must answer for your time. I had to admit that I loved my free days. Sometimes after walking the dog with a group of people with whom I'd become friendly, we'd go to breakfast. Sometimes I'd go to Target, which never failed to lift my mood. Sometimes my friend Hillary and I would go to the diner for a Greek salad, or I'd go to the Short Hills Mall with Liz. But then I'd feel guilty because I wasn't doing enough after I dropped the kids off at school, walked the dog, went to the gym, shopped for dinner, cooked dinner, and helped my son with his homework.

I went to the gym five days a week. I did this for two reasons: I was forty-nine and wanted to be fit and not look fifty, and I was trying to keep those endorphins up—keep that creeping depression away. Not in that order. I looked like I had it together. I managed to keep it together enough to shower, cook a meal or two, and spend lots of time searching for just the right remedy to make myself feel better. One day I had downed some kind açaí berry health drink, which tasted like dirt, that my trainer gave me promising all around well-being. Maybe it gave other people a sense of sublimity, but me, I couldn't stop scratching. The only thing that came out of drinking the açaí berry was hives, which kept me from the yoga class that I love.

Maybe, I thought for the umpteenth time, I just needed to hire help—someone to shop, cook, pick up the kids, help with the homework so that I could be in my office from the time I dropped them at school until shortly before dinner and I could write another book. I wanted that helper to be loving, smart, and know how to take charge without being told what to do, and I wanted my kids to really like her, but not too much. I felt guilty for wanting this, for not being able to survive on four hours' sleep, for not being able to "do it all" like my mother.

I remembered a day, years before, when my mom was leaving for the evening after babysitting Baldwin so I could finish the edits on my first book, *Good Hair*. I was incredibly grateful then, and now I know for sure that finishing my first novel, indeed my first two books, would've been a lot more difficult without her help. Cliff and I didn't have enough money to hire anyone, and I was way too nervous to leave my child in the hands of a stranger. On this day, I'd walked my mother out the back door to the deck. Mom was standing on the top step on her way out. I was holding Baldwin, gently nudging my nose against her chubby cheek, feeling that warm, emotional bubble rise inside me.

"I just love her so much," I said.

My mother looked at me and said, "The way you feel about her is how I feel about you."

I can still see her, holding on to the banister, walking down the stairs of the weather-beaten wooden deck. I can still feel how her comment stopped my heart.

12

Daddy

Mom and Dad with one of his shipmates (*center*), 1989.

SEVERAL YEARS after I married Cliff, my dad gave a speech at Mount Teman A.M.E. Church after being named Father of the Church. The title was an acknowledgment of his service. I can't recall ever seeing my dad give a speech. It was always my mother. But on this Sunday, Matthew Little walked up to the altar and began with the words:

"I am a survivor."

The church became hushed as my dad, in a strong, confident voice, went on to tell what it was like growing up in segregated Anderson, South Carolina, and of the horrors to which he had been a witness. "Black people were still being lynched as a regular occurrence," he told the congregation, "and after a hanging, White people would sell off pieces of that rope as souvenirs." There were also the daily insults like White men referring to grown Black men as "boy."

"That's probably why I don't talk much today, 'cause I just didn't want to hear that kind of talk. I just keep my mouth shut."

While my dad was describing things that had happened to him more than fifty years ago, his tone of voice and the expression on his face let us know that the memories were as fresh for him as if they had been yesterday. His anger was contained yet palpable. My brothers and I looked at each other. I was in my late thirties; they were in their midforties. We were all stunned by these stories that we were hearing for the first time. After the speech we asked Daddy why he'd never told us about his childhood. He said, "Because I didn't want to teach you all to hate."

Even before the dementia took hold of his mind, Daddy didn't say much unless he was talking about being in the war. We'd heard him tell about the USS *Franklin,* the aircraft carrier he was stationed on, which had been attacked by Japanese warplanes; how the hull had been filled with fire and black smoke, and he'd made his way up the stairs from the lower level, where the Blacks were posted, to the deck, grabbed a mounted heavy machine gun, and started shooting enemy planes. He would talk about how many men were killed that day: twenty-three hundred men. The seven hundred who survived called themselves the 700 Club long before Pat Robertson took the name for his Christian television show. Daddy recalled how he got a basic accommodation medal and the captain, who had stood right next my dad as they fired into enemy airspace, got a Purple Heart. He never used the word "unfair," but it was certainly implied; the sense of that particular injustice was always on his face whenever he spoke of it.

In the town where my dad grew up, Starr County, now incorporated into the city of Anderson, South Carolina, my father's family was among the lucky ones. They owned twenty-five acres of land, which had been inherited by my great-grandmother. Her daughter, my paternal grandmother, Elease Vandiver, and each of her four siblings had five acres, where they lived with their families. My paternal grandfather, Hallie Little, was a farmer who had a taxi business and other entrepreneurial ventures. Like many Black folks at the time, the Vandivers lived off their land. Back then, Black people literally built their own schools, churches, businesses, and hospitals and staffed them with Black doctors and nurses, teachers, ministers, and shopkeepers. They were self-sufficient. But none of that shielded them from the virulent racism at the time.

When my dad went back home after WWII, he found out his mother had died. He wasn't notified while he was in the service. His father died the year after. Both were in their early forties. Like most Black men who served, my dad believed being a soldier in his country's war would gain him a degree of respect and freedom, but he was consistently turned down for jobs when he went back to Anderson. Black men, some in their uniforms, were still being lynched and sometimes castrated. They were still being passed over, still not being treated like American citizens. After the war my dad went back to finish high school—he'd had to leave school when he was drafted to join the navy. He wanted to go to college and play football at Clemson. He applied and was accepted, but upon their learning that he was a "Negra," he was told he wouldn't be able to go to school there. He'd have to attend one of the "colored colleges."

I never got to ask my dad why he didn't do that. What I did learn was that he had wanted to stay in Anderson, even with all degradation; he was a son of the South. Eventually it became clear that he'd have to leave home to find a job with decent pay. I assume that, unlike my mother's family, he would not do field work. He moved north, to Newark, where his aunts Lisher and Doll and his uncle TB had already moved. At the beginning of the twentieth century, 90 percent of all African Americans were living in the South. Between 1915 and 1970, six million Black Americans were part of the Great Migration out of there to the North, Midwest, and West Coast.

After working as a truck driver delivering liquor and fruit, and assorted other jobs, my father got hired at General Motors, a premium job in those days. He began his twenty-five years there on the assembly line at the GM plant in Linden, New Jersey. Eventually he was promoted to materials coordinator. Over his years there, the company often offered to promote him to foreman, but Daddy turned them down each time. Our parents never talked to us about their actual work. We'd hear things about the people they worked with, but that was about it.

I went to Howard with a lot of kids from Detroit whose fathers also worked in the car factories, and a lot of them had been foremen. Once a friend from Detroit who was in law school, and whose father was a lawyer, asked me what my dad did for a living. I told him he worked at GM. He assumed Dad was a foreman. I let the assumption stand. I was trying to impress this guy, even though I never could decide whether I actually liked him, or liked that he was a popular guy and he liked me. The next time I was home from college, I asked my dad why he never accepted a promotion to foreman. He told me that he was a proud member of the UAW (United Auto Workers) union and that being a foreman would have required that he leave the union. Even worse, he said, it was like being an overseer: "I didn't want any part of that."

Like my dad, I didn't want to burden my kids with any feeling of what they couldn't do or be because of racism. What I wanted most for my children was what I felt I got from my parents and from my Black neighborhood: to be free to love and accept all of my Black self. Being surrounded by people who looked like me gave me a solidity that I used to take for granted. I never had my nose pressed against the glass of the house of White folks, believing that "the White man's ice is colder." In my formerly all-Jewish Weequahic neighborhood, everybody was Black except some of my teachers. Most of them were Jewish, and in those days they considered themselves Jews first, Whites second. There was still an allegiance over our shared history of persecution. Toward the end of the Civil Rights movement and with United Nations ambassador Andrew Young's support of the Palestinian cause, the once symbiotic relationship between Blacks and Jews was fractured, but when I was growing up, that hadn't happened yet.

My kids weren't growing up in a segregated neighborhood like mine; rather, we moved to our town because it had a healthy mix

Ford and Baldwin watching Black Santa dance.

of all kinds of people. But it quickly became clear that while there was a rainbow of colors, sexual orientations, and economics, the area was still primarily affluent and White, and there was still a subtle (and sometimes not so) "ice is colder" vibe. Cliff and I fought against that vigorously. But rather than doing a lot of talking to our kids, we showed. We always took them to Black pediatricians and dentists. Baldwin was allowed only Black or Brown dolls, as well as a few Asian-looking ones.

The year after Baldwin was born, the beautifully rendered American Girl dolls were created. Each doll represented a part of American history and was sold with a book chronicling that doll's story. There were dolls that represented the Colonial and Revolutionary periods, slavery, the Depression, WWII, women's rights, and so on. Baldwin got Addy, whose story was that she was born into slavery but escaped with her mother and moved to Philadelphia, where she lived as a free person. The doll was a gift for her first birthday from my college friend Lynne Scott Jackson. When Kaya, the American Indian, came out, we bought her that one and later added on Josefina, who was Mexican but living in New Mexico. When Baldwin was in the third grade, a new doll was introduced, a blonde surfer name Kailey. The introduction of a new American Girl was a very big deal to this demographic of eight-year-old girl.

Because Baldwin and her friends were so into American Girl dolls, Baldwin and I decided to host a doll tea party and each of her friends would bring their American Girl doll. We did it on a Friday after school. They all got dressed up, and we had tea and sandwiches and juice and cupcakes. Even Ford was there, dressed in a sports jacket. A discussion of who was going get Kailey followed. Two of the girls, Allie and Nora, who were White, were definitely getting Kailey. Two who were Black, Daria and Indu, weren't sure, and Baldwin was sure she was not getting her.

"My mom doesn't let me play with White dolls," Baldwin said.

"Why not?" Allie asked, innocently brushing her doll's hair.

Baldwin said, "'Cuz my mom won't let me. She wants me to play with dolls that look like me."

"Well, your dad is White," Allie said.

Baldwin looked at her and thought for a moment and laughed. "No, he's not."

At that, as children do, Allie said, "Oh," and the playdate continued.

In trying to give our kids a strong sense of their identity, we have often taken stances that might seem harsh. The culture shows them in too many ways that they don't count as much, that they don't matter as much, that there's something aberrant about being Black. My choices were designed to fight against that, to build them up, to help them see themselves positively, more accurately. Baldwin didn't ever voice anything about Cliff's light skin color, or her own, because we didn't discuss it. We didn't discuss it because I believe when you do, you give those distinctions power, and I didn't want that to be a part of their thinking. That was then. Now, with the rap culture, and *all* culture, references such as light-skinned, big lips, good hair are everywhere, and my kids throw around that stuff, much to my dismay.

I've also gone against common wisdom in the Black world: I don't believe in teaching our kids that they have to be twice as good to get half the credit that White people do, although, too often, it's true. I've always thought that passing on that thinking could create another form of mental slavery. One that says, the world is hostile and stacked against you and you better be a Super Nig to survive. Instead, I focused on my kids' emotional lives, believing, as my mother did, that loving them hard and accepting who they were would shore them up. I tried to teach them about the roots of their people, stolen from Africa, and about being enslaved, not "slaves." I learned early in my mothering journey that I have to teach them these things in a way that's accessible and interesting, such as pointing out our people's contribution to the larger contemporary culture.

Whenever "Respect" would come on the radio, I'd ask them, "Who is the Queen of Soul?" From their car seats they'd recite, "Aretha Franklin." Without this, they'd think the answer was Adele. I let them see her and all the other British and American singers give all praise to Aretha. I did the same thing with the Godfather of Soul, James Brown. And when Ford was little, I found a book in our wonderful local bookstore about the Beatles and the Rolling Stones and how they acknowledged that they came to America to meet their idols, Muddy Waters, Howlin' Wolf, and Chuck Berry, whose music they readily admit that they copied. Cliff always pointed out Black inventors: Garrett Morgan, who invented the traffic light; Benjamin Banneker, who took over the architectural design of Washington, DC; and Lewis Howard Latimer, who improved the lightbulb. I didn't stress, or even say, "White" or "Black" as an identifier around my children when they were young. I'm not sure why I did this, but I knew they'd get acquainted with this country's race obsession soon enough. As it happened, Ford found out about it with much more force than Baldwin did.

13

Betrayed

WHEN FORD was in preschool, his closest friend was an alpha male we'll just call J. Once there was some discussion about who the leader of his preschool group would be. According to one of his teachers, Ford was the class favorite.

"It's as if they can't start until Ford gets here in the morning," she had said.

I'd witnessed the elated cheers myself when dropping him off.

"Ford's here! Ford's here!"

I remember him in his little navy-blue quilted jacket, his little face showing no emotion. Just being his cool, slightly introverted self, which at fourteen, he still is. During the group discussion, J told Ford that he couldn't be the leader because he didn't have flat hair. Ford came home and told me this, and while he wasn't upset, I could tell it was something he didn't understand. I explained what J had meant by flat hair, and assured him that his classmate was completely mistaken. Two years later, when Barack Obama was elected

Ford in his lion costume, with Cliff.

president, my son said to me: "He's the leader of the country and he doesn't have flat hair."

"Yup, he has hair just like yours."

I assumed that by then he knew that Black people come with all kinds of hair textures and in all skin shades. Cliff and Baldwin are lighter-skinned, while Ford and I are darker-skinned, but I had never seen the purpose of introducing a discussion about our family's range of complexions. Colorism is a poison that continues to hold Black folks shackled. If there were a reason it came up, we'd discuss it, although the first time I heard sixth grader Baldwin saying something about being light-skinned, as if it advantaged her in some way, I went ballistic. Her godmother, Joni, who was visiting from California at the time, had the same reaction but was able to explain calmly to Baldwin the history of such delineation and how that kind of thinking was designed to divide and conquer.

Skin color hadn't been discussed in my family of origin, either. I didn't really notice difference in complexion until I was almost out of high school.

The kids knew that Cliff was Black; at least Baldwin knew that. Ford . . . ?

He was now in the fourth grade and they were learning about slavery. We keep a wall of pictures of ancestors in our family room. The pictures have been there as long as we've been in our house, fifteen years. Ford, who was nine at the time, had never seemed to notice the pictures, much less ask questions about them. One day I found him kneeling on the couch, which sits below the area where the photos hang, to get a closer look. He started asking questions about his grandparents, wanting to know if Grandma, my deep pecan–colored mother, had been a slave.

"No, sweetie, Grandma wasn't enslaved, she's not that old. When did President Lincoln sign the Emancipation Proclamation?"

He hunched and then beamed.

"1865."

"So let's do the math."

We wrote it down and subtracted the year my mother was born, 1925, from 1865. "So how long had slavery been over when she was born?"

"Sixty years."

I pointed to a photo of my maternal great-aunt Estelle, my mother's aunt, who lived healthily till a month shy of her one-hundredth birthday and died only because she decided to stop eating. I had once gone with my mother to visit her aunt, whom she hadn't seen since the family had moved north when my mother was nine or ten. My grandmother had died before I was born, so I was anxious to meet her sister. I interviewed her and audiotaped our conversation.

"What was it like growing up for you?" I asked her.

Her voice was scratchy with age, but her mind was sharp as a hatpin.

"Well, for the chaps, that's children, we had to work too," she told me. "But I went to school." Lots of Black children, she reminded me, either didn't go to school at all or had to miss during cotton season so they could work in the fields. "Our mama died when we was young and our father married Geneva. She was so mean to us. Eighty years later, her hurt still visible. When she had her own daughter, she got to have patent-leather shoes, and we had to go barefoot. I'll never forget that."

When I asked her questions about picking cotton, she seemed insulted.

"I ain't picked no cotton. I ain't that old." (Although there were people her age and way younger who had.)

"We slept on a mattress made outta straw. We pumped our water. I don't know what you wanna know. It was just life. We was just livin' life: church, work, school, cooking, all that. There was a outhouse. I be scared to death to go out there at night, so we'd keep a slop jar by the bed." She had laughed at the memory of that.

Ford moved on to the pictures of Cliff's family. Most of them look racially ambiguous. Both of his paternal grandparents were biracial. Cliff's paternal great-grandparents met in Hell's Kitchen in New York. He was a Black veteran of the Civil War and she was a German immigrant named Esther Stein. Their daughter Emily was Cliff's paternal grandmother. His paternal grandfather, the first Clifford, was the only child of a Black woman named Caledonia and an unknown White man. From what we know, she was a fierce woman who had moved with her son to New York from Macon, Georgia.

I looked at Ford's face and could tell he was confused.

I went on to explain that, long ago, some of these unions between Black women and White men were why Black people had such a range of colors. I thought he was too young to explain that often these "relationships" weren't consensual.

"So if you were born in slavery and you had a White father, couldn't he take you out of slavery? If you had a White father like Daddy?"

I laughed, mostly nervous laughter, because until that moment I'd had no idea that Ford thought Cliff was White. He's light, but I don't think he looks White.

"Daddy's not White," I told him. "Daddy's parents, Nana and Papa, are Black. Their skin is just very light." My mother-in-law's parents were also racially ambiguous. In their wedding picture, my mother-in-law looks like a dark-haired Italian beauty.

By the time I got to explain that part of American history, Ford was drifting away. I saw that he'd decided that he had learned enough for one day.

About a year after his lesson about slavery and miscegenation, Ford was called the "N" word. It happened on the field in the back of the school he had gone to since he was in a BabyBjörn on my

Our family on Christmas 2003.

chest. Baldwin had been a student there before him. He had been there so often with her that he was, at age two, included in Baldwin's *Lion King* performance during the annual school talent show. In his Halloween lion's costume, he jumped onto the stage and roared at the end of her song. He'd been officially enrolled since he was five and had felt as comfortable at the Edgemont School as he was at home. He was eleven at this point. In general, he didn't cry much, but after that word was hurled at him, he became so overcome with emotion that a buddy, a biracial boy named Matthew, put his arm around him and ran him to the nurse.

Is it easier to receive pain if you know it's coming? Can we gird our kids, toughen them to slights, hurtful comments, bigotry?

The boys who had called Ford this word were his friends. I don't mean casual, on-the-same-baseball-team friends, I mean part of his main birthday party crew, sleepovers, trips to the beach, and trick-or-treating together kind of friends. He must have felt as if an exposed nerve had been struck. He must have felt betrayed.

When I came home on that February day, Ford was sitting on the paisley chenille couch in the family room, ironically beneath the ancestors' photo wall. He was playing a game on the iPad. I stood in the entranceway. Something about his slouched posture caught my attention.

"How was your day?"

"Good," he said, taking his eyes off his game only briefly to look at me.

I walked into the room and wedged in beside him on the couch.

"What'd you do at school?"

"Nothing."

"Anything usual happen?"

"Nope."

"Well, why do you look like that?"

"Look like what?"

"You look sad."

"I'm not sad," he said, almost indignantly, and kept at his game. I sat next to him for a minute longer, hoping he'd offer something but knowing that he wouldn't.

"Okay," I said and got up from where I was sitting next to him. "I'm going upstairs."

My son is seldom talkative, especially when it comes to his feelings. My Baldwin, on the other hand, can dissect a feeling to dust. I would've known about her day before she got in the door from school. She would have called me, but it would have also been emotionally telegraphed. We are that in tune. It's what I had always wanted our relationship to be. It's what I'd experienced with my mom.

I went upstairs to my bedroom. I sat down on my bed and the phone rang. The caller ID said "Montclair Board" and the phone number was Ford's elementary school's. It was his principal, Mrs. Hopper. We exchanged pleasantries and she asked me if Ford had told me what happened at school.

"No, what happened?" I asked, suddenly feeling anxious.

She told me that there had been some name-calling on the field during a soccer game at recess. She kept talking, using the phrase "name-calling" every few words. I have to admit the "N" word didn't ever enter my mind as one of the possible names. I hate sounding Pollyanna-ish, but it just didn't. I had drunk the Kool-Aid about our progressive, hip little urban suburb. Enlightened, intelligent people don't use that word—especially not here. Montclair has always been a home not just for Black and White, but everyone, Asian and Latino and everybody else—two moms, two dads, nesting divorced parents, divorced couple and wife's boyfriend under one roof. Baldwin has a best friend who is Indian and Russian, who was raised solo by her dad. We've also surpassed Minneapolis in having the largest number of interracial marriages. I finally asked the principal what the names were, and when she said the "N" word, my mouth literally dropped. It was open long enough for my mouth to become dry. The word was not just a word to us, despite rappers and fans throwing it around like beads during Mardi Gras. It was like a thousand-pound weight filled with centuries of hate had been hurled at my child, shattering my sweet boy's innocence.

"I know, I know," she said in response to my silence. "I've lived here twenty-two years and have never heard that word or heard of anyone saying it."

"You have to tell me the names of the boys who said it."

She told me without hesitating. She also told me what she had said to the one who admitted he had said it. The other one had denied saying it, and his parents believed him. Ford maintained that he did.

"I have a feeling that there was something else going on, something that happened outside of school," the principal said.

I shared with her what I knew. Ford had made the "A" baseball team and one of them had not. Ford had not invited that boy to his birthday sleepover a few weeks earlier. At the time, when we were doing the guest list and that boy's name wasn't on it, I'd asked Ford why, and he'd just said, "He's annoying."

While the principal's news left me feeling as if I'd been hit in the stomach with a fifty-pound kettle bell, I also felt empowered by my mother radar—the thing that had led me to look at my son's face and know, despite his insistence otherwise, that something bad had happened to him that day.

I got off the phone and went back to where Ford was still playing on his iPad. I needed to be with him and get him to talk about how he was feeling and what had happened.

"Ford, come downstairs with me. I want you to talk to me while I put ice on my sore hip." We had a sectional in the basement, which would allow for both of us to lie down but not face each other. I knew that boys tended to handle talks better when not looking you directly in face.

I told him that Mrs. Hopper had explained what happened in school.

"What'd she say?"

I recounted our phone call. I asked him if that was accurate.

He said yes.

I asked him if he knew that word. He said yes, another punch in the gut.

"Tell me what happened," I said.

He relayed the story as Mrs. Hopper had, except he said two, not one, of the boys had called him the "N" word, and the one who denied uttering the word had been angrily chasing him when he said it. Now, my head was on fire, but I knew I had to remain calm to get the whole story. Mrs. Hopper had already told me that Ford had burst into tears and that Matthew had put his arms around Ford and taken him to the nurse. She also told me that Matthew had come back to the playground afterward and confirmed to every adult in sight what had happened.

I told Ford that that word wasn't about him, but said more about the people who used it. He nodded his head. I told him that people use that word when they feel bad about themselves, to try to make you feel bad about yourself.

I know that I can sometimes be too nuanced, so I asked him at each turn if he understood what I'd said.

He said he did. Ford is quick to tell me when he doesn't understand something.

I asked him if he wanted to say anything else.

He said no.

He was fidgeting, so I knew that meant I had to stop, that we were done.

I had called Cliff as soon as I had gotten off the phone with the principal. By the time he arrived home a few hours later, Ford's mood was lighter. We were at the kitchen table, having dinner. It was just the three of us because Baldwin was at SAT prep. Cliff tried to engage Ford in a conversation about what had happened.

Ford looked at Cliff and flatly said, "I already talked to Mom about this."

Translation: We'd processed it—"Mom'd" it, as he and his sister call my emotional and psychological excavations—and we could move on now.

That night, the mother of the boy who admitted saying it—let's call him Mark—called to say that she was sorry.

"I'm mortified and I don't know what to say," she began the conversation.

This was someone I had interacted with regularly for years. I could hear the agony in her voice.

"I know, it's horrible and there is nothing that can be said," I responded.

We talked about how Ford was doing and about her son. I thanked her for calling and I meant it. I was calm and I believed her when she said that she'd never seen her son so distraught.

The other boy's parents never called and never responded to the principal's calls. Several weeks later, I ran into the boy's dad in the park after walking with my friend Deb. I'd just told Deb the whole story, which by now was about a month old. She and I were in her car and she was about to pull out of her parking space. "Stop," I said, putting my hand on her arm. "That's the boy and his dad." They were pulling into the parking space directly in front of us.

I got out of the car. The boy looked scared. The dad greeted me warmly, as he always had. I asked him why they'd never responded to the principal's request that we all meet to talk about what had happened. He fidgeted and looked at me and began a rant: "I'm sick of all the baseball politics in this town and who's in the country club and who has money and who doesn't and who lives on the South End, and I grew up on the wrong side of the tracks in Berkeley, and all my friends were Mexican and Black, and I would never use that word and I know my son didn't . . ."

I listened as he went on until I didn't want to anymore. While it was clear he had a lot of strong, hurt feelings around the elitism of travel baseball, I said firmly and calmly, as I air circled my face with my pointer, telegraphing my brown skin, "And what does that have to do with me?"

The Trayvon Martin killing had recently happened, and I pointed out to him that it was much more likely that my son would be randomly shot and killed because of his race, even with his country club membership and higher economic status, than that his son would. "I'm not your problem," I said, a cold slap to his hysteria.

The conversation moved on to one between compassionate human beings. I said what I needed to say, how hurtful that word is and how much it had disturbed Ford. He maintained that his son didn't, wouldn't ever, say it. He said that his son had said that Ford had teased him about not being a good ballplayer and had teased him about his weight. His son not making the "A" team had been a blow, but Ford maintained that he'd never even brought it up and that he'd never teased the boy about his size. They are no longer friends. Ford said he had no interest in talking to either of them again. Shortly after the incident, we saw the boys and Ford looked through them as if they were invisible.

But a year later, I heard Ford on his Xbox headset playing Black

Ops. He was saying, "Mark, do it now, do it now." I walked into the basement game room, which had become Ford's Xbox room, the place where he would happily live if we let him.

"Is that Mark from Edgemont?"

He looked and me, headphones on, and nodded his head yes.

"You're talking to him again?"

He actually took off his headphones and looked at me.

"Yeah, we're cool. He said he was sorry and I said okay."

And I said, "Okay," and left him to his game.

The day after the "N" word incident, we made our almost daily stop at Dunkin' Donuts on our way to school. That morning, the green icing on the donuts signaled St. Patrick's Day. We got our stuff, an apple fritter for him, a small light coffee, light sugar for me (yes, I sometimes let him have a donut for breakfast; he's the second child).

In the car, I said, "You know why there's St. Patrick's Day?"

"Nope," he said between bites, devouring his apple fritter.

"Well, when the Irish came here, nobody liked them, and they were called names. St. Patrick's Day was created to make them feel better about themselves and have pride in their ethnicity."

I saw him through my rearview mirror, looking up now. I had his attention. He considered what I was saying, hunched his shoulders with an *uh-huh*, and went back to his glazed treat.

"You know there's a horrible name for every racial and ethnic group?"

"No," he said in a whisper from the backseat.

I told him the slurs for every group that I knew: Jews, Mexicans, Italians, Puerto Ricans. "Now you've heard them," I said, "don't you ever, ever use them."

14

The Trouble with Miss Ann

A YEAR before her and my father's fiftieth wedding anniversary in August 2003, my mom told me that she wanted to celebrate it by having a wedding—a genuine wedding with a white wedding gown, bridesmaids with color-coordinated taffeta gowns, flower girls, and a ring bearer.

I couldn't believe what my mother was saying and actually thought she was really just talking. I should've known better. As the months passed and she started going to places like David's Bridal and reception halls, I tried to talk her out of her plan.

"Mom, it's too much."

"Whaddya mean, too much? It's not going to cost that much. I have the money."

"I'm not just talking about the money. It takes a lot of energy to plan a wedding and . . ."

"I'm doin it, Neal."

I thought the idea ridiculous and came close to saying so, but I knew better. I had to either get on board or get out of her way. I'd had no idea, until she told me, that she'd always wanted to have an actual wedding. When she and my dad had originally gotten married, she'd worn a black wool sheath with small gold designs on it. They went to city hall. Seeing her now in full wedding-planner mode, I felt a little sad for her, but that changed to admiration (as usual) as she went about getting what she'd always wanted, no matter what I or anybody else thought about it, no matter that it was fifty years later.

The day came. My mother wore a white bridal gown with a headpiece. I was the matron of honor. Her bridesmaids were her remaining sisters, Aunt Marion and Aunt Grace; Wendy, mother of Kamal, Duane's first child; and Keisha, mother of two of Duane's younger children, Sumayyah and Amir. We all wore light blue, short-sleeved gowns. My brother Larry's granddaughter Jasmine was a flower girl, along with Baldwin and Sumayyah; Amir and Ford were ring bearers. Larry walked Mom down the aisle. Marc was the best man, and Cliff and Kamal were the groomsmen. The ceremony was at Mount Teman A.M.E., the church my grandmother had joined when she'd moved her family from the South to Elizabeth, New Jersey. The reception was at a hall in nearby Roselle.

My mother beamed like a first-time bride, and Daddy, upon entering the reception from the wedding with my mom, raised his arm and announced: "This is the happiest day of my life."

When I thought about it later, I realized that long marriages like my parents' are filled with complex feelings. You fight and you love, you push each other to the very end of human patience, and somehow you stick in out for fifty years as my parents had, and you live for the moments of grace.

In some ways my own marriage to Cliff mimicked the stock market. We'd had high-flying years when we were groovin' on the same page, and we'd had years when we didn't get along, and I'd wanted to bolt. Thankfully, Cliff has always been the steady one. Of course, I knew that my life as a wife and mother wouldn't look anything like my mom's, but I never actually pictured what it would look like, other than that I would be a working mom. Never in my most extreme dreams did I picture myself making dinner, organizing playdates, carpooling, and supervising homework full-time. During those years, I kept thinking I'd get back to writing; I just needed to get my kids settled first. Month after month, that's what I told myself.

My mother was a den mother and used to have her Boy Scout meetings in our unfinished basement. I remember the boys coming in the back door and going down the stairs in their blue uniforms with the yellow-gold ties, my brothers Marc and Duane among them. I hated the time the scouts got with my mom. I used to listen as they gathered around the pool table working on some project—my mother loved a paper towel craft—so jealous that sometimes I'd sit at the top of the basement steps and shout, "Why don't you go home to your own mommies!"

One of my brothers would tighten his lips, the other would show me a fist, but my mother would stifle a laugh and pretend to ignore me.

She was also president of the Block Association. She was able to do all these things because she didn't sleep. I couldn't do what she did, even if I wanted to. At one time, I imagined filling twenty hours a day as she had, but I'd planned to do it by finding a great nanny who would be with us the entire time my children were young, and I would go off every morning to write, travel, go to dinner with my husband. Although by my midtwenties I recognized that I wanted to be a mother, I had thought I would still live in New York City, with the simple addition of a child, an accessory or more like a goldfish—a low-maintenance kind of pet. I clearly had no idea.

I was never one to gush over children or really pay much attention to them—other than my nephew Kamal, who'd been born when I was eighteen. I loved him immensely and took him on outings, but he was my nephew, sometimes like the younger sibling I'd never had. And because he was an only child he was preternaturally mature; not like a kid at all. I had always wanted children, but I saw myself as the kind of mother who was like an older camp guide. I never saw myself as someone who would nag about homework or cleaning up. I didn't grasp what a Herculean task it would be to instill the importance of self-discipline in a child. My actual mothering bears no resemblance to what I'd imagined.

"You don't just mother, you inhabit their skin; it's very interesting to watch," said Lynne, who has been my friend since our firstborns were babies. She was right: I tried fiercely to protect my kids' emotional and psychological lives. Lynne's observation helped me to understand why I find mothering so exhausting. When you listen to, process, and analyze everything that happens to them, it's straight-up draining. If something happens to one of my kids, it's as if it has happened to me. I don't just empathize; I feel it in my body.

When Baldwin was new to middle school, I was near her school during dismissal one day and decided to pick her up instead of having her ride the bus. She didn't have a cell phone, so there was no way for me to let her know that I was there. I saw the buses lined up and went through throngs of eleven-, twelve-, and thirteen-year-olds to locate her. As I looked around, trying to remember what animal her bus was named for—red swan, green rabbit, blue monkey—I heard a girl from a window of the bus I was standing next to say in a nasty tone "Baldwin is a . . ." and before a noun came out, I felt heat rising to my head. I went to get on the bus, but the door was shut. The driver was midway up the aisle, I assume trying to quiet the kids before driving off. I saw a boy who had been in Baldwin's class all through elementary school, quietly sitting in the front seat, near the door. I waved my hand and got his attention and told him to open the door. He did, and I got on the bus, squeezed past the driver, and headed directly to where the girl was sitting. The two girls—one of whom had been Baldwin's friend in elementary school—saw me coming. One tried to hide her head in the other one's chest. I jabbed my pointer finger into her shoulder. She looked up at me, confused and a little terrified.

"Don't you ever, as long as you live, say anything bad about my daughter."

The two of them nodded their heads at me, as if in a trance, in unison.

I walked off of the bus and resumed looking for my child.

Our family when Baldwin was in middle school.

I never imagined I'd be like this, and I guess that's part of what veteran parents try to tell you when you're pregnant. You'll never love anyone else like this; you'll do things you can't imagine.

I was craving a drink after lunch. *At least it's not noon,* I rationalized, even though I'd promised myself that I wasn't going to have a drink for a week. I was taking a break just to show myself that I could easily do so. By the night of day three I ached for this drink like I used to crave chocolate right before my period. I got out of bed, where I'd been reading a novel, and went downstairs. I squeezed the juice from a lemon, then a lime, and poured it into a glass with tequila and agave, added some ice, and voilà, I'd made myself a margarita. I savored it, standing at the kitchen counter. It was good. Did that mean I was an alcoholic? I'd just had one. I didn't want another, and I went back to my bed and book. I had a glimmer of insight that I drank mostly because I was bored. Thinking up the drink, mixing it, sipping it gave me something to do that was just for me, but I also felt that I needed something to take the edge off the mind-numbing demands of domestic life.

This was year three of not writing, of being a stay-at-home mom. Here is what my life looked like on any given day:

- Call the sprinkler guy, Brian (we're on a first-name basis).
- Wait for "door specialist" to come and fix the garage door for the third time.
- Wait for handyman to hang silk valances in Baldwin's room.
- Have firs replanted after intense spring snowstorm dropped a foot of snow on them and forced them to the ground.
- Shop for end-of-year class teacher gift (last year witnessed disappointed face of Baldwin's teacher when she saw the brown velour hoodie; volunteered to do better job).
- Paint Adirondack chairs in yard.

My week-in, week-out list was more relentless:

- Walk the dog, feed the dog, and put in eye drops for cataracts after wrestling twelve-pound dog wearing oven mitts to prevent him from taking my skin off.
- Pick up Ford from school, take him to tae kwon do. Sit and wait for the half-hour lesson. Repeat twice a week.
- Take Ford to soccer practice one day, baseball two other days.
- Take Baldwin to the math tutor two to three times a week, depending on whether she has a test.
- Pick Baldwin up from bimonthly hair salon appointment.
- Take and pick up Baldwin from lacrosse practice. Sometimes tutor, hair, and lacrosse fall on the same day, but never get the hair done before lacrosse. Can't sweat out the new do.
- Clean up breakfast dishes to make room to cook dinner.

As I'd plan dinner, feeling weary, pissed, and bored from my day, I'd get a lift just looking at the clock and realizing that it was five-thirty and I'd completed my driving responsibilities. I could have a cocktail. Usually it was a glass of wine, but sometimes it was a Cosmo or a margarita, something fun and youthful, something to make me feel like the girl I'd been when I was single and living on Manhattan's Upper West Side, alone in my one-bedroom, rent-stabilized apartment, hanging with my girls Eleanore and Shannon. Just like Carrie and her crew. I'd inhale *Sex and the City* episodes, the escapades often mirroring those of my girlfriends and me, such as being broken up with via a Post-it. The best one, which actually happened to one of my best friends, was finding out that the guy she was dating was about to be a father when his baby's mama's voice came over the answering machine announcing that she was in labor while my friend was underneath him in his bed. None of this had been fun at the time, but the memories were now a hilarious distraction.

After about six months of my solitary Happy Hour, Cliff told me that he was concerned that I was drinking too much. I started to clean up the bottles and glasses before he came home. I didn't want to hear what he had to say. He was worried. Shit, I was worried, but not about my drinking. I was resentful and afraid that I was losing my fucking mind, but I felt as if I couldn't really complain because I lived in a beautiful brick Colonial partially covered with ivy and had a big, gorgeous yard with a garden of climbing Pink Peace, thistles, pink dogwoods, yellow forsythia, blackberry bushes, peonies, and clematis over an arched Walpole gate. I drove a Mercedes SUV, and my kids were cute and bright and nice, and my husband was cute and bright and nice and brought home the bacon. I was aware that only a small percentage of women—and an even smaller percentage of Black women—shared this life, and very few of them ever acknowledged ennui. Which made me feel worse, lonelier. I knew many would hear my complaint and wonder what the fuck was wrong with me.

During this period, an after-lunch margarita wasn't my only distraction. My shopping addiction was also getting a little out of hand. Twice a year, Cliff and Baldwin would go on a father-daughter camping trip sponsored by the YMCA. Ford and I were on our own. I remember we were walking from his soccer game toward the town center in our neighborhood one day when I saw a sale sign outside Coco, one of my favored boutiques in town. It was right next door to my most beloved store, a vintage spot called My Inheritance, owned by my buddy and "colleague" Carrie. Ford and I were holding hands, and I steered him across the street. Even at six, my son detested shopping, so I took him into My Inheritance first, where I could distract him with the bowl of Jolly Ranchers that Carrie kept on the counter. Nina was working that day. I told her I wanted to peek in on the sale next door at Coco. She offered to watch Ford for me. She was a social worker during the week and moonlighted at the store on weekends. I felt very comfortable leaving Ford with her. I went next door and proceeded to try on jeans, then a top and then a dress. In my shopping zombie trance, I had no idea that a half hour had passed. As I was stepping out of the dressing room, I looked toward the entrance and saw Nina holding Ford's hand.

"He has to go to the bathroom," she said kindly.

"Oh, sweetie, I'm sorry."

I told them to hold on to the clothes, slinking out of the store to take him to the bathroom.

The look on his face made me feel as if I'd been caught by a neighbor drinking brown liquor in the morning. He just said: "Can we go home now?"

Some of the things I bought during this manic shopping phase from Coco were a Chan Luu bracelet (before everyone starting wearing them and knocking them off—I should've waited); a Paul & Joe leather bolero; Red Engine jeans; a silk polka-dot halter dress that could be a tunic or a dress, which I'd seen in the window and coveted but didn't buy until it was on sale. From My Inheritance, over time, I bought a black classic lambskin Chanel purse; Gucci sunglasses; La Perla sunglasses; an Hermès belt; a fox boa; a red bouclé Adolfo suit; and too many other things to remember.

At my shoe store in town, Piazza Del Sole, I scored a great pair of brown suede '40s-style pumps, a pair of pointy-toe Donna Karan boots (that I don't wear anymore); a pair of over-the-knee La Canadienne boots (that I do still wear pretty much all winter). At Tory

Janes: a pair of Tory Burch ballet flats, high-wedge sandals (neither of which I wore more than a half-dozen times—the flats became way too ubiquitous); Cordani wedge sandals. From Ruby, my other favorite: Vince T-shirts and Vince cashmere sweaters, J Brand jeans, Seven jeans, earrings. You get the picture.

This is not counting the department-store booty bought during mindless mall shopping: Nordstrom, J.Crew, Neiman Marcus, H&M, Zara. I can't even recall all the costume jewelry, cashmere wraps, wallets, and handbags I bought from Jillian, who held private sales two to three times a year. After this went on for three years, Cliff started to turn up the complaints.

I decided that it was my marriage that must be the problem. This was after having my chakras realigned in October; seeing a naturopathic doctor and having hair strands tested for metal in

Mom and Dad on their fiftieth anniversary, dancing
at the wedding ceremony they'd always wanted.

my body in November; and drinking green-ocean scraps for a year. When I still felt like shit, I called a therapist for Cliff and me to see. The psychiatrist came highly recommended by some friends in the city. Over the telephone he asked me how many children we had and their ages—Baldwin was fourteen then, and Ford was eight. The doctor asked how old Cliff and I were; when I told him that we were both fifty-one, he made a sound, something like *humph*.

"Why'd you do that?" I asked him.

At first he said, "Oh, no, no, no reason."

He quickly realized that I'd caught him having a reaction, and he relented. He knew that I wasn't going to stop pushing him until he said what it was.

"Well, I was just thinking that most people at this age might be free of raising children, that your children would be almost grown and you'd be taking care of yourself, and not still have children as young as you do."

Yes, I thought, *this makes perfect biological sense.* I booked the appointment and anxiously looked forward to meeting this man.

Dr. Henry McCurtis's voice was a combination of Morgan Freeman's and what I imagined God might sound like—if God were a man. The doctor's accent was a mixture of Oklahoma and Texas. In sessions, he offered down-home compassion—"Bless your heart," he would say, upon hearing something especially horrendous—and utilized the intellectual training he'd received at Columbia Medical School, riffing on human needs and dissecting Siddhartha. Cliff and I saw McCurtis for five or six sessions. He sent us on our way with tools to better understand each other's stressors and triggers, and a good marital prognosis.

So now I knew the problem wasn't my marriage, but I still couldn't find my footing; I couldn't shake the feeling of teetering on a precipice.

"Girl, you need to relax and go on and live Miss Ann's life," said my hair colorist and pal Joy Harris one day as I sat in her chair. Meaning just enjoy the house, the car, the club, and being a stay-at-home mom.

"Miss Ann" wasn't a positive term for Black people. Miss Ann was the lady of the plantation, weak, mean, and prone to fainting spells. These proverbial Southern White women relied on their Black maids to do everything from breast-feeding and raising the children, to cleaning the house, cooking, and submitting to rape from her husband if said husband/master requested. An updated version of Miss Ann is portrayed in the bestselling novel and movie *The Help*. White people couldn't understand why Black people resented, hated *The Help*. We understood that our foremothers had toiled for Miss Ann, who was still the heroine of the story.

That didn't mean that we were above honest work, only that we meant to preserve our dignity. When my mother was a young girl, high school age, she worked as a nanny and a maid for White women after school in the Elmora section of Elizabeth, New Jersey. In the summers she would go with them to their vacation homes on the Jersey Shore. After a few summers with one Jewish family, she and the woman she worked for managed to get beyond the social expectations of the time and became something resembling friends. When the summer was over, the woman, Susan, invited my mother to visit her at her home in Washington, DC. My mother took her up on the offer. When my mother arrived at the tasteful, elegant home on a tree-lined street in Northwest, a Black maid, "the help," let's call her Esther, answered the door. This was the late '40s, below the Mason-Dixon, where Jim Crow was still law.

"Hello, is Susan home?" my mother said.

Esther appraised my mother and told her yes, but she'd have to go around to the back door.

My mother with her Northern ways told Esther no, she wasn't going around back.

Esther insisted.

My mother insisted that she would not.

After a few moments of a standoff, Susan appeared behind Esther to see who was at the door. Upon seeing my mother, Susan screeched, "Clara!" and stretched out her arms. Esther moved aside as Susan and my mother embraced.

Remembering this story from my mother's past, I knew that Joy was basically advising me to just chill, to be the proverbial lady of the manor. But my mind was jammed and my soul felt tangled. All of me was unaligned, though I didn't fully understand this at the time. I only knew that my normally iron will to keep moving had started to rust and was beginning to give.

"Why you drinking so much?" my mother said one day as we sat at my kitchen table during a visit. She said she'd noticed that I often had a drink in my hand.

I blew her off.

"Ma, I'm not an alcoholic. I just like to drink right now."

She took her concern to Joni, my oldest friend, the sister I never had, who now lived in LA. Joni, the most balanced person I know, was like my mother's other daughter. They had their own relationship apart from me. When I went away to Howard, Joni continued having dinner with my mom two or three times a week after her classes at Seton Hall and before heading to her job as an assistant manager at Bamberger's. Joni convinced Mom that there was nothing to worry about. She told her that the motherhood thing was just difficult for me right now, especially since I wasn't writing.

"She'll be okay," Joni assured my mother, and I think my mother believed her. At least she stopped bugging me, or maybe she was becoming consumed by health concerns of her own.

A few nights after Joni allayed Clara's fears about my drinking, I had a small breakthrough. Homework, dinner, bath time were over. Ford was in bed. Cliff and Baldwin were talking in her bedroom, and I was in my dressing room with Charlie at my feet on the chaise. I pulled out my new MacBook Air, the beautiful laptop that my husband had surprised me with for our anniversary the previous June, and began some writing. The audio guy was banging in the basement, installing the kind of TV sound system that I'd soon learn I would need a PhD to operate. I was typing away. I was writing. It occurred to me what I was doing; I was like a kid who realizes he's riding a two-wheeler without training wheels. I stopped typing to observe myself: Maybe writing through noise and when everybody was home was the new normal. Maybe I wouldn't have six hours undisturbed in my office away from the family rhythms like I used to. Perhaps what I had to learn was to write around tending parents as well as children—the stuff of life—not alone in a quiet room. It wasn't perfect, but it was clearly doable. I was writing.

15

Mom's Malady, My Menopause

THE OCTOBER evening had taken on a blustery fall chill. My mother was scheduled for open-heart surgery the following day. I was sitting next to her hospital bed, listening to her sum up the state of her health and the litany of her recent encounters with medicine.

I can't walk three feet without losing my breath. They finally figured out what was wrong with me. My cardiologist, that handsome Dr. Lappa, found out that one of my valves is leaking. I told him I'd had another valve replaced six years ago. They put a pig part in me. My other cardiologist, Dr. Mahdi, turns out was the daddy of one of Ford's friends. They always took good care of me, but after he found out I was Ford's grandma, he took extra good care of me. When they recommended surgery, I didn't think twice about it. "Let's do it," I said. But everybody was all worried. You even said to the doctors, "But she's eighty-two. How're you going to do that kind of operation on somebody her age?"

Dr. Mahdi said, "Other than her heart, she's in perfect health."

I have to admit I thought that was funny. "Other than her heart," like you can live without one. I want to get better. I want to be able to do all the things I used to do. I don't like sittin' around. It was bad enough that Matthew took my car keys from me, just because I got a little confused one time and we got separated at the mall and the police was called. They thought I'd escaped from the old folks' home or somethin.' They didn't believe me that me and my husband came there together and had got mixed up about where we were supposed to meet. I told them call Neal, but you weren't home so here comes Cliff to get me. He had to drive all the way down to the Woodbridge Mall from Montclair.

Well, the night before the last surgery I remember you stayed later than your usual time, past visiting hours. Lookin' at me all sad, telling me, "You've been a great mother. I was so lucky to have you." How you love me and appreciate everything I did. I think you thought I wasn't gonna come outta that surgery. But I knew I would. I'd made up my mind that I wasn't ready to go yet, even though I was sick to death of hospitals. I've been in and out of the hospital in the last few years, had to be six or seven times. Before I got into my late seventies I didn't have any problems. I had never been in the hospital. Before all this mess with my heart, my regular doctor, Dr. Haggerty, thought she saw a mass on my pancreas during an X-ray and was sendin' me to all these specialists. I remember how you broke down right in the elevator after we was leavin' one of 'em. I looked at you and told you, "I'm not worried about this. I don't have no cancer or nothing. I gave it to God." I wasn't ready to go. I used to walk three miles every day, cut out salt, went on the trips for Matthew's navy reunions, visited with my brother Fred and what sisters I had left. I had my kids and grands. I had managed to make to it see my grandson Kamal graduate from Brown, like I always promised him I would. I might even make it to Baldwin's weddin' if she get married at twenty-one. I'd be ninety.

I can tell you tryin' to work up a cry, Neal. You always was a crybaby. I'm not one for a whole lotta mushy stuff, but I've changed as I've gotten older.

You better go home now, sweet pea. It's late and you know this neighborhood, it's kinda rough. Get the guard to walk you to the parkin' lot.

Mom had no idea what was raging inside me as I left the hospital. All I could think about was losing her, and I wasn't ready yet. I'd actually convinced myself that someday I would be ready. It just wasn't now.

I had walked these streets—Osborne Terrace, Lyons Avenue— every day to and from high school, hanging out at Area Board 9, the community center that used to be down the street. I understood that the place had changed since I'd lived there, but it was still my neighborhood. Still, my mother had cautioned me to have a guard escort me to my car, so I walked up to the two Black twentysomething security guards talking at the entry desk. I asked if one of them would be willing to walk me to my car. One of the men assessed me. His look felt harsh and negative. I said something about being from the neighborhood. I told them that I once lived here thirty years ago. I heard myself and realized how long ago that was and remembered how I used to feel when someone, especially someone Black, used to say that to me. I'd feel resentful at the term—"used to"—like they'd gone on to something better than here. I could see the same thing in the guard's eyes. I wanted to say, "No, that's not at all what I'm thinking," but I didn't. Suddenly I was the older, clueless person needing assistance. The other guard, the one without the edge, said sweetly that of course he'd walk me.

The next day, after my mom was prepped for surgery and given the anesthesia and her chest was opened up, they checked her blood and realized it wasn't clotting. She had been on Coumadin, but the doctors thought they'd stopped it long enough before the surgery for her blood to clot. They were wrong. She wouldn't stop bleeding—too many years on blood thinners. So her chest, which was entirely opened, was bandaged, and she lay in an induced coma for two days while they tried to get her blood to bulk up. Baldwin came with me to see her and sobbed and fell on Mom's bed at the sight of the ventilator breathing for her. I had to leave the room.

Three days later my mother came through the surgery even better than the doctors had predicted. Mom was already sitting up two days after her surgery when her surgeon came into her room. He was a large and vigorous man with thinning blond hair, a medical star that Beth Israel had hired away from the Cleveland Clinic. My mom reached out to hug him and he leaned in. "I can't believe you're sitting up already," he said.

Mom beamed at him like a teacher's pet.

The nurse on duty turned pink, and after the doctor left said to my mother, "I can't believe you hugged him."

"Why?" Mom said, with all her bemused surliness.

"Because, he's, well, no one does that."

"*Humph*," was all Mom said, but the nurse got her meaning: *I'm not like everybody else, and he puts on his drawers same way I do.*

The surgeon, in addition to repairing the main leaky valve, ended up performing a bypass and patching up a hole in my mother's heart that she'd had her entire life but that no one knew about because it was behind a ventricle. He also shaved down her heart muscle, which had become enlarged from years of overwork. The metaphor of my mother's overly large heart couldn't have been more appropriate. She seriously believed that we are each our brother's keeper; that we are here to take care of one another. My mother was better than me. She was better than most.

She was the sort of person who went to Jamaica on vacation, became friends with some impoverished locals, got their addresses, and came home and bought new jeans and mailed them. She would not only give panhandlers money on the subway when she was visiting me in the city, but she'd also talk to them. To her, they were no different than the people in business attire riding the train home from work. One day when I reprimanded her for talking to a homeless man, she scolded me, "Don't be telling me who I can talk to." Left unsaid: *He puts his drawers on same as you.*

After two weeks in the hospital, she was finally released. She had to go into a rehabilitation/nursing home for three weeks. Still weak, she was primarily in a wheelchair. When she walked the halls with her physical therapist, Jason, it was with a walker. I hated seeing my mother like this, but not as much as she hated "the damn walker." Sometimes I watched her work with Jason in the weight room. She grunted and groaned but got up the weight that was strapped around her ankle, lifting it in a slow kick.

Jason looked at me. He said, "She's amazing."

Another fan.

Me, Baldwin, and Mom visiting her at rehab.

Around the time of my mother's multiple heart procedures, I thought the difficulty in my life had peaked. I remember I kept losing things. Some I'd find, others would simply vanish never to be seen again, like my cell phone. One day it simply disappeared. Cliff and I were traveling the next day for a week in Anguilla, sans children, to celebrate my fiftieth birthday. I thought that I'd just happen across my lost phone after a long-needed rest. But when I got back a week later, still no cell phone. I never found it. Another day we needed a few things from the A&P. Cliff handed me three twenties, and I put the money in my jeans pocket. I got to the store and no money. Sixty dollars, just gone. Then there were the misplaced glasses, purses, keys, and simple words and names that I no longer seemed capable of recapturing. Later, I also lost my diamond engagement and wedding rings. They simply evaporated. I'm still hoping that they're somewhere in my house.

I complained to my husband.

Hardly listening, he said, "Too much stress."

I felt so sorry for myself that I called my mother, knowing she'd feel sorry for me too.

"Oh, that's terrible," she said. "I hate when I do that."

"Ma, you're eighty-three, of course you can't remember things." She cackled.

Soon, my full-time activity became trying to figure out what was wrong with me. My mom was making steady progress in rehab, but I seemed to be falling apart. Like so many women my age I was scatterbrained, depressed, had carbohydrate lust and alcohol craving, all of it pointing to the big "M." At the time, Oprah was doing many shows on menopause. She devoted entire segments to Dr. Christiane Northrup, author of *The Wisdom of Menopause,* the menopause bible. I bought this book and devoured it. On the same subject, the hilariously brilliant writer Sandra Tsing Loh wrote the following in an *Atlantic* magazine essay entitled "The Bitch Is Back":

> Northrup notes that before this time in history, most women never reached menopause—they died before it could arrive. If, in an 80-year life span, a female is fertile for about 25 years (let's call it ages 15 to 40), it is not menopause that triggers the mind-altering and hormone-altering variation; the hormonal "disturbance" is actually fertility. Fertility is The Change. It is during fertility that a female loses herself, and enters that cloud overly rich in estrogen. And of course, simply chronologically speaking, over the whole span of her life, the self-abnegation that fertility induces is not the norm—the more standard state of selfishness is. . . . [I]f it comes at the right time, menopause is wisdom.

Tsing Loh broke down our adult life trajectory like this: if a woman gets married in her twenties and has all her children in her late twenties or early thirties, by the time she reaches her menopause years, her kids are leaving the family home and she is free. But for me and most of my contemporaries, it hadn't worked out that way. We put college, grad school, and careers first, which meant we weren't even thinking about marriage until thirty. By the time we found *the one* we could be thirty-five, and if we wanted to have a little time just with our spouse, that meant we were thirty-six, thirty-eight, forty by the time we had our first kid.

I had adventures in dating and traveling while living the single life in Manhattan. I'd wanted to be settled in my career before I got married and had kids. I didn't marry until a month shy of my thirty-fourth birthday, had Baldwin at thirty-six and Ford at forty-three. I was doing what most of those in my milieu were doing at the time. However, by the time we got to having it all, we were right up on perimenopause. It was the scenario Dr. McCurtis had observed on the phone.

Okay, so I was in menopause, and it was hell. I had to do something about it. I couldn't just throw frozen meat at my kids as my mother did to me when I was fifteen and was sassing her while she defrosted the freezer. She was forty-eight. I had been standing in the kitchen telling her how I wasn't going to do whatever it was she was telling me to do; she was quietly removing packages of frozen meat wrapped in white freezer paper and placing them on the table; back and forth, back and forth. All of sudden I sensed something coming at me and had the good fortune to move my upper body slightly to the side as the bricklike pack of ground beef whizzed past my ear. I looked at my mother, and I honestly can't remember if she'd even bothered to look up at me. I walked out of the kitchen and didn't say another word.

I decided to try bioidenticals, the estrogen and testosterone creams and the progestin pills that are purported to be safer than synthetic forms of hormones. This treatment was supposed to be plant-based, and didn't travel through the liver; therefore, there was no risk of breast cancer.

A friend referred me to a doctor whose office was in a part of New Jersey I'd never heard of, even though it was a half hour from my house. I drove along the Passaic River, taking twists and turns through neighborhoods that went from a cookie-cutter *American Beauty* set to something out of the movie *Deliverance*. I met with Dr. Gomez,* a kind man who talked to me for over an hour about his personal story with male menopause, a lack of testosterone, which he thought cost him his marriage.

"You will feel better, I promise," he assured me.

He took eight vials of blood and told me to come back in a week. When I went back, he ordered estrogen and testosterone creams and progesterone in a pill. He sold me niacin and CoQ10 supplements. I walked out of the office almost happy, or as happy as I was capable of feeling at the time, at the prospect of finally feeling better. I'd heard dozens of women on *Oprah* and elsewhere testify about the wonders of hormone replacement and how it had given them their lives back.

"How long will it be before I feel better?" I had asked him.

"It usually takes anywhere from one week to three weeks," he'd said. "You will feel better."

I went to sleep that night, dreaming about feeling better. The first week I took the pills and applied the creams, I felt nothing but extreme sleepiness at night. By nine thirty I would be so sleepy, I had to pull my leaded legs upstairs to bed. I'd shut down like I was on codeine. The second week, the same sleepiness but no other changes. I called the doctor. He assured me that the treatment would work; give it time. I was calling him three times a week, and by the third week, still nothing. I felt sleepy, hungry, grouchy, and still had only enough brain bandwidth to go to CVS and remember two things. I called him again; he was away at his father's funeral. When he returned, I offered my condolences. Perplexed as to why the pills and creams weren't working, he said the problem was probably my thyroid. He prescribed Synthroid. I pushed back and said I'd never had a thyroid issue, but I was desperate so I got the pills. The first day I took one, I felt like I was turning green and my chest and arms were bursting out like the Incredible Hulk. The second day, I felt the same, plus so hungry that I could've eaten my own leg. By the third day, with those symptoms persisting, I stopped taking the pills. I continued with the bioidenticals and talked to Dr. Gomez three times a week.

"We'll just keep trying," he said, although I sensed he was becoming as frustrated with me as I was.

After four months, I stopped calling and stopped taking the meds.

For the money and time I spent on this process, I could've bought a spa weekend. The big question for lots of women during this stage of life is whether to take synthetic hormones. I couldn't figure out what I should do. I was certainly finding many other ways to cope, including drinking, shopping, socializing, and sleeping. I didn't try having an affair or running away, and obviously I didn't commit murder or suicide.

Eventually, at Cliff's urging, I began going into Manhattan once a month to see Dr. McCurtis. Walking down the tree-lined street to his Central Park West office was part of the therapy that worked for a while—but it was short-lived. It became apparent that this "storm of murk," as William Styron described depression, would not let go with talk therapy alone. So McCurtis prescribed Wellbutrin and later added Prozac. I took the two pills, eventually only taking Prozac, for about a year. I did feel better, enough to join a gym, hire a trainer for three months, and begin a rhythm of extreme exercise: hard workout classes four days a week and jogging on the weekends. I'd read that thirty minutes of serious cardio exercise can be as effective as antidepressants for mild to moderate depression. I decided that was me, and that exercise was all I needed to manage my moods. I had stopped shopping and drinking so much, limiting it to weekends, even though I found myself still looking forward to it too much.

I wanted to get off the meds and I did. I was doing a little better, was a little calmer, not getting too overwhelmed and cursing out too many people. I upped my yoga practice and read spiritual self-help books. I usually felt the presence of sadness waiting at the door, but I used all the will and strength I possessed to keep the door shut. I was working full-time at keeping it together.

One afternoon, as I sat at my wooden kitchen table, surrounded by newspapers and the mail, Charlie started barking. I looked out from the kitchen window and saw my children holding hands, walking up the driveway. My heart liquefied. Baldwin had happened to pass as Ford's school bus letting him off and the two of them walked home together. My fourteen-year-old daughter and my eight-year-old son held hands as they talked to each other. Right then, I was so glad to have been there, to be a witness. A calm came over me and, for that moment, all was well.

16

Shame

IT WAS the Monday after Thanksgiving. I dutifully went to the gym then went for coffee with three women friends afterward. Two of the women had been secretly having an affair and they'd told me about it. My trainer Lisa, the "out" lesbian, said something to the group. The other woman, let's call her Kelly, who was married to a man, said, "You're so bossy."

"Fuck you," Lisa said.

"Fuck you," Kelly said and stormed out of Starbucks.

Up until Kelly walked out, we all thought the two of them were just joking. I told the one who was left that this was just a bad day for them both; things would calm down, *blah, blah, blah*. Now Lisa was furiously typing into her BlackBerry. They were texting "Fuck you" back and forth. I sighed and sat there, too tired to move, but wanting to.

I'd often fantasized that lesbian couples didn't behave like this.

Whenever I spent time with my friend Linda and her partner,

Jana, and their gay couple friends, I was always envious of how peaceful they all seemed. It made sense to me that there would be more harmony among women, given that they shared the same feminine sensibility. Rethinking that Starbucks dialogue, I was reminded that I owed Linda a call. I always felt better after talking with her. She was calm and sensible and understood me. We became best friends when we were the "baby" senior editors at *Essence*.

I laughed till my sides hurt as she told me about her latest book project and her subject, who wanted Linda to be her mother, her therapist, and her maid. "She actually had me waking her up to go to church and waiting in her house for three hours until she came back," Linda told me. Linda had a daughter and a son, and while we always talked about our kids, our conversations veered all over the place. That day we reviewed an article in the *Times* about the women in Obama's cabinet. The White women were all married, half of a power couple. Linda pointed out that only one Black one, Susan Rice, was married and she had married her White college sweetheart. The other Black women were all single or divorced. Even Valerie Jarrett, who had been called Obama's secret weapon. She was fabulous: smart, attractive, spoke several languages, had a great fashion sense, a daughter at Harvard Law School. She'd been divorced for decades.

I knew I was one of the lucky ones who had a husband, a Black man, who was well employed, took care of his family, and was loving and generous. But despite all this I still felt unhappy. I could only talk about this to a very small number of Black women. Linda was one of them. I was very careful whom I let see behind my pleasant demeanor. In retrospect, this hiding who I was inside wasn't only the fallout of having been bullied. I had also been sexually abused as a child, something I hadn't told anyone until I was thirty, the first time I was in therapy. Once I told my therapist, Dr.

Chisholm, I told everyone with whom I was close, so Linda knew about the abuse. The next day she sent me an updated copy of Betty Friedan's *The Feminine Mystique*. She also sent me Leslie Bennett's contemporary version, *The Feminine Mistake*, a book critiquing a woman's decision to give up her career in order to stay home and raise children. I confess that both of them sat mostly unread on a counter in the butler's pantry.

During this period, I was still seeing McCurtis. I went into the city for a three-hour session with him that yielded lots of insights. I felt like he was on his triple-A game, maybe because he was getting ready to move to Sierra Leone to work in the refugee camps for a year. We talked about the sexual abuse by a family member that I'd experienced when I was ten. While there was no penetration, I came to understand that it was still abuse and that it changes who you are. I had eventually written a letter to my abuser letting him know I forgave him. Not for him, as Dr. Chisholm, my therapist at the time, had explained, but for me. McCurtis offered me an additional insight: After that incident, everything had started changing for me. The bullying got more intense and by the fifth grade, some kids were also kissing and fondling. By sixth grade I knew about a few who were even going all the way.

I wasn't doing any of it. I'd had a "play" boyfriend, Chris, pretty much since third grade. He'd walk me home and we'd talk on the phone; one Christmas he gave me three little bottles of toilet water. In sixth grade he started bugging me about going all the way. I thought it was absurd that he was even asking me. I was still secretly playing with Barbies. No one in my neighborhood was still playing with dolls at twelve years old. A new girl named Karen* came to our school, and she liked Chris. Rumor had it that she was willing to go all the way with him. He gave me an ultimatum: either I did it or he was going to break up with me. I didn't budge from thinking it absurd to have sex at twelve, so we broke up, and he went with Karen.

But then I met Greg. He was a fine, bowlegged bad boy, a year older and many years faster. All the girls wanted Greg, but he started noticing me, flirting. One day after school when everybody had gone home for the day, he and I were alone outside the building. "Come here," he said, and took my hand, pulling me to him. He was leaning on a brick school wall. He pulled me into a hug and put his mouth on mine. Chris and I had close-mouthed kissed before, but Greg stuck his tongue against my lips, pushing it, trying to pry open my mouth. I gagged and pulled away. I had no idea what he was doing. He laughed at me, and I felt like the stupid child I was. We started talking on the phone, and he would walk me home from school. We were now a couple, and I felt like I'd won the lottery—the finest, most popular boy, an upperclassman, liked me. After about a month, he started pressuring me to have sex. He had already done it with a few girls. This time, unlike with Chris, I convinced myself that it wasn't absurd. My desire for him to be my boyfriend overrode any good sense.

After weeks of him trying to talk me into it, promising his enduring love, playing the Temptations song "Just My Imagination" over the phone, I said okay. On the agreed-upon day, we met after school. I had no idea where we were going. We walked two blocks from school, holding hands, stopping in front of a house with an open side door that led to the basement. He walked me down the stairs, carefully holding my hand like I was made of crystal. We were in someone's dirty basement, a filthy mattress on the floor. We kissed a little and he leaned me onto the mattress. He was on top of me and he unzipped his pants. As he lay on top of me, he pulled down my pants and then my panties. He felt around for my vagina; his fingers felt large and scary. He held his penis and pressed it on my vagina, then attempted to insert it. It didn't get past my labia. It hurt—being pinned on the nasty mattress with him greedily fumbling against me. I felt nauseous and grimy. After a few tries with no success and me complaining that it hurt, he stopped. He got off me, sat up, zipped up his pants, and stood. Looking down at me, he said, "Get up."

He walked me home, only this time we weren't holding hands, and he wasn't even walking next to me, but several feet ahead. When we got to my house, my dad was getting out of his Buick Skylark station wagon, just coming home from work. He smiled as he always did, and waved when he saw me. I waved, but I was so ashamed. I literally felt shame wash over me like I was a cartoon character changing color from green to blue, starting at the head and running down to the feet. I knew that what I had done with Greg was wrong, but I'd honestly felt helpless to stop it. I was crazy about him, but right at that moment, the possibility of my dad knowing what I'd done was far worse than losing the popular boy. I have no way of knowing if my dad sensed what had happened that day, and up until this moment in McCurtis's office, I'd never allowed myself to consider it.

McCurtis observed that that feeling of shame was a bit of wisdom that I could tap into, because that's what happens when you go for the dopamine high—the shame comes after. He told me that I was both blessed and cursed with the unusual ability to amplify feelings into images. "You must be aware when you feel the need for the high, for the dopamine, that you cannot give in to it," he told me. "The waves of shame will follow." And then he added, "Cliff provides oxytocin, which is comfort and a safe place to heal. That's what Cliff has given you. A safe place to heal."

17

*The Clock Has
No Meaning*

AND THEN my mom got sick again. This time it looked terminal, and I found myself on the edge, toes curled over a canyon.

Mom had been in a continuous loop of hospital stays: in for three, four days, out for two weeks, back again, a dozen times, maybe more. She'd also had three stints in rehab. In February 2008, when Joni and I brought her cupcakes on her eighty-third birthday to Robert Wood Johnson University Hospital Rahway and told her to make a wish on the candle, she'd said, "I don't ever want to go to the hospital again."

The hospital where she had stayed the October before had admitted her after she'd been delirious for a few days because of a lack of oxygen. The delirium continued at the hospital. Her physician, Dr. Kang, was from Korea, and he had a very heavy accent. He told me that my mother had heart failure in addition to stage-four lung disease. "Her lungs like Swiss cheese," he said.

"She very sick lady." I asked him to repeat himself, not quite able to take it in.

The next day, Baldwin and I drove the fifteen miles to the hospital to see my mom. I was thinking that this could be the last time. The Bill Withers song "Lean on Me" came on the car radio, and we both started singing along.

For it won't be long
Till I'm gonna need somebody to lean on

I felt my throat getting tight, but I kept on singing, tears rolling down my cheek to my lips. Baldwin looked at me and reached over and rubbed my hand, which was on the gearshift.

When we got to the hospital, Mom was sitting up, holding court with my dad; my cousins Bern, Barbara, and Denise; my nephew Kamal, his then wife, Eva, and baby, Lucia; and family friends Eric and Lori Rountree. All of them were standing and sitting around her bed, hanging on her every word. It appeared to be a miracle.

I told her what bad shape she'd been in the day before, and she eyed me suspiciously, but smiling.

"Really, Neal? I was wonderin' why everybody kept making such a big deal over me today."

Apparently the lung specialist had given her a heavy-duty steroid that had brought her back to life.

She was with us on Mother's Day the next May. Every year I hosted a celebration for the mothers, which was always held at my house. Cliff was in charge of marinating the chicken wings in a hot Jamaican sauce that he got from his former Egyptian American intern, and cooking them on the grill. They were delicious and always a little burnt. My parents, Clara and Matthew, and my in-laws, Joan and Big Cliff, came. Big Cliff was actually only about five

Daddy and me, with a young
neighbor in the background.

foot nine. I'd given him the nickname to distinguish between him
and my husband. Cliff's extended family called him Cliffy, which
I could never bring myself to do. I adored my father-in-law and
eventually Big Cliff was an affectionate sobriquet only I called him,
although at some point, I think my mom adopted it, too.

We passed the day sitting at a wrought-iron table under an
olive-green umbrella, drinking red wine or margaritas on the patio.
We talked about light things—how the kids were doing in school:
Baldwin on the honor roll, Ford not happy about having left his
womblike, fun preschool for "real school." This year my brother
Duane brought a new girlfriend. He'd already introduced her to
Cliff and me the day before, and I could tell he was anxious for our
mother to meet his new love. When they told my mother that they
had met online, she said: "Where? What line?" My brother, his girl-

friend, Cliff, and I laughed until our eyes streamed. My parents and Joan sat clear-eyed, having no idea about online dating sites. Only my father-in-law, an engineer who was building his own computer from scratch, was versed in the internet. He remained quiet.

My mom believed in also celebrating me on those days. She always bought me some kind of creative, thoughtful gift. Her last Mother's Day gift to me was chair pads for my Adirondack chairs and an umbrella to cover them. She and my dad set it up one day when I wasn't home. On my first Mother's Day, I had become so upset at my mother-in-law for not giving me a card. I came from a big card-sending family. When Cliff attempted to explain to her that my feelings were hurt, she said, "What? She's not my mother."

My mother cackled when she heard.

"You know when I'm gone, you're gonna need a mother."

This was fifteen years before she died. I had no idea why she said this then. What did she know? I was silent. I couldn't imagine a time when she wouldn't be here.

"Do we have to talk about this?"

She cackled again.

"It's gonna come, sweet face. I'm not gonna live forever."

Of course, I knew that was true, but when it came to my mother I indulged in magical thinking, as if she had special powers and would somehow live forever, or at least until I didn't need her anymore, which was the same thing as forever.

"Well, I'll deal with it, then," I told her, trying to keep it light.

The Tuesday before Thanksgiving 2008, we were in Mom's small, eat-in kitchen. I had come to spend the day learning how to make her collards and her stuffing. I unloaded all the supplies—four bushels of greens, three large green peppers, four cans of College

Inn chicken broth, Wesson oil (never Crisco), and Indian Head cornmeal.

"Good, good," she said, examining the groceries I'd purchased per her exact instructions. My mother's Thanksgiving spread was legendary—her stuffing, her greens, her yams, her cakes, pies, gravy. Everything she did, she did well. Growing up with that caused me to not try; the standard seemed too high.

"Get a knife, get two. Like steak knives."

I obeyed and sat down on the pine and hunter-green spindle chair across from her at the matching wooden table.

"Get the big pot," she said, pointing to the right-hand cabinet. Her weak lungs kept her seated.

Just as it had been in our house growing up, everything in this apartment in the retirement community my parents had moved to was arranged perfectly: her pot, pans, tops; there was no haphazard storage, like at my house in Montclair.

She picked up the greens. "First, you gotta cut the stems off. Some people leave them on, but that makes 'em tough."

There was a precise method to this.

"Here, hold them like this," she said, holding one leaf at a time and ushering the knife down the side of the stem on each side. We did this for each leaf. I have no idea how much time this took but know it was long.

Then she showed me how to roll up the leaves and to cut them in strips, making for the perfect-sized morsel to eat.

"Then you gotta clean them. You gotta soak 'em at least three times to get all the grit off."

I didn't bother pointing out that, these days, not coming directly from the field, the greens weren't tinged with dirt. It probably wouldn't have made a difference to her anyway.

We cut up the green pepper to add on top, put in the chicken broth, and finally the greens were ready to be put in a cauldron and cooked. It was a great day with my mother. I wish I had it on tape, but it's forever in my mind for me to turn over, like a precious heirloom.

That year was the first time Big Cliff and Joan weren't with us for Thanksgiving dinner. His prostate cancer had already metastasized to his bones and brain. He was too sick to ride in the car for the close to an hour it took from their home in Mount Vernon. Joan sent her fabulous homemade rolls, turnips, macaroni and cheese, and creamed onions for Cliff, as well as a chocolate mousse. The rest of the family was there: my parents; brother Duane; nephew Kamal, his wife and daughter; his mom, Wendy; her husband, Robert; Cliff's aunt Miriam and cousin Em Sue.

At Christmas, Mom insisted that we drive to Westchester so she could see Big Cliff. We had to take both of our cars because we couldn't all fit in one. Cliff drove my dad, and I drove my mom and the kids. As she sat next to me in the passenger seat, I could hear her breath rattling in her lungs. When we got to their house, she had to hoist herself up the ten stairs, gripping the wrought-iron railing as she went.

Joan was her usual buoyant self, although the long days and sleepless nights of caretaking were showing on her face. She'd cooked a full holiday meal and had set the table. Big Cliff sat in a wheelchair, a gauze patch taped over his left eye from a recent procedure. He couldn't smile much, and we couldn't hug him because it would hurt. He was exhausted, but I knew he was happy to see us, and we were thrilled to be with him. I was so glad that my mom had insisted we make the drive. Maybe she had had a premonition. Big Cliff sat and had dinner with us at the table, able to stay up until before dessert. A month later, on January 23, 2009, he was gone.

Mom was in the hospital, again. This time I'd been the one who found her sitting in a La-Z-Boy chair in their apartment, barely able to speak. One side of her face drooped, as if she'd had a stroke. She was holding her right wrist with her left—it turned out to be broken. She recognized me but not Joni, who was visiting from LA. My father was at church but had left my aunt Marion, my mother's sister, with her. Mom had complained that her hand was hurting. She'd apparently broken her wrist days earlier during one of the three times she'd fallen that week. My father hadn't told me about the falls because he'd forgotten to. Neither of them knew she'd broken her wrist. This is when it became clear to me that my dad was no longer capable of taking care of her.

About a decade earlier, my parents had sold the house in Newark where they'd lived for over forty years. My mother could no

Mom, Daddy, and me on my
thirtieth birthday, July 7, 1988,
in my New York apartment.

longer climb the stairs. They hadn't wanted to move but felt they had no choice. She just didn't have the heart or lung capacity to get from the basement to the second or third floor, where their living quarters were. At eighty-three, they were both unraveling, albeit in different ways. I used to say, when people would ask me how they were doing, that they were a good match because mentally she was sharp, and physically he was perfect; but he didn't know how to cook, and she couldn't stand long enough to do it. She also didn't have an appetite and got annoyed at him for insisting that she eat and take her medicine. She said he was the cause of much of her stress; just his presence seemed to send her to an angry, frustrated place. This wasn't new; it had just become clear enough for Ray Charles to see.

I was frustrated by her frustration with him. The same things that annoyed her had always done so. I told her she had to let it go. She got annoyed with me and told me that I didn't understand just how difficult Matthew was: "You don't know what he's like." I knew my dad was far from perfect. He was cheap and could be moody, but he loved her and had always taken care of his family, and he was one of the kindest and gentlest people I'd ever known. Most people shared that view. He worked for twenty-five years at General Motors, mostly on an auto assembly line making Buicks. He left the house every single morning before the sun came up, with a paper bag containing a Spam sandwich, a Thermos of tea, a piece of fruit, and maybe something home-baked. He came home every single day at four thirty—you could set your watch by it. Every two weeks, he would hand my mother his paycheck. Wherever my mother wanted to go, we went. We spent all holidays with her side of the family, we traveled to see her friends, and we went to the shore because that's where she wanted to go.

When we got her to the emergency room, the attending physician, Dr. Rothman, said Mom was suffering from congestive heart failure. I told him about the open-heart surgery she'd undergone two years earlier, and that she'd had her leaky valve replaced, along with a bypass and a ventricle repair, and that her enlarged heart had been shaved. To my mind, that meant her heart was like new. He said that unless she drastically changed her situation, the stress could still cause more damage. He told us that her failing lungs were the reason for her falls and the condition I'd found her in that mimicked a stroke. By the next day she was much better; a CAT scan showed no brain damage, no bleeds, and no evidence of a stroke.

It would be easy to say I got lost when my mom got sick, but that's not quite what happened. It certainly made things worse, pushed me closer to the edge, but I was already standing at the periphery, just hanging on. Mom getting so sick was simply the match thrown on a pool of gasoline that surrounded me. I'd discovered if I had too much free time, torture was my form of exercise. I don't mean physical torture, but rather round and round mean, bad thoughts about myself and how worthless I was; how guilty I felt for, oh, fill in the damn blanks—not always packing healthy kids' lunches; sending Ford to aftercare; not making Baldwin a full breakfast before she left for school; not working and making my own money; not calling my mother enough. I felt guilty for being overwhelmed. I fantasized about the mother in *The Hours*, based on the Virginia Woolf novel *Mrs. Dalloway*. She packed up and left her little boy and girl and husband and moved to someplace far away. She never saw them again. But while I used to fantasize about a rich ex-boyfriend rescuing me, putting me up in a luxurious Manhattan high-rise, I could never, even at my most desperate, imagine leaving my kids.

On February 10, 2009, the day before my mom's eighty-fourth birthday, I moved her into our home. My plan was just to bring her to my house for a week to strengthen her up, allow her to relax and not have to worry about cooking; she still cooked every meal for my father. They both needed to get some good nights of sleep, and my dad needed a break. I saw him getting thinner and worried that, in taking care of Mom, he was going to get ill. I turned our family room into her bedroom, where I put the rented hospital bed, commode, and oxygen tank. A walker and a rented wheelchair were all set and ready for her, although she was never again well enough to use them.

I had to fight with Daddy, who didn't want to relinquish what he believed in his bones was his responsibility to care for his wife. But she'd told me that at night when she needed help to walk to the bathroom, he couldn't hear her calling for him. At eighty-four, he was overwhelmed with the demands of taking care of someone so sick. He relented only when I promised him that this arrangement was only temporary. At that point, they'd been married for fifty-six years and had never been apart, other than the times she traveled to her PTA conventions.

He and my mother had been living fifteen miles from me, but Daddy came to see Mom at my house every single day. He would sit with her, and they'd watch their favorite soaps, *The Young and the Restless* and *General Hospital*. They'd nod off or bicker, just like they did at home. He was always trying to get her to eat more than she wanted or could, convinced that if she'd just eat, she'd get better. More than once, he literally pushed food onto her pressed-together lips. One Sunday Joan, my mother-in-law, came over to help out. She had cooked a big meal of fried chicken, mac and cheese, and string beans, and my father, who never yells, had it out with her about the richness of the food. He was frustrated that my mother didn't want to eat and took out his frustration on Joan. Cliff and I were in the basement watching TV, but really hiding. I felt so sorry for my dad because he just didn't know what to do, and for Joan too, because she'd just gone through two years of caretaking and had buried her husband only two months earlier.

The first five days after she came to live with us, Mom was able to eat regular food and communicate fine, and didn't need the portable commode. She was her usual sharp, funny, brutally honest self. A physical therapist came once but said she wouldn't come back because there was no point. Mom's will was strong, but her limbs were just too feeble. We also had a young, super competent visiting nurse, Keisha. When she first came on a Monday, she said mom's vitals were good, that she was doing pretty well. Wednesday, Keisha came back and said she wasn't quite so sure why Mom's vitals had declined from the two days before. By Friday's visit, Keisha looked stricken.

"She's doing bad, really bad," she said. "Her pulse and her blood pressure are at the point where, legally, I have to call an ambulance."

I shook my head. I'd promised.

"You can turn them away, but I have to call."

My mother was lying in her bed, looking frail, but her voice was strong and determined: "No hospital. I don't want to go back to the hospital."

The paramedics came, and I sent them away. I'd made that deal with her when I convinced her to come to my house to recuperate. She was tired. After the paramedics left, Keisha asked me if I'd considered hospice.

Hospice? We weren't there yet, were we?

"It doesn't mean that the patient is going to pass right away," she explained. "You can have hospice for six months, a year, even longer."

Could Mom have that long?

I didn't think so, but I'd take six months.

After a week of Cliff helping me take care of my mom and me feeling like I had a newborn again—Mom would wake up in the middle of the night—I hired a hardworking, loving Ecuadorian woman named Sonia to help. God sent Sonia to me. I know that for sure. She came through a friend of a friend. I interviewed her a week after my mother moved in; I looked into her deep-set, light-brown eyes and felt a kindness and compassion emanating from her that led me to hire her before I'd even checked her references. I just knew she'd be perfect, and she was. Our hospice nurse Joe even commented on how lucky I was to have found her.

He'd been through thirteen caregivers himself in trying to care for his father at home. I'd hear this story over and over—they were unreliable, untrustworthy, or just didn't do the work. Sonia cared for my mother, "Miss Clarita" as she would call her, as if she were her own kin. Watching them filled my breaking heart. Sonia came Monday through Friday from 8 a.m. till 7 p.m. Cliff and I were on duty nights and weekends. There were nights when Mom wouldn't sleep between calling me and yelling for Jesus to take her. She'd moan sometimes but more often these would be loud, begging de-mands. We'd bought a baby monitor, but on some nights, toward the end, I would turn it down. I was losing it. Some nights I'd sleep on the couch next to the hospital bed, just to be closer if I needed to give her one of the two hospice-provided medicines: one to calm her down, the other, morphine, for the pain. Often, she just didn't want to be left alone and would scream for me to not leave, even though I was only going to the bathroom, which was right by the room where she lay.

The clock has no meaning to someone who is chronically ill. On the weekends Cliff and I couldn't go out at the same time. We couldn't leave Mom alone or with just the children in the house. If we both had to leave, Daddy would be in charge. He knew how to administer her breathing treatments in the nebulizer, but he didn't know how to change her diaper and couldn't prepare the kind of food she was able to eat, nor would he accept that she couldn't swallow unmashed food. One Saturday morning—it turned out it was her last Saturday morning—I got up at six thirty to change her and put ointment on her butt, just like I used to do with my children. I washed her up and was preparing to give her breakfast and her medicines (at one point she had nine different prescriptions) when she said: "Neal, sit down. You've done enough. Take care of yourself. Go tend the children. You don't need to do anything else for me."

"But I still need to give you breakfast," I said.

She, literally on her deathbed, was still trying to take care of me. I didn't know it then, but she'd already begun to show symptoms of the death march. Her pupils were dilated; she was more upbeat but with a kind of flat affect, slightly detached from reality. I was dressed in my nightgown; my hair was a wreck in two big, loose, sloppy cornrows. I was fixing the sheets on her bed, rearranging her pillows.

"You look so pretty," Mom said. "Who did your hair? You look so nice."

At the time, I thought it was odd, but between sleep deprivation and grieving for what I knew was coming, I didn't put any stock in the craziness of what she was saying. I was grateful that she'd never lost our connection. She never said mean things to me as she did to my father, her sister Marion, and sister-in-law Etrulia. Sometimes even the hospice nurse, Joe, and Sonia got the wrath of Clara.

One day Joe was trying to examine her, and she regally told him: "I'm not receiving visitors now." Her tone was enough for Joe to stop what he was doing and come and sit with me in the dining room, where I had been waiting for him. We'd needed to talk about what to do. Cliff and I were at our end. Mom was bleeding internally; buckets of blood would pour from her rectum. It had happened three times. We had no idea why—the doctors had theories but had ruled further tests unnecessary.

"You could have her taken to the hospital and have her examined," Joe pointed out, "but it would be invasive. What would be the benefit? You would know what's causing it, and then what? You're not going to fix whatever it is."

The first time, her blood soaked into the carpet, but that was nothing compared to the scent of the blood, a combination of rotten fish and burnt metal, that wafted through the entire house. It was one of the worst odors I've ever smelled in my entire life, and there was no escaping it. I could smell it in my office, three stories from her room. It was winter, so opening the windows or going outside wasn't an option. By the third time the bleeding happened, I was convinced I couldn't take it anymore, that I'd have to move her.

Joe said that we could send her to their hospice facility. "But there are a lot of people on the ward, and she won't get a lot of attention," he said. "She probably wouldn't survive the ambulance ride."

I decided to keep her with me, and Cliff agreed that we'd just have to push through. We'd just deal.

She died the next morning.

18

Aftermath

I PLUMMETED.

Cliff called my friends the day Mom died, and by that afternoon several of them just showed up: Lynne, Andrea, Adrianne, Iqua, Jeanine (please forgive me if I'm leaving you out). Joni got on a plane from California as soon as Cliff called her. That night, as I lay in bed, lights off, not sleeping, not awake, Cliff brought Joni home from the airport. She walked into our bedroom, took off her coat and her shoes, and got in bed with me. We lay facing each other, hugging and sobbing, faces pressed together, tears mingling. My mother had loved her; she'd loved my mother; and Joni knew how much my mother and I had loved each other. She'd witnessed our bond; she "got" that Clara was different, special in a way some people just missed.

Joni had been here for Cliff's dad's memorial service. When she came for Mom's funeral, she was planning on staying a week or two with me, but after my mom died, she found out that her mother,

Barbara Brown, who lived nearby in Roselle, had pancreatic cancer. Her mother had kept the news from her for almost three months, not wanting her to worry. From her diagnosis to her death was four months. We still have a hard time believing that we both lost our moms, twelve days apart. Joni ended up staying with me for six weeks.

For the first days after my mom died, I hardly got out of bed. Cliff got Baldwin out of the house to the school bus and drove Ford to school. I didn't even walk Charlie; he'd simply curl up with me in the bed and wouldn't leave until the afternoon when Sonia would walk him to go and meet Ford's bus. Joni spent most of her days visiting her mom in the hospital in Elizabeth, while I'd stay in bed until seven, when it was time for Sonia to leave. Although I'd hired Sonia to take care of my mother, after Mom died, I just couldn't bear to part with her. She'd been there; she'd been a witness. She'd been with my mother during her dying weeks. She had also been there for me, and I needed Sonia's kindness, her tending to the kids and the house along with my soul. When Cliff would come home from work and find me in bed, he never acknowledged it. He'd just talk to me about work and report on who'd sent condolences to me or to him.

In dealing with his dad's death and then two months later my mom's, our home had been hit by an emotional earthquake, both of us walking around with gaping holes in our hearts. We were each dealing with it in different ways, however. Cliff had worshipped his father, whom he (and many others) had considered a genius. I'd loved him, too. "I miss my dad," was all Cliff would say, sometimes out of the blue, sometimes in response to unfolding events. When BP's giant deepwater rig blew up and oil and toxic chemicals gushed into the Gulf of Mexico, engineers scrambled for weeks with ideas of how to contain it. "If my dad was here, he could've figured out how to fix it," Cliff said. "We would have had some good talks about what happened."

Even as we tried to cope with our losses, our financial lives were also unraveling. The year before, on September 30, 2008, Cliff and I had sat next to each other on the couch in the family room watching MSNBC as reports of the world's financial markets collapsing played over and over. He knew all the abbreviations by heart, so as the crawl went by, he knew exactly how badly the companies were performing. I recognized only a few. Apple, or AAPL, had dropped from over $700 to $106 a share. The bottom of our financial bucket fell out almost a year to the day later, on the night of Rosh Hashanah, just months after Cliff's father and my mother passed away. Ironic, I later thought, since that holiday is said to mark sweet beginnings. For us, it was the acknowledgment of the end of an era and of a lifestyle that had been flush. We weren't rich by any stretch, but we had what we needed and a lot of what we wanted. I'd bought clothes and things for the kids without much thought, but we were now close to liquid broke. We could no longer afford the way we were living. We could barely afford our enormous taxes once we paid for our mortgage and food and insurance. At least our relationship at that moment was solid. We just hunkered down and held onto each other.

We pinched off our savings to pay monthly expenses that had previously been covered easily by Cliff's commissions, because the large check Cliff was given to move from Salomon Smith Barney to UBS was actually a loan and required an immediate payment that took a huge chunk of our monthly income. Everyone was suffering. Most people lost money, but lots of people, including my two best friends, also lost their jobs (they were unemployed for four and two years, respectively, and one is still very much underemployed). Some clients didn't follow when Cliff moved to another firm, and the ones who did just weren't investing the way they once had. Since the market had crashed, people were more cautious. Clients who had previously invested in stocks and funds now were choosing to put their money into real estate and other less volatile investments. My husband was now bringing home a quarter of what he had in the past, and the very nice money from my books had also mostly dried up. Most people hear my husband works on Wall Street and think we're rich, part of the 1 percent. We aren't, and in the New York area, we never were.

Right around this time, our dog Charlie started going blind. Our perfect storm continued to build, and even worse weather was on the way. Three months later Cliff was diagnosed with prostate cancer—which was how his father's cancer had started. Unlike me, Cliff isn't emotional. He's calm and processes mentally, but hearing the word "cancer" momentarily rocked him. I was rocked too, but tried to remain steady for him. He called me right after he'd left the doctor's office, where he'd gotten the news. Weeks earlier, his PSA (which stands for "prostate-specific antigen") had been high—not to the sky, but elevated. It was a red flag, but both of us were sure that it was nothing. When Cliff told me that the cause of the elevation was cancer, I sat down with my hand over my mouth, as if that movement would trigger my brain to say something intelligent, something meaningful, something to make him feel better. Nothing came.

"I'm coming home," Cliff said.

I googled "prostate cancer" and found what I pretty much already knew, that it was a "good cancer," and that it was highly treatable as long as it was caught early, which this had been. We talked about it, and Cliff began reading everything he could find. The most helpful was a book called *Invasion of the Prostate Snatchers,* which was about the overabundance of prostatectomies. A friend told us about a chiropractor in Westchester County who specialized in vitamin treatment for the prostate. Cliff came home with about seven different bottles of stuff, including vitamin D, curcumin, turmeric, Zyflamend, and açaí berry. He had the name of an oncologist at Sloan-Kettering from when his dad had been sick. We were told by the surgeon that his cancer was in the very early stage and was located in a small quadrant. Prostate cancer was most commonly treated in one of three ways: surgery, radiation, or active surveillance, which means getting the blood checked every three months and a biopsy and MRI every other year.

After thinking, reading, and consulting with his urologist in New Jersey and the cancer surgeon at Sloan-Kettering, Cliff decided the best option for treatment for him was active surveillance, even though getting the prostate biopsied every other year is in-

My parents-in-law, Joan and Clifford Virgin.

vasive and very uncomfortable. His local doctor agreed with his choice, although he said most people can't handle the uncertainty of cancer in their body and want to just take it out. "But most people aren't like you," he said. Cliff's decision, which for me at the time was nerve-wracking (I wanted him to have it taken out), was the right one. Four years after the initial diagnosis, they haven't been able to find any cancer in Cliff's body. The doctors won't actually say the words "cancer-free," but so far there has been no visible sign of cancer anywhere. Grace.

My longtime yoga teacher, Susan, had organized a yoga trip to Mexico. A poster featuring women doing downward-facing dog on a beach in Los Cabos hung in the elevator that led to the yoga studio. I'd noted the dates of the trip and mentally decided I couldn't go. They would be there on my mother's birthday. It was several weeks before it dawned on me that I wouldn't be busy with my mom, celebrating her birthday, because she was gone. I was available to take the trip, but could I? I was still groping around on the dark floor of a cave of grief, and besides, we couldn't afford it.

"You can't afford not go," Susan said. "I'll do whatever to help you." Although the deadline had passed, she got me a room at a discounted rate, and I got myself packed and on the plane. I was armed with the thick Jonathan Franzen novel *Freedom* that I'd wanted to read but hadn't been able to concentrate on. In my room at the Westin, I finished it sooner than I'd expected and found myself with time to read a second book. On my iPad, I toured the suggested readings on Amazon. The yellow and lavender cover of *The Help* kept popping up on the screen. I'd sworn I wouldn't read it because I didn't want to hear from another White woman rhapsodizing about her Black maid, with the maid merely being an angelic prop and not a fully realized character. But then, I thought, how could I criticize something that I hadn't read? So I read the sample chapter. I was pulled in by the story. The writer did get the dialect right and captured some of the women's inherent dignity and determination. Reading about the main Black character, Abiline, I kept thinking about my mother and the girl she was when she had worked as a nanny and a maid. Reading this book confirmed for me how clever these women had to be to survive, to push past the daily assaults on their humanity.

The next day was February 11, Mom's birthday. I sat out on the terrace of my hotel room, looking over the Sea of Cortez. I was glad to be sealed away from the other tourists at the resort, as I held up my vegetable juice in a solitary toast to Mom. She would've loved it here; she loved to travel anywhere, even Utah to see the Salt Lake Temple. I smiled as I recalled one of my favorite memories of my mother.

For five years, Cliff and I had rented a house for the month of

With my girls in Sag Harbor: (*from left*) Wendy, me, Joni, Eleanore.

August in Sag Harbor, where we met. We'd rent in either Azurest or Sag Harbor Hills, which I called the colony. We'd usually invite my mom for a weekend to spend time with the kids and us. My mother, who'd passed on to me her love of the beach, would happily come, always agonizing about what to pack. I'd assure her the bay beach was small and private, that it wasn't fancy; it was just family and friends. After my mom would put her bathing suit on, she would pull out two small disc-shaped jars and begin dotingly applying the contents to her legs. It was leg makeup.

One day, Cliff and I were outside of our bungalow when we ran into Chester Redhead, a noted Harlem dentist. We got to talking and doing "Negro Geography" and it turned out that Cliff's father and Dr. Redhead had gone to City College together. Cliff pulled out his cell phone and called his dad so the two men could speak. After that, Dr. Redhead invited us over for a drink. My mother, Cliff, Baldwin, and I strolled to his house, which was just a few feet from where we were renting. Inside it was a world away: beautiful Black art, Persian rugs, and lovely mahogany everywhere, including the glass cabinet. The place was not babyproofed and Baldwin was only two, so after one drink, I took her home, leaving Cliff and my mother to talk and have more drinks. When they got back hours later, Baldwin and I were chilling on the rattan couch.

My mother had clearly passed her two-drink vodka-and-cranberry-juice limit. I went to her bedroom to help her out of her bathing suit.

I asked her if they'd had a good time. She was beaming.

"Oh, yeah. That's some house. It's somethin.'"

"Yeah, it's really nice."

"And facing the water like that . . . *umph.*"

My mother's voice sounded funny, and I looked at her. She was crying.

"What's the matter? Why're you crying?"

Unlike me, Clara rarely cried.

"Neal," she said, now in full sob. "I never thought I'd see Black people living like that!" Seeing that place and the others lined up beside it, *Black Enterprise* magnate Earl Graves's place on one side, the late attorney Johnnie Cochran's on the other, had filled her with pride. It said to her, we had overcome.

Now, sitting on a terrace in Mexico and looking out at the Sea of Cortez on her birthday, I was happy I had been able to share that with her.

She had given me so much.

19

Lawrence

AS PAINFUL as it had been, my mother's declining health and finally her death left me with an unexpected gift: my oldest brother Lawrence. My mother got pregnant with my brother Larry when she was sixteen years old, and she'd married his father.

I used to like to dig through my mother's things, her papers, jewelry, underwear, and her quilted box filled with crème lambskin, lavender suede, and black cotton gloves. One evening while she was making dinner, I was in her bedroom on the floor, going through her bottom dresser drawer. She used to have a large black leather clutch bag with all kinds of official-looking papers tucked inside. I came across a divorce decree. I couldn't have been more than seven or eight. I read the words and didn't understand them, but there was something in the weight of the paper, the seal, the ink, that told me this was important. I got up from the floor with the paper in my hand and went to my mother, who was in the kitchen stirring a pot on the stove.

I held it out to her.

"Mommy, what does this mean?"

She looked down at what I was holding and looked sort of amused.

"That's from Mommy's divorce."

Divorce. I only barely knew the word. What I knew more strongly was how it made me feel. Like something illicit, like the four-thirty movies I liked to watch after school, the ones that starred Susan Hayward—*Back Street* and *I Want to Live!*

"How are you divorced?"

"I was married before, to Larry's father. We didn't get along, so we got a divorce." She said it just like that, measured, matter-of-fact. I decided if it wasn't a big dark secret to her, it wasn't to me. What struck me as much as her response was how she'd let me just go through her things; it was as if there were no secrets between us, or at least it seemed that she didn't want there to be.

I didn't really know Larry when I was growing up. Eighteen years was too much of an age difference, and whenever he did come around, Marc and Duane acted like he was a superhero and dominated his time. I do remember one Christmas, I believe I was thirteen and in the eighth grade, he bought me several dresses and a coat. I, a picky, style-conscious girl even then, hated all of it, and told my mom. Somehow, he said okay, ignoring my brattiness, and we went to the store together and picked out something that I liked. I don't remember what happened after that. The rest of the memory has evaporated.

Over the years I didn't see him much, and he didn't come to my wedding. When I asked my mom why he wasn't coming, she said it was because he had to work. I thought that was strange, that he wouldn't take the day off, but I left it alone. I'm sure there was more to his decision. Years went by and I didn't see Larry until I'd been married for a few years and invited him to the surprise party I gave for my mother when she turned seventy. It was the first time I really felt that he was my brother, not just my mother's son. When my parents decided to finally sell their house in Newark, they moved to a community in Rahway that Larry had told them about, a place near his house.

"I guess he wants to be near his mom, after all this time," my mother said to me, couched as a joke.

Before my parents moved from their house in Newark, I had spent two years off and on looking for adult living places for them closer to Montclair. My mother would reject them as too expensive or "for old people" (this was when she was eighty). I think it brought her some kind of peace and closure to be near Larry. I got to know him better during this time, too. I'd see him when I'd visit my parents. He dropped by their place a lot, usually bringing something, a TV, an answering machine, outdoor chairs for them to sit out on their terrace. I also saw how close he and my dad were. Theirs was a loving relationship that my brother Marc says has always been there. "Daddy used to take Larry to work with him when he drove that delivery truck," Marc told me. "He wanted Larry to come and live with us, but Mommy said no." Neither of us knew the entire story. Larry later told me that Daddy always introduced him as his son. "Matthew was always a good man," he said.

I got closer to Larry when Mom got sick. We were both at the apartment the time I'd found her, when it appeared that she'd had a stroke. He and I had waited outside the radiology department while they did the CAT scan at the hospital. We made small talk. I was wracked with worry, and it was clear that he was, too. It made me love him. When I got her to come and stay with us weeks before she died, it was Larry and Daddy who brought her. She was in a wheelchair and using an oxygen tank, insisting that she didn't need any of it. Larry would come often to sit with her, and one week he even helped to pay the nurse I'd hired. I didn't ask him for money, and he didn't make a big deal over giving it to me. He simply wrote out a check and handed it to me. Until then, Cliff and I were the only ones paying. During the planning and leading up to the funeral, and after, I talked to him on the phone often; he was feeling that deep cut like I was.

Two of my brothers spoke at the funeral. Larry and I sat mute. My brother Duane, whose voice broke at one point, said the gift we could give to our mother was to love one another as she had loved each of us. I have tried to stay connected with my brothers, but it's hard when the mother dies. With my dad having dementia, there can be lots of resentment over who is doing more caretaking.

The year after my mother died, I called Larry on his birthday, August 7, exactly one month after mine. I'd only just learned when his birthday fell. Larry and I chatted about the kids, his health, taxes, and a possible move out of the state or at least the county where he lived. After we hung up, I flashed on what Duane had said at the funeral. I felt warm inside, like Mom had approved. Larry told me a month later that my birthday phone call was the best he'd ever had.

Mom and I used to talk about her life after she had left Larry's father, which was shortly after they married. She told me that he'd hit her twice, and that was twice too many times. She packed up her baby son and moved back to her mother's house even though it was already crowded with family. While I knew that his paternal grandparents had raised Larry, I was never clear about why.

On a warm day, almost a year after Mom had been buried, Larry and I stood and talked in the cemetery parking lot. I asked him how he'd come to live with his grandparents.

"One day my grandfather came to Grandma's [my mother's

extended family's house] and got me because I'd gotten sick with some kind of bronchitis and I wasn't getting any better. He felt like nobody was really taking care of me over there. Mama was working a lot. He picked me up and took me to his house, and that's where I stayed. It was fine because my grandparents were very loving."

Mom told me that once Larry went to live with his grandparents, she would take money to them for Larry every two weeks, when she got paid. "That man [her ex-husband] would chase me down the street, every single time, trying to catch me so he could beat me up," she said. "I'd haul ass. He never could catch me."

Larry told me, "When Mama married Matthew, I'd go and visit. I was so happy when Marc was born. I had a brother. I would come and visit on the weekends and we'd play. When we were older, we would play in the playground across the street; they were on Rose Terrace at the time. Anytime a kid did something, if there was a fight, Mama always accused me of starting it and she'd beat me, whether I did it or not. One time Aunt Grace was babysitting us; she was always mad because she was only a teenager and just wanted to hang out. Grace told Mama that I'd called Marc a bastard. I hadn't, but she didn't believe me. I got the worst beating from her that I've gotten in my life. But I still never wanted to leave, to go back home. I was sad. I couldn't understand why I couldn't live with them, with my brother."

Larry's words made my heart hurt. I hugged him. I wanted to apologize for my mother, but what would that mean?

I said it anyway. "I'm so sorry you had to go through that."

"No need," he said.

Still, I felt compelled to explain her. I told him that she was young and in pain and that it wasn't him she was angry at; he just happened to be there; that she was angry at getting pregnant with him so young, at having to put all her dreams away in a drawer.

"It's okay," Larry said. "I got a lot of love from my grandparents, and me and Mama, we had fun, too. It wasn't all bad."

Still, I hurt for him.

To Marc and Duane, Larry was someone they were proud to call "my big brother." To me, Larry was a big, dark, and strange presence. Growing up, I didn't understand his connection to our family, how was he my brothers' brother and not mine, and if he was mine, too, why didn't he live with us and why didn't he look like us? It's embarrassing to write this now, to admit it, but it's the truth.

Now that Mom's gone, we don't keep in touch like we did when she was sick and shortly after she passed, but I've gotten to know my big brother as man of his word, as a former marine; as someone whom I respect, and on whom I know I can always count.

Mom working a mouton fur coat (*right*) in
the 1940s; couple in photo unknown.

20

Code Switching

ANOTHER WALLOWING day. How did this get to be my life? School drop-off, walk the dog, go to the gym, go home, think up dinner, make dinner, pick up one kid or meet his bus, serve snacks after school, help with homework, listen to stories of life in middle school—who's smoking weed, who is *a complete slut*—have dinner when husband comes home, get some time alone while kids play with Dad, then either I put Ford to bed or Cliff does. I kiss them both good night, then watch TV with my husband till I fall asleep. Day ends. Repeat next day.

None of it was enough to drown out the constant loop running in my brain: *I'm going insane. I'm so sad all the time. If I don't get some mental stimulation soon I'm gonna lose my mind. I have to find work, write another book, do something. I'm so tired of complaining. A book, maybe an article about women like me. I know there are hundreds, thousands. Of course, for Black women, these are Miss Ann problems 'cause most of us work 'cause we have to; I'm going to have to if the stock market doesn't turn around soon, which it doesn't look like it will, which means I should be looking for work now. Cliff's commissions are down, and so is our income. I seriously can't figure out what else to do. How did this get to be my life??*

There were of course a whole host of reasons why going back to work would be challenging—but that was exactly the muscle I needed to flex. I was not challenged. The biggest thing I faced daily was working out and keeping myself from sinking into a pit of depression so deep I might never pull out of it. The blackness was always there, waiting to envelop me, waiting for me to show one bit of weakness, the tiniest crack, and then I'd be sunk.

I decided to try an analyst who came highly recommended by a therapist friend. I got lost going to his office, which was right in my neighborhood, five minutes from my house. I couldn't visualize in my mind where his house sat. I knew the street but couldn't conceptualize the block. I drove back and forth along the street, passing his office several times. I called him twice from the car. I finally showed up, frazzled and frustrated by how difficult everything had become. He opened the door, and I saw deep-set, soulful eyes, disheveled hair, and a very wrinkled shirt. The fact that he was an analyst meant he had training beyond a PhD in psychology. He told me to call him by his first name, James.* I tried to make small talk, inquiring about his ethnic background and he shared that his family was of Greek extraction. He then asked about my background—family, husband, kids, the work I did. As he probed further, I told him about my mom's death. His condolences seemed genuine, heartfelt. He asked questions about our relationship, and I managed to get through most of the session before my sobs became so intense that I could no longer talk. But I'd liked his face and the gentleness of his demeanor and decided to return.

At our third or fourth session, when I was questioning whether what I was feeling could be "just grief," he told me yes. He said the overwhelming grief that I felt was completely understandable. "In some cultures a professional mourner is hired because the grief becomes too great," he told me. I couldn't help but wonder how a professional mourner would be able to lessen my own grief. Would they climb inside me and somehow excavate this pain?

I saw James a total of six times. His method was prodding and Jungian, much like that of the first therapist, Dr. Chisholm, I ever saw when I was thirty and thriving in my career as a magazine editor and living in Manhattan. In those days, my only unhappiness was about my choice of men. I saw Dr. Chisholm once a week for three years, and our sessions were hugely beneficial. But with James, I knew that I didn't have the stamina to delve into my subconscious. In our sessions, I could barely focus on what he was saying and instead found myself obsessing about the fee of $175 for forty-five minutes. I'd asked him his opinion about antidepressants, and while he didn't come right out and say that he was against them, he said, "I believe talk therapy works."

I asked him if he thought talk therapy would work for what was ailing me, and he said yes. But I knew better. He was kind and clearly an excellent therapist, but his heavy, methodical approach was beyond what I could manage at that point. Another time, I would be all in for exploring the depths of my psyche, but not now.

Not long after, a friend of a friend who'd struggled for years with depression and was eventually diagnosed with fairly tangled brain wiring, suggested I see her therapist, who was also a nurse practitioner. Diana* was a lanky Black woman from Mississippi, and after several weeks of me just sitting on her leather couch and crying like a lost child, we both understood that talk therapy alone was not going to work. I couldn't get through a session without dissolving into sobs. My internal scaffolding had completely collapsed.

Diana diagnosed me as clinically depressed and suggested that I might need medication. But even though therapy alone wasn't working—and I was convinced it wouldn't—for months I resisted the idea of taking meds. After six additional months, it was clear that I needed prescriptive help. I would've tried hot coals on my exposed flesh at that point.

My depression didn't respond to the first drug we tried, Prozac, even with the addition of Abilify. Next I tried Wellbutrin, but that just made me feel fuzzy and aggressive. I'd been on Effexor a few years earlier—when the severe ennui with a side of perimenopause first hit—and it had worked, but after a few years, I hadn't wanted to take it anymore. Believing that consistent cardio exercise could be just as effective in treating my mild depression, I became a gym rat and weaned myself off Effexor. I was freaked by how severe the withdrawal dizziness was; that was why I hadn't wanted to take drugs when Diana first suggested it—I didn't want to become dependent again. But this time was different. I didn't just want to be happier; I needed help so that I could perform basic life tasks.

Cliff was also desperate for me to feel better. He knew that I'd always wanted to go to Italy, to Tuscany. A short while after my mother died, I managed to get myself to our annual Montclair Art Museum gala. I'd cosseted myself with a wide leather belt, wrapped around a floral silk coat. When I got there, I immediately ordered something that I never drink, a vodka martini. As I stood sipping it by the bar, Cliff went off to look at the silent auction items. I found out later that he had been bidding during the live part on an Italian villa—and he got it. Meanwhile, I stood in one spot, not wandering through the crowd, as I normally would have done. The only people I talked to were those who made their way to me. Most of them knew that my mother had died. They all readily shared their own stories of losing a parent. One writer pal, Dottie Frank, looked into my eyes and said in her South Carolinian drawl, "I'm so sorry." She grabbed me into an embrace so powerful that I will never forget it. Her hug told me that she got the awfulness in full; that losing her own mother had been the worst pain she'd ever endured. I still think of her urgent, firm hug as my initiation into the motherless daughters club. We were now comrades.

I had wanted to go to Italy for twenty years and now, as the trip approached, I couldn't pull myself together. I didn't want to go.

"Let's try something else," Diana said.

I began the prescription for Lamictal about a month before the trip. Usually it takes these drug about six weeks before they kick in and, given my nonresponsiveness to the other meds, I wasn't all that hopeful that this would lift me enough so that I could at least go. Thankfully, it did. I was able to be present with Cliff and the kids, and experience the trip. The sunshine on the Amalfi coast on the Mediterranean was magnificent, as was the Hotel Caruso in Ravello, where we stayed for two nights. From there we went to the villa and stayed eight more days. After six weeks, I could actually smile without faking it. Every morning when I took the pill, I said a prayer of gratitude that such a medicine existed.

Middle school is bar and bat mitzvah season, and Baldwin went to ten of them during seventh and eighth grades. I believed, as my mother taught me, that being exposed to other cultures and being open to people different from one's self was one of the keys to a rich and meaningful life. When Baldwin would come home, after asking if she'd had a good time—the answer was always yes—I'd ask how many other Black kids were there. She'd look at me with an exasperated *Why do you want to know that?* look, and say, "Just me." Sometimes the answer would be "The nanny and me." This didn't seem to bother her. She accepted this representation, or lack thereof, as the way it was. No judgments. I often learn from her.

There was a time, during middle school, when Baldwin had only White friends. She had her first crush on a boy who was White.

Cliff was alarmed.

"She needs to be hanging out with some Black kids," he would say regularly. I wasn't concerned—well, not as much as Cliff was—because I knew she would find Black friends eventually. She'd open her circle as she delved deeper into herself. I knew we'd given her the tools.

Close to the end of middle school, Baldwin told me that she didn't want to go to our town high school. She said that after being über-social in middle school, she was afraid all that socializing would be an impediment to academics. This was a month after my mom had died, although while she was sick, I'd discussed with her Baldwin's reluctance to continue in public school. My mother had advised me to let her do a year at the high school first, and if it didn't work out, then to move her.

I wasn't so sure. The deadlines for the private schools that could've been a good fit had passed, and I didn't know what to do. I was then only a month into my grieving season. I saw an ad in the paper for an open house for an all-girls Catholic school a few towns away. I went one evening and listened to the presentation, although looking around at the other moms and daughters, I knew that these were not my people. I convinced myself, however, that the school would be fine, that Baldwin would make it work. In my right mind, I would have fished out my keys from my purse and left before the end of the presentation. But I wasn't in my right mind. I enrolled her.

From the first day, after drop-off, at the "mothers' coffee," I felt like I was the new girl at the wrong school. Some of the moms were decked out like New Jersey Housewives—big Gucci pocketbooks, big gold jewelry, frosted hair extensions, and tanning-salon-colored skin. I tried making small talk with a few of them. Some tried to be friendly, but we each realized that our tribal tongues were just too foreign for us to be able to communicate. One, who lived a few towns from mine but had to pass through Montclair to get to where the school was in Caldwell, even suggested carpooling. I thought at the time that it was a sweet gesture, one that I knew I'd never take her up on, and later, when I saw her zipping through the parking lot in a Maserati, I realized she probably didn't expect me to. A few others, decked out in Lilly Pulitzer or Talbots, were Catholic girls' school alumnae and were happily speaking in the same vernacular.

The head of the school, a six-foot one-inch nun, was one of the scariest people I've ever encountered. The woman never attempted to look at me, much less say hello—well, not counting the time I went to get Baldwin after she called for me to pick her up because she wasn't feeling well. When I arrived at the secretary's office, Sister Principal was at the desk. I made a joke that she'd taken on a new job, even as my heart was beating overtime, and I'd just been in the car crying about Cliff's prostate cancer. She glared at me. I shifted into business mode and explained that I was there to pick Baldwin up because she wasn't feeling well.

The next thing she said: "Well, if she called you from her cell phone, we will have to confiscate it because she is not allowed to use her phone at school."

"Wow," was all I could say, under my breath. I wanted to call her on the insensitivity of her comment and to let her know that I'd just found out that my husband had prostate cancer. But I was too afraid of her—and having grown up with brothers and Newark bullies, I don't scare easily.

There were many other harsh interactions with administrators, some of it perhaps just the way of Catholic schools, I don't know. Baldwin soldiered through. She had a great math teacher, and her English teacher was very good. The nuns she had for biology and religion were also good teachers and kind people. Of the school's motto, "Empowering Young Women," Baldwin used to say that they should've added, "after they squashed you into the ground."

Baldwin figured out her place in our country's ethnic sociology during her year at Catholic school. In Montclair, in middle school, she could be just Baldwin. She didn't need to explain herself. But many of the girls at her Catholic school were working-class and first-generation college-educated Italian or Irish; there were only six Black girls out of sixty in her freshman class. It was very different from Montclair, where the ratio is 35 percent Black and there was a vibrant mix of religious and socioeconomic backgrounds. After her first week, she asked me, "Where are the Jewish kids?" To her, "Jewish" was a culture, not a religion, even though she'd gone to enough synagogues to have learned some prayers. She tried making new friends, eating lunch with some of the girls and even attending a few football games at a brother Catholic high. She went to two house parties and came home early, horrified at the rampant drinking and sexual experimentation, and also after hearing that some of the girls planned to get married right out of high school, with no plans to go to college.

She had her Jack and Jill friends to hang with on the weekends. She'd been in Jack and Jill since she was six and had always been ambivalent about it at best. One Friday, when I was driving her home from school, she said out of nowhere: "I love Jack and Jill." After years of forcing her to go to Jack and Jill activities, I couldn't believe what I was hearing. For her, it had done what it was founded to do: provide a safe, comfortable place for Black children with similar family values to be with one another. Most of the kids in the group spent their days at private schools, which at worst could feel hostile to Black students, and at best tolerant.

Sometime in the middle of the school year I was having a glass of wine at the home of my neighbors Pete and Colleen. I was telling them about some of the crappy stuff Baldwin had been dealing with at school. Pete and Colleen grew up in one town over from the school and knew the kinds of folks who send their kids there.

After they listened to me go on for who knows how long, Pete said, "It sounds like they don't want you there."

It was a clarion call.

"Yeah, I think they don't."

When the year was half over, the school sent a contract requesting a commitment to return the following year. I didn't bother to send it back. A few months later, they sent a short form survey asking why Baldwin wouldn't be returning. I typed a four-page letter documenting all the awful things she had experienced. Not all of the awful stuff was reserved for her, but the meanness and the attempt to demean and belittle the girls was something I wouldn't tolerate for mine. I'd worked too hard at building her up.

I never heard a word back.

Baldwin was happy to go to Montclair High after her disastrous time at Catholic school, although the weeks before she was to start tenth grade, she was so filled with anxiety she couldn't sleep. She was nervous about the social scene. I was nervous about the academics. Our high school was a tale of two institutions: the kids who were on the AP/high honors track went to good colleges; the ones in the lower classes were left without much guidance. My concern wasn't that Baldwin couldn't be in those top classes, but whether she was going rise to the occasion and give it her best. She did.

That is not to say the three years at the high school weren't without a whole lot of bumps. I cried huge tears of relief at her high school graduation because I felt that, while she'd done the work, I'd had to be her advocate every step of the way, making sure she got the grades she'd earned in those upper classes, where too often relationships with the teachers were not supportive. I'd channeled my mother, rolled up my sleeves, and gone in there. It was fascinating to me how a teacher's attitude changed toward a child when the parents showed up. With a Black parent and child especially, there was often an "Oh, you care about what's going on," or "Oh, I didn't know Baldwin came from that kind of family."

It was exhausting, but I knew I had to do it. My mother had certainly done battle for my brothers and me and lots of other kids. But as Baldwin was preparing to enter public high school, I started having flashbacks and dreams about my own high school drama with bullying girls. In therapy I told Diana about it. She asked me if I'd encountered any of them recently. It had been many years since I'd seen or talked to any of my high school group. I had run into one of them in the mall late one night when I'd been searching for a pair of special tights for Baldwin's kindergarten school picture the next day, and she had been on a similar mission. We'd hugged and chatted cordially, and then she'd said, "You know, everybody is mad at you because of your book." She was talking about my novel *Good Hair*, which had been published three years earlier. I was surprised because I couldn't think of anything in the book that would offend, because it was a novel and there wasn't much about high school. She enlightened me: It was the part where Alice, the main character, talked about being in a sorority of *obnoxious* girls in high school. At the time I wrote it, I wasn't thinking of the word in its literal definition. I only meant to convey that our presence was an affront to some of the other students, especially the girls. We were a pack who wore matching jackets, dressed in the most fashionable clothes, and did all the stuff that the popular girls do.

Decades later, these high school experiences had left deep imprints.

Suddenly I found myself back in "mean girl" world. I dreamed one night about being left out of a grown women circle of friends, a group I didn't even want to be part of, but in my dream we were all living in the same apartment and they were all getting dressed up to go out together but no one had invited me. I analyzed the dream with Diana, and I realized that it reflected my anxiety about Baldwin, not me. Intellectually, I knew that I'd have to let Baldwin work out her own stuff, in her own way; that it was part of her growing and becoming her own person. But emotionally, I hated it. Hated the watching it and having to relive it. Diana suggested that the more I worked out my issues around self-acceptance—not giving a crap about what other people thought of me—the more I'd be able to help Baldwin.

But Baldwin was learning her own important lessons independent of me, for example, how to code switch. When we went on our trip to Italy, we were wandering down one of the many tiny, curved cobblestone streets in Florence one day, when Baldwin spotted a leather jacket in a store window and begged to go inside. Before we had left home, we'd agreed no shopping. Europe was so much more expensive because of our depleted dollar, and there wasn't much there that you couldn't also find in New York. But when she tried on the jacket, it fit as if it were custom-made for her. She had to have it, and Cliff bought it for her. She loved that jacket and wore it all the time when she got back home.

Two years after she got the jacket, she walked out of her high school classroom and left it on the back of a chair. By the time she remembered it and went back to the classroom, the jacket was gone. She didn't tell me for several days, hoping she'd find it. She even filed a report with school security. When at last she told me,

I yelled at her, but I didn't tell Cliff. I just didn't want to hear him ranting about how irresponsible she was.

She was now in her junior year of high school, and we'd begun college tours. Veteran's Day weekend we went to DC. She was interested in George Washington and American. I insisted she look at Howard while we were there. We had an okay tour of GW, and a good one at American. Howard was closed for the federal holiday, so we didn't get a real look at my alma mater. After a great stay with our friends Carmen and Maxie, who had recently moved from Montclair, we headed home on the train. When Cliff picked us up from the Newark Penn Station, he got out of the car to help us put the bags in the trunk. He randomly asked Baldwin why she hadn't worn her leather jacket. We looked at each other and got into the car. I was silent, wanting to see how she'd handle telling him. She began with a long lie about how it had gotten stolen out of her locker. I said nothing, even though my stomach was churning as I listened to her lie. I abhor lying. I counted down in my head—five, four, three—before he began.

"Why would you leave it in your locker? How could you lose a jacket? I never lose anything. I've had things for twenty years. You begged me for that jacket . . ."

The next day Baldwin went to school and saw a girl wearing the jacket. The girl was three times her size on the bottom and had on bamboo hoop earrings with her name spelled out inside.

Baldwin went up close to her and said, "Excuse me, but where did you get that jacket?"

The girl stepped back and looked Baldwin up and down.

"My sista gave it to me."

"Um, well, can I see the label?"

The girl said, "Hell no," and turned to walk away.

Baldwin followed the girl, tapped her on the shoulder, and said,

"That's my jacket." The girl was now walking faster to get away from Baldwin, but she wouldn't let it go.

"We can do this nice or we can do it nasty," Baldwin told her. "I've already reported it stolen to security, and there are cameras around."

The girl gave Baldwin a malevolent look, at this point probably not sure she wasn't crazy. She rolled her eyes, took the jacket off, and handed it over.

When Baldwin called me from school to tell me the story, I was incredulous.

"You did what?"

I called Cliff at work and told him. I was proud of the way she'd handled herself. Cliff was worried that there might be a crowd of girls waiting for her after school, something I hadn't considered, something that would have happened at my school. I called her back and she assured me that everything was cool, that there was nothing like that to worry about. She was right. When she came home and retold me this story, I held my arms out and bowed as if reciting Dana Carvey's famous *SNL* line, "I'm not worthy." I knew, right then, that she was going be okay, better than okay. I knew we'd made the right choice in sending her to public school, because she was learning how to navigate the complicated reality of being Black in America. She understood what it meant to be able to code switch, to be bicultural.

It's often necessary to be schizophrenic in order to be healthy and Black. You have to be able to speak affluent suburbia, hood, and neutral. Baldwin knew the necessity of being able to roll with the many versions of Black girl, among them: the Black/White, the BAP, the Pookie. The Black/White girl is nonracially identified. She prefers rock, folk, and Maroon 5 to Trey Songz or Drake. The BAP (Black American Princess) prefers Cartier, private school, and Martha's Vineyard. The Pookie might have a baby and lots of burgundy hair extensions. It's been said that our children are born to us to be our teachers. While I've been various combinations of Black girl, at different points in my life, I learned my best lesson in code switching from my child. Baldwin showed me that the key is knowing the code, but not switching who you are.

21

A-1 Daughter

MY MOTHER'S friend Amy Jones called me on my first Mother's Day without my mom. Amy is at least twenty years younger than Mom but had been one of her dearest friends in the last decades of her life. They'd met while serving on Newark boards together—the Status of Women commission or the rent board. Amy was one of the many people who simply wanted nothing more than to bask in Mom's specialness. It had been a hard week leading up to Mother's Day. Walking into CVS, I'd avoided the card section but still ended up leaving the store without whatever I'd gone in there for. The whole month had been wrenching, especially the late realization that I didn't have a gift to buy. I'd always stressed over whether to buy something practical or sentimental, unless Mom had use for another sweater or shawl and said so. When Amy called that morning, Cliff and the kids had made breakfast and brought it to me in bed, as they always did. They were lying across the bed as I sat propped up with pillows, eating but without an appetite.

Amy said, "I just wanted to tell you that you were an A-1 daughter. I know this day is going to be hard for you, but I want you to know that your mother was so proud of you. She used to talk about you all the time. She loved you so much, and she loved your children. She never complained about you; the only thing she said was that you couldn't cook a Thanksgiving meal."

By now I was crying, especially when I heard the bit about the Thanksgiving dinner. I couldn't stop crying and smiling. It was classic Mom.

I thanked Amy, who released me from the phone call before I had to go searching for an excuse to get off. Cliff and the kids left me alone, knowing I needed to cry—the kind of crying that had to be done in private.

In early June, I had one of my worst days as a mother since my mom had died. It was a rainy, dark day that looked like nine at night at 8 a.m. Baldwin had gotten herself out of the house but called almost as soon as she got to school, asking me to pick her up after third period. She wasn't feeling well but said nothing specific was wrong.

"No, I'm not coming. Stay in school until the end of the day and I'll pick you up." I hung up and rolled over in my bed.

I knew that she was tired because she had stayed up too late. I no longer had the strength to fight with her: *Go to bed, get up, do your homework, eat something, eat your vegetables, pack your lunch, take your EpiPen, wear your bracelet* (her MedicAlert bracelet stating that she had a nut allergy). I hated everything; I didn't know how I was going to make it.

The next morning I saw I'd gotten another sympathy card. I found it lying on the kitchen counter. It had been three months. I opened the envelope. The card was from the head of Ford's nursery school. I cried just at the sight of Gingi Donohue's name. I'd heard that she had just lost her ninety-plus-year-old mom. I knew what her grief felt like. I knew it didn't matter how old they were. We each knew in our bones the specific pain of losing one so close, so vital to who you were. Since I'd lost my mother, I'd begun putting people into two categories: those who had lost mothers and those who hadn't. Generally, the ones who hadn't experienced the loss were the ones who didn't call or send a card or come to the service. Some even called to complain about mundane problems and "forgot" that my mother had died.

I put the card down and started making my pot of coffee. Cliff was standing in the kitchen, readying to leave for work, and he was taking Baldwin with him. She was taking forever to get dressed. I turned back to the coffee and began to cry again. The smell of the grounds reminded me of my mom, an inveterate coffee drinker.

"I don't think I'll ever get over this," I whispered.

Cliff looked at me, knowingly.

"It takes a long time."

I went outside to get the paper from the driveway. I was dressed in a robe and the beach cover-up I'd worn the day before when I took Ford to the pool. I'd slept in it. I'd developed a habit of sleeping in my clothes, of falling into a deep stupor without the routine of washing my face, brushing and flossing my teeth. I looked down the street at the young men who worked on the garbage trucks. I began to think about who they were. Most of them were Black; many had grown up right here in Montclair, had gone to high school right here alongside kids who went off to Brown and Williams and Princeton and Morehouse and Rutgers. I again flashed to my own high school: Number one from my high school had chosen to go to Howard, number two to Yale; some were doing okay, but too many were not. I'd gone to college because of my mother. I hadn't become a teenage mother because of my mother. I had the kind of life I had because of my mother. I'd been no model high school student. She'd never given up on me. College had been the golden ticket in my mother's eyes. Growing up, my brothers and I all understood that college wasn't an *if*, simply a *where*.

I heard the noise of the garbage truck churning smelly waste that people tossed out without a thought as to how the refuse disappeared. I thought about those city jobs, coveted among some people where I grew up, the ones who didn't have parents who could advocate for them in school and who therefore ended up with few options. I could've been one of those kids if I hadn't had Clara. People who knew me as an adult would be shocked to hear me say that, and might even debate that idea.

"Not you, you're so ambitious, you would've succeed on your own," they'd argue. Maybe. It was hard for most people who didn't know my mother to grasp the role she'd played. I would try to tell them what a force I'd had pushing me at every stage.

The phone was ringing when I came back into the house. It was Jacquie, a fellow suburban wife who was also on a journey to figure out how to be happy, calling to invite me to South Beach in two weeks, when school was out. She had two nights free in the just-opened Mondrian Hotel.

"Do I wanna go?"

I looked around my kitchen, the sink still filled with last night's pots and pans, counters sticky, floor needing to be swept, and I knew I'd be willing to go anywhere right about now; an overnight to Dairy Queen alone would be a thrill.

For three days we lounged in our all-white, smallish but oh-so-chic suite. We ate Thai rice with avocado and sushi at Nobu. We wandered around town, drooling over the home furnishings in Jonathan Adler, Roost, and Nest. We drank sweet cocktails and lounged by the pool. By the time I came home, everything was looking better. Much of my listlessness was gone.

I came home for two days, and then the family was off to Anguilla for the wedding of the daughter of our friends Reggie and Stephanie, the latter of whom had once been my boss at *Essence*. I'd watched her daughter Anique grow up, so this wedding was special. The Caribbean setting, the deep fuchsia dresses the bridesmaids wore, and Anique, a gorgeous professional dancer in her beautiful bridal gown, were just what we all needed. We had a great family time, staying in the same beautiful villa where we'd stayed twice before. The first time I'd seen it had been when Cliff took me for my fiftieth. I stood in the foyer, looking at the galley kitchen and the sunken limestone-floor living room that led out to a wraparound patio and a private pool. I turned to Cliff and said, "Where's the lobby?" I couldn't believe this place was just for us.

My travel had distracted me, but the distraction had proven to be just that. Before my tan had faded, the emotional blackness was back, stronger than before.

⁂

It was Sunday. I'd felt so good all day. The way I'd love to feel every day. I kept trying to figure out what the exact ingredients were. I'd slept in a little, then gotten up and had my coffee while I read the paper in the family room as Ford watched cartoons. Maybe it was the carrot, cucumber, celery, apple, and ginger juice I'd had as breakfast. All day I was just in a good mood, actually felt optimistic. I was on the fence about staying on antidepressants, and today I felt strongly that I didn't need them.

That night I hadn't been able to sleep. After hours of switching from side to side, I realized it was the allergy medicine I'd taken earlier. I rolled, turned on the light, and read the sticker on the bottle of Singulair, which said it can cause depressive moods and sleeplessness. "Write your way out of it," my husband and some of my friends used to tell me, and I could on a good day.

Why did I watch *Revolutionary Road*? Baldwin had begged me to, and I relented. It was depressing enough the first time I watched it. The one person in the movie who is insane is the only one who sees things as they really are: He asks the husband, the main character, Leonardo DiCaprio, "Why do you work at a job you hate?" And DiCaprio says, "So I can have a nice life." The other guy says, "Oh, I know, the nicer the house the more you hate your job." It's a story, set in the 1950s, about a couple who, when they meet, are against the bourgeois suburban life. After they find themselves living that life, the wife convinces the husband that they should move to Paris. They begin packing and planning and telling all their very skeptical friends. Then the wife, Kate Winslet, gets pregnant. DiCaprio wants to stay in the States because of the baby. Winslet loses her mind and dies after trying to give herself an abortion.

I know why this movie gets to me. I, too, find much of the bourgeois suburban lifestyle to be stifling. "Why did I let you make me watch this again?" I said to Baldwin, who loved the movie.

"Mom, you just need to start writing again, then you'll feel better," she said. She was fourteen at the time and not yet a writer herself.

The movie made me think maybe we should move back to the city. My longing for it had never really died. When I left it for the suburbs seventeen years ago, I hadn't wanted to move. I used to tell people that the scuff marks from my shoes were still on the pavement in front of the Lincoln Tunnel entrance.

"If you're going to write full-time, you can do that anywhere," Cliff had said. He was right of course, but I didn't want to become a suburbanite. It just didn't fit my self-image. I wore black all the time, loved to walk all over the city, dropping in at an art movie house in the middle of the afternoon, or sitting outside in a café and people watching. I loved leaving my apartment on a Saturday or Sunday without any plans and just wandering the streets of Manhattan, alone or with a friend, stumbling upon a street fair, being out all day, from having brunch at Popover Café, to going to the Village and hearing some jazz, to having dinner someplace good and cheap. These things felt fundamental to who I was; how would I duplicate this in the burbs?

It was now six months after Mom had died. I lay awake on the third floor in the old au pair's room. It's a tiny room with blue and white toile wallpaper and eaves that I love. You can hear the rain in that room and feel as if you're in a cozy cave in an Amazonian forest. I had gone there because Cliff was snoring again, loudly enough to hear from a floor away. It woke me up and pissed me off. There was a running list in my head of what I had to get done today and how was I going to get it all done? Not that it was so much—get a new printer cartridge, meet Carmen for lunch, register Ford for fall soccer, call my nutritionist to see if my order of green dirt had come in yet, return jeans that stretched out too much to the Gap, and return an overpriced cargo jacket to J.Crew.

That night, I met my novelist friend Laurie Albanese at the train to head to Cobble Hill in Brooklyn. We were meeting my writer crew, Christina and Pam. Pam had an assignment from *More* magazine to find the next hot cocktail, the Cosmo for a new generation. She'd invited us to go along to offer our opinions. Laurie and I planned to ride the train together from Montclair. Cliff, who drove me to the station, waited with me on a park bench until Laurie arrived. I was feeling happy to be going on an adventure but a little nervous because I had no idea what subway to take to Cobble Hill once we got into Manhattan. I felt inept for having to rely on Laurie, but in my depressive state, my mind was clouded and I couldn't process any new information. We got to the place, known for having a most innovative bartender, and I greedily perused the list of unusual and yummy-looking cocktails and appetizers. We had booked a car service take us home so that we could drink until we had no memory of what we talked about other than which drinks we liked.

I got up the next day a little before nine, groggy from not having had a solid night's sleep. I got Ford off to baseball camp, and with a breakfast that wasn't supplied by Dunkin' Donuts. I dropped him off at Edgemont Park and sat in the car for a moment, surveying how I was feeling—*a little more in control of what I have to do.* I got home, opened the *New York Times,* and it said it was Wednesday, not Thursday as I'd thought. Now I was in panic mode. For at least a solid ten minutes, my head was spinning, heart beating fast, as I wondered about all the things I must have missed, all that I hadn't done. It took a while longer for me to remember that I'd picked up another paper off the driveway this morning and that it was still in its blue plastic wrapper. It was simply that I hadn't read yesterday's paper. I was getting thrown like that way too often.

22

Waking Up

ANOTHER NIGHT. I was lying in bed trying to fall asleep, my brain scanning. Ford was about to start sixth grade and I needed to get . . . I sat bolt upright at the thought that Ford was about to start middle school. I realized with a shock that I'd been home for his entire elementary school career. Six years. Had I been asleep for six years? How could this be?, I asked myself, surveying my brain for some kind of explanation. I was like a character in a novel or a romantic comedy who bumps her head and wakes up to find she has a completely different life.

But I didn't have the luxury of lamenting the six years I'd lost in the domestic dungeon. My father would be moving in with us soon—he had dementia—but first I had to move him out of his apartment. Duane got Goodwill to come and take most of the furniture. There was no time to figure out what I could give away to relatives or friends. Jessica, the caregiver I'd hired to help with Dad, was at the apartment helping me pack up. Duane and Larry helped some, but it was mostly on me. My friend Will was a godsend who offered his assistance and his truck. He and I, along with Mo, another dog-walking friend, moved a bed, a nightstand, and a lamp into a room in our house that had been an office/sports equipment storage space.

My dad is a lovely man. He is tall and movie star handsome, Southern, and very polite. However, his emotions are muted, and I've often wondered if it's because he was traumatized by his time on the USS *Franklin*.

My dad had had nightmares throughout my childhood. He would wake up screaming at least once a week. When I was young, I would be asleep when the dreams came, but as I got older and was able to stay up later with my brothers on weekends, we'd hear him yelling, screaming. We never could make out the words. When my mother was home from work, and Daddy was having a dream, she would go into the bedroom and shake him awake, telling him that it was only a dream. Daddy would lie in bed for a little while and get up and go to the bathroom, his face stricken. He never mentioned his nightmares until decades later, after he retired and started going to reunions with his shipmates.

He and my mother loved traveling to different parts of the country, every other year, for the ship reunions. Mom eventually got my dad to see a psychiatrist, or, as my dad called him, "my head doctor," at the VA hospital. The dreams went away. I asked him recently what the doctor was like, if he liked him.

"He's nice, he's real nice. He's a young man, I guess in his forties. He just asks how I'm doing, now, especially since Mom is gone."

I was proud of him for going, but after my mother died, he eventually stopped.

"Nothing really to talk about," he said when I asked him why.

I told him that maybe this was a good time to check in with

the doctor to talk to him about grief and depression, but my dad grunted and let me know that he didn't care what I had to say. He wasn't going to go back and that was that.

My father moving in with us hadn't been the plan, but it became the only option. After Mom died, my brother had, surprisingly, relocated to New Jersey after thirty-plus years in Jacksonville, Florida, to look after Dad. My brother was a great help when he was here, taking my dad to the doctor, being his companion. Daddy was so lonesome without Mom. They'd been married for almost sixty years, and I frankly thought he'd die soon after her. Marc would help keep him active in the adult community where they lived. Without being pushed, Daddy wouldn't participate in anything in the building. The first year Marc was with him, Daddy seemed fine, but by the second year Marc began to notice things, like Daddy's obsession with the mail, especially lottery swindles. When he sent five thousand dollars to a scam lottery out of Australia, via Jamaica, we knew he was losing it. He'd even called me one day saying he had "great news. I'm going to get four million dollars."

My heart ached. He sounded so happy; I didn't have it in me to tell him that the whole thing had been a con. Then he started getting up on a Thursday night and putting on a suit. He'd come out of his bedroom fully dressed, and Marc would ask him where he was going. Daddy would think it was Sunday morning and he was going to church. Marc even thought once that Daddy had been in the hallway of his floor dressed in his underwear. It became clear that our father couldn't be left alone when Daddy stayed with me for a month while Marc went back to visit Jacksonville. We saw just how far he'd deteriorated in his dementia. My brother had initially planned to come back and stay in New Jersey to help out with Dad's care, but ultimately he decided to move back to Florida. My dad still talked about the four million dollars that he thought he'd won. Sometimes he thought it was coming; other times he said that they lied to him and were keeping the money.

Most of the time he lived with us he never said my name. Sometimes, he referred to me as his daughter, sometimes I was the young lady. Only once or twice he asked me who I was and how we were related, but those times were enough. They were like sucker punches.

After a year, I moved him into an assisted living facility and he was put on an Alzheimer's drug, Namenda. He knew my name after that and even introduced me as "my daughter, my baby."

※

My exercise routine was no longer working as a mood-lifter. I felt myself being progressively sucked down into a hole in the ground. I tried everything to fight it, but I didn't have the strength. I knew that I should be happy. I had such a good life. *But.* It was almost as if the more stuff we acquired (and I had to take care of)—the bigger house, the gorgeous yard and garden, the architecturally designed basement—the unhappier and more disconnected from myself I became. I know this now, but didn't then.

Cliff kept saying, "You need to write, you'll feel better. Just go upstairs and write, 'I hate my husband, I hate my husband, I hate my husband.'"

He is a riot and very funny, but right then he was deadly serious. He knew that I needed to get back into a creative routine. I felt like I couldn't.

The next morning after I dropped Baldwin and Ford off at school, I met up with Carmen. She and I walked with Charlie until our legs hurt and we found a bench. Carmen was an acupuncture practitioner and was deeply interested in wellness and holistic living. She listened to me go on and on about my malaise, the deep

sadness that I couldn't seem to shake, the anger and resentment I couldn't quite understand. I'd been walking around with this image in my head of the writer I was, who was cool and successful despite the banalities that made up life in the suburbs. I was clearly no longer that person, but I had no idea who I had become.

Carmen said calmly, "Stop resisting. You have to let go of what you used to be; don't fight it. Just be. You are in a different place now. Just let what is be."

I listened; it had never occurred to me not to resist. I came from a long line of fighting women. I reflected on my warrior mother, my busy, strong, always moving mother who, while she never said it, led me to believe that my sensitivity, my "feeling too much, thinking too much," was a bad thing. As much as she loved me, and as deeply as I felt her love for me, she was never a cuddly, emotional kind of mom, and I always felt that my sensitivity was a disappointment for her. Once when I was a child, she was putting me to bed and leaned over to kiss me, and I pulled her down onto my chest and said, "Do you love me?" She'd never said it; no one in my house had ever said it. I'm sure I alarmed her. She said yes. Fortunately, she lived long enough to open herself up and become very affectionate. She began saying "I love you" all the time, and then so did my father and my brothers.

Maybe Carmen was on to something. I flirted with giving non-resistance a try, but not even two weeks later I was back to resistance and anger. I had decided that I didn't want to stay in this marriage, and that it was my mind-numbing suburban existence that was causing me all this angst. I needed to escape all this conventionality that I had forced on myself for the sake of being with Cliff. I'd been refusing to acknowledge that this was not the life I wanted anymore. I'd been so afraid to say it out loud. I'd tried anything and everything to get my head clear, to get happy, to pick up my

mood, talk myself into staying. I realized I wasn't afraid of being alone; I actually relished the idea of quiet time, to be in my head, to read my stacks of unread books. But leaving my marriage would also mean splitting up the time my children spent with Cliff and me, and I didn't want that.

On a day when my lingering grief and midlife malaise were especially intense, I had to drive Baldwin twenty miles for a lacrosse tournament. She picked up on my bad mood and tried to talk me out of it. I told her that I wasn't mad at her, but that so much of this part of mothering just felt like too much. Of course, the real problem was that I had stopped doing my thing—my writing, meeting with my circle of writer women, activities that would stimulate me and elevate my mood. I must have said something to the effect that I didn't think I could tap back into the artistic side of myself while still living in the suburbs. Baldwin listened to what I had to say, then announced, "If you divorce Daddy, I'll never speak to you again." I told her that I was not going to divorce Daddy, that I was just frustrated at not being able to figure out how to fix what was bothering me.

But Baldwin's statement rocked me. Reflecting on our exchange later, I realized I'd always considered her mine alone, my girl, my daughter, in much the same way that my mother felt about me. Without thinking about it consciously, I'd assumed I was the favored parent, especially since I thought that Cliff was sometimes too hard on Baldwin. Obviously, she had a different take. Just the night before, Cliff had taken away her iPhone and her laptop—hell for a teenage girl. He had been raging at her about not working hard enough on homework, doing it on her bed instead of at her desk, talking too much on the phone. She had been freaking out, yelling back at him—she could be rough with him, too. Listening from another room, my mother-bear instinct was strong. *What does*

Cliff even know about teenage girls? I fumed inwardly. *So what if she wants to do her work on her bed?*

They were screaming so much and so loudly that I actually thought I would call the police. I'd gone to the basement to remove myself from the ruckus, knowing it would end, as always, with Cliff trying to explain his position to me. I settled down to watch the giant-screen TV with the controls one needed a PhD to operate. The TV got all staticky just as Cliff appeared in the basement and sat down next to me on the sectional that I'd been living on for the past weeks, watching old episodes of *Sex and the City.* I'd watched them so often I knew dialogue by heart. I also watched *Oprah* and *The Dog Whisperer.* And I watched *The Real Housewives* of New York and Atlanta, trying to figure out why. I watched it all so I didn't have to think or feel. I watched and I cried.

"I know you're just down here pushing buttons," Cliff said.

He'd pushed one of my buttons. I was so angry I was burning inside.

"Stop it right now," I growled.

It would be some time before I understood that much of Cliff's behavior during that time was his response to losing his Dad. He didn't cry or take to his bed as I had, but he was also wounded deeply. And he was also frightened and confused about what was happening to me.

Before I got married, I'd promised I wouldn't have a relationship like my parents'. My mother often growled at my dad.

I am back in the kitchen of the frame house where I grew up. The cabinets are redone in a dark wood veneer, the counter and backsplash are bright yellow Formica; the fridge, also in yellow but paler, is built into what used to be the pantry. My mother knocked out the door and wall by herself and got Milton, our backyard neighbor and jack-of-all-trades, to frame it out. The wallpaper is a brown floral print that she hung herself, and the linoleum tile is beige and brown.

There was always dinner cooking. She'd start around lunchtime and would have dinner on the table at five. My dad or I would clean up the dishes, and she would go to sleep for four hours. She'd jump up at ten fifteen, warm up her leftover black coffee that she'd percolated that morning, sip some, pour the rest into a Mason jar to take with her, dress in her uniform, support hose, white shoes, and be out the door in fifteen minutes to arrive at St. Michael's by 11 p.m. How did she do that every day for thirty-two years?

I'm remembering the afternoon my father came back from the A&P, where my mother had sent him to buy a bottle of Heinz ketchup. It was one of the rare times we ran out of something and needed to go to the supermarket midweek. Clara was a scrupulous homemaker: food shopping was done on Fridays and she never went without her lists and her special coupon billfold. She'd hit three different markets: A&P, ShopRite, and Foodtown, often with me in tow. I loved going to the supermarket with her. *Foodtown's got McIntosh forty-nine cents a pound; A&P got rump roast for eighty-nine cents. Paper towels are on sale at ShopRite.* She'd buy enough to pack the pantry and the fridge.

That day, Daddy bought the right brand but the wrong size, too small. I can still see him standing in the hallway, pulling the ketchup from the brown paper bag. When she saw the size, she exploded, ripped into him as if she'd caught him bed with another woman. I must have been nine or ten. After she stopped yelling, I heard myself verbalize what I'd always thought.

"Why do you have to talk to him like that?"

I don't remember what she said or if she, my brothers, or my dad said anything. I don't know if my comment even made her think. I hated when she was so harsh with my dad. To me he was only sweet, loving, and patient. He was the dad who'd always drive my friends and me to the mall and wait in the car for three, four, five hours reading his newspaper or listening to a ballgame on the radio. He never complained about taking us or about waiting for us. The only thing he'd say when we got back to the car was: "You girls have a nice time?"

"Yes, Mr. Little," my girlfriends would say in unison.

I'd scoot into the passenger seat, lean over, kiss him on the cheek, and say, "Thanks, Daddy." His warm smile would be breaking across his face; a peck was enough for him.

When I got older, early high school, my mother attempted an explanation of why she spoke to Daddy the way she did. She said that when Marc and Duane were little babies, twenty months apart, she'd found the life insurance policy Daddy had taken out in the event something happened to him. Daddy had put his brother Curtis as the beneficiary on the policy.

"I couldn't believe my eyes," my mother said, the pain still fresh on her face. "That that man would do that, would leave me with two little boys to take care of. I could never get over that."

It was a discovery that cut her to her core, and every few years, I'd hear the story again. She'd had him change the policy as soon as she saw it, but she couldn't seem to ever let it go. Was that really the thing that stood between them? Was that the only thing in the way of her being kinder to him? She's gone now and I'll never know. I never thought to point out that Daddy, being the old-school chauvinist he was, probably thought Uncle Curtis should administer the money, that Mom wouldn't be able to handle such things. I knew that thought wouldn't ever have occurred to her, and it might have made her angry in a different way if it had.

I watched her when she was sick and weak and dying, just being annoyed by his presence. I felt so sad for her, for him. It was hard to imagine that she had held a grudge for almost six decades. The one time she ever voiced an appreciation of my dad was when she was about eighty. There was some conflict between her and her remaining siblings about the family house, and they'd had to see a judge about taxes or something.

"Matthew dropped me off at the courthouse, walked me inside so I could sit down," she told me later. "And then he went to find a parking space. I shouldn't even have been there. I'd just got outta the hospital again and to have to be bothered with that mess over that house they let just get all broke down. I wanted to just sell that mess and be done with it. While I was just sittin' there, waitin', I realized how Matthew has always been there for me, right by my side."

She'd repeated this same thing to my brother down in Jacksonville. We were both so shocked. Marc had even called me just so we could talk about it, neither of us trusting our own ears. We had an hour-long conversation about that one comment. Maybe she had appreciated Daddy all along. What I know now having had my own long-term marriage is that no one knows what goes on between spouses, not even people living in the same house. Often not even the couple.

23

For Better or Worse

IN THE very beginning of our marriage, when I'd taken the chance of quitting my job to write full-time, knowing that Cliff didn't want me to, I had figured he'd leave me. I think he wanted to, but he didn't. His mother told him to give my dream a chance. I loved her for that. We stayed together and we built a life, even with me kicking and screaming a lot of the way—by which I mean resisting. For Cliff, bickering is communicating. His mother was the same, but his parents were demonstrative and loving toward each other, too. I pretty much saw only bickering in my parents' marriage, and I hadn't wanted to duplicate that, yet I often did. I started to wonder if this might have been where my resistance to married life was coming from.

By late September, I was so at the end of my patience with Cliff that I literally got down on my knees and begged for an answer as to whether I should stay in my marriage or leave. I got up and decided that I didn't want to be with Cliff anymore. I was so tired of him just flipping off at every little thing that came up, and then later saying he was sorry and wanting to talk. I was over it. There was so much tension between us, our exchanges increasingly clipped and curt, punctuated by my poisonous silences that were charged with resentment.

We had been invited to a wedding on Martha's Vineyard, and the idea of being in a car with Cliff for over four hours, plus a forty-five-minute ferry ride, filled me with dread. We were staying at the Mansion House, a lovely B&B. The woman who checked us in was indifferent, even hostile. Even though I had booked months in advance, she gave us a tiny room with a barely working air conditioner. To make it more painful, she was Black. My bad mood worsened. We had to get changed to get to Tashmoo, where the dinner for out-of-town wedding guests was being held. The party was a fabulous yet low-key tented affair on the grounds of a spectacular house right on the bay's edge. We drank champagne and ate lobster and fresh corn. My mood was lifting. Cliff and I avoided each other and talked to the several other people we knew who were also there from Montclair.

The next day we had hours to fill before the wedding. I felt anxious and restless, like we were supposed to do something on the island, but it was misty and off-season, and there wasn't a lot happening. We decided to take a drive. I couldn't settle myself. Cliff was trying to understand, but I had no words to help him or myself. Later, we tried to take a nap, but I couldn't get comfortable in the warm room. I was relieved when we were finally picked up in a van with other guests to be driven up island, where the wedding would be held. We were among the last three couples to be picked up. The other two couples were slightly older than us; we knew them casually. The four of them, all WASPs, had clearly had a few by the time they got into the van. They were loudly teasing one another about having fishy breath from eating tuna, and I heard something too about passing gas. Their conversation was lively and free. They were like Cliff. I was not, and though I was put off by their behavior, they helped remind me of what had attracted me to Cliff. He says what he thinks and does what he says he's going to do, and truly doesn't care what people think about him.

And he'd always been there for me.

The marriage ceremony was perfection. It reminded me of ours. The entire wedding was held in one place: the vows were exchanged and the reception was set up in the garden. Ours had been at a flower-draped gazebo; theirs was under an arbor covered with lavender hydrangeas. At ours, cocktails were on the lawn and the reception was inside. The weather was gorgeous, the food excellent. They had a great band—I danced the entire night, exactly as I'd done at my own wedding. I remembered how happy I'd been at our wedding. I felt like I'd waited a long time to find Cliff, and that he had been worth the wait. At the time, I'd known that he was a perfect match for me. I felt happy and free. I was able to be all of who I was, knowing that my husband loved and accepted me completely.

That was still true.

At the end of the weekend, we drove home, happily singing along to the old R&B songs on satellite radio.

It was Sunday. I went for a run and was able to keep from sinking into the depressive state that now marked most Sundays. Maybe this day of the week left me vulnerable because everyone was home; I felt like they were all looking to me to be like Julie, the cruise director on *The Love Boat*. I had hated Julie almost as much as I hated the show. Even at ten or twelve or however old I was when it was on, I knew it was stupid, vapid, filled with empty people trying to fill up their lives by getting on a boat and traveling somewhere away from their own pathetic lives, only to get out to sea and want nothing more than to return to those lives.

The night before, we'd gone to the Crossroads Theatre in New Brunswick for opening night. Cliff was the president of the board. He loved the theater as much as my mother had; I liked that about him. He also loved giving them money, and having people look at him as the man who could make things happen. The play, *Fly*, about the Tuskegee Airmen, was a moving, historically important work. But I found myself sinking into a dark mood and I had a vague idea why. I knew Trey Ellis, the co-playwright, from twenty-five years ago when we were both young, aspiring writers hanging out with other creative types like Nelson George and Warrington and Reggie Hudlin, who, like Trey, had gone on to have major creative careers. A bunch of us would hang around Trey's large, inherited Upper West Side apartment, broke but cute, with big ambitions. This was before Trey's novel *Platitudes*, or Nelson's big book, *The Death of Rhythm & Blues*, or the Hudlins' breakout movie, *House Party*, and way before my novel *Good Hair*.

After the play, I was talking with Trey as we walked out of the theater. Ford started pushing me and demanding that I hold his shirt and jacket, which he had removed because he said it was hot and he was thirsty. I was angry and embarrassed that his behavior was taking me away from a desperately wanted writers' talk with Trey. I still wasn't really working on anything, so I didn't have anything specific to talk about, but that didn't matter. I wanted to talk to someone who had known me from another time and in another context. Ford probably sensed that I was morphing into that other person, my writer self, and he didn't like it. Did he react in that uncharacteristic way because he sensed something was different about me, something he hadn't seen and therefore didn't like? I'll never know the answer; I only know the feeling I had at that moment. I was frustrated that I couldn't have a conversation, but it was more than that. I felt like something had been taken away from me or that I'd given away too much.

It was then that I started saying, "I don't do wife very well." I can't smile and say thank you when people congratulate me for something Cliff has done. Instead, I say, "For what?" I mean, why congratulate me? When people persist or try to explain, I say, "Oh yeah, well, it's his passion." Translation: he has interests and so do I.

But I didn't say this to Trey that night. Instead, I mumbled something and walked away. I just wanted to leave but knew we had to stay a little longer. Cliff is highly verbal, is quick on his feet, and loves to hobnob. He needed to stay to schmooze the state arts person and the bank manager, the kinds of people who held the fate of the theater in their hands. I don't like the part of him that enjoys being seen as a big man. It always makes me uncomfortable, but what I've learned in being married this long is there will always be things about your spouse that you're not going to like, some of them fairly central to who they are. I'm moody and I'm prickly and usually too psychologically probing—things Cliff dislikes about me but rarely mentions. He just accepts those parts of me.

I slept on the way home, because I was tired, but also because I didn't want to be snippy with Cliff. He didn't deserve that. He was a good man with a good heart, and he loved me and he loved the kids and he just wanted us to be happy and have a good life, and for me to say it was great. I couldn't say that, so I slept.

The next day I ran two miles. It was either that or stay home and yell at my kids and my husband. That afternoon I also had an acupuncture appointment. It was my fifth session, and I left there feeling tremendous—light, not angry, depressed, or anxious, none of that. The problem was I couldn't seem to make it last more than three, maybe four days.

I've had periods in my married life when felt I was wrong, as if I didn't fit, didn't match any group, said the wrong things in the wrong way, felt too deeply about everything. But whenever I was ready to throw in the towel, convinced that Cliff didn't get me, we'd have a conversation about something or he'd say some random thing, and it would be so on the head of a pin, I'd realize that he *does* get me. Instead of jumping in and instructing me when I'm talking about being supersensitive, he just listens. And I get him, too. He is filled with anxieties just like my mom, and like her, he thinks he's hiding them. I've learned that the way to deal with him when he's anxious—like my mother scrubbing, scrubbing—is to simply hug him. His shoulders come down from around his ears and his body falls into mine.

A week later, I got an unexpected lesson in just how fortunate I was to be with Cliff. I was in the produce section at our local A&P supermarket, where I'd run into our neighbor Marcellus. We were chatting about what we were each going to make for dinner and the state of Black America and the country in general. He's an economics professor from West Philly who has great stories, three Ivy League degrees, and a great mind. I'd just come from the pool. I had on one of those cheap, long strapless dresses with the elastic smocking. My wet hair was in a knot on top of my head, my skin was dry, and I was barefaced. I was talking to Marcellus when I saw him from behind and recognized the head—my ex-boyfriend Bruce. *Fuck*, I thought, and for a second I figured I could just keep talking to Marcellus and he wouldn't see me, but mysteriously he turned around, almost as if he felt my eyes on the back of his head. A big smile crept across his face and he came walking toward us.

"Hey." He leaned in and kissed me on the cheek. He was grinning as if we were friends running into each other at a garden party.

I introduced Marcellus to him.

"So if I'm seeing you in the A&P, you probably live here," I said.

"Yeah, we just moved in today."

I was as cold to him as a dairy aisle. After a very few minutes of small talk, he went on his way. Marcellus looked at me.

"What was that about? I've never seen you like that—you were like ice."

I was furious. I didn't understand quite why at the time, but it was like I'd released in that moment all that I'd held on to for decades. I'd put Bruce on a pedestal and allowed myself to believe that I wasn't good enough for him, and that ultimately the person he'd choose would be better than me.

I told Marcellus a little about the background:

Bruce had called me out of the blue to tell me that he and his wife were thinking about moving to Montclair.

It had been five years since we'd last spoken. After I'd heard that at age forty-five he was getting married, I had tracked him down through the last email address I had for him. I'd written: "I hear you're getting married. Congratulations. You have to tell me everything . . ."

He called me right away.

At the point at which I'd run into him in the A&P, we'd been broken up twenty years. The three years we were together, off and on, were some of the most intense, exhilarating, miserable years of my romantic life. When it was good, it was grand, but when it was bad, it was hell, and it would shift from one extreme to the other in minutes. We were in touch intermittently over the years, mostly in the first years after I got married, when he was trying to convince me to leave my husband for him. When we were together, he hadn't ever said, "I love you." He had never wanted to meet my parents or for me to meet his, even after I'd practically begged to do so. Yet after I'd gotten married, he insisted I had been the love of his life.

The first time we broke up, he'd moved from New York to Boston. I had tried to move on with my life, eventually settling into a stable relationship with a nice, low-key guy I'd known at Howard. A year later, Bruce got in touch with me. We met for lunch, and he poured his heart out, saying he wanted me back. Just like Carrie with Mr. Big in *Sex and the City*, I went running back to him, dumping the nice Howard guy in the process. Bruce was an immigrant with an immense drive that led him to become very successful in his career. His manner could sometimes be high-handed, and while I hated that aspect of him, to me he was sexy and handsome. Deep down, I had felt that I was not enough for him. I was too emotional (or right-brained, as he used to say). I hadn't traveled the world as he had. I hadn't gone to "an Ivy." I just wasn't accomplished enough. He would tell me decades later that, in fact, he had felt insecure and unsophisticated compared to me.

I finally broke up with him when I realized that he was dancing around making a real commitment to me. I figured that he wanted someone who had multiple degrees, spoke at least three languages, and looked like a model. This was why when I heard he'd was actually getting married I just had to know who this spectacularly accomplished woman was. I envisioned a combination Valerie Jarrett and Condoleezza Rice, with Halle Berry looks. I even wanted to meet her, so that I could give him and her props. My opinion about what he'd been looking for would have been validated—but he married his administrative assistant, who was eighteen years his junior. No Ivy or any degree, no fluency in the Romance languages, no world traveler.

When I asked him what she was like, he said, "Really beautiful."

A year earlier, when he'd called me out of the blue to pick my brain about Montclair, I was not happy and told him so. I didn't want him to move to my town.

"I really want the diversity. I don't want my kids to grow up like I did, being the only Black kid."

"I get that, but there are other towns."

"But the schools are good."

"I know you, and you're not going to be happy with public school and you'll end up sending them to private school."

He fell back into a pattern of trying to charm me to change my position.

"Look, I just don't want you to live here. I don't want to run into you while I'm out walking my dog or running to the supermarket or just living my life."

He told me that they were looking at other places too and that Montclair wasn't his wife's first choice. Obviously, that was before I ran into him in the A&P.

"There are lots of other nice places with diversity. There's South Orange/Maplewood, New Rochelle, there's Englewood . . ."

He wasn't interested.

I'd held the phone to my ear and looked at myself in the mirror and remembered the hot girl I'd been when I was with him. I didn't realize that he thought me sophisticated, but he told me that the fact that I was seeing a therapist had seemed the ultimate in refinement and was threatening to him. *Sheesh*, I thought.

Now, while I still looked good, I was a middle-aged woman, complete with dry hair and a muffin top in my oh-so-cute Citizens boot-cut jeans, with feet that hurt and required some kind of comfortable shoes (though never Merrells or Rockports or any of those "Mom" shoes, as Baldwin calls them).

When I told Eleanore, my ride-or-die girlfriend of twenty-five years, about Bruce's move to Montclair, she said, "Why do you care?" She'd had a front-row view of our past relationship, knew the play-by-play, but pointed out that it was long ago.

I knew she was right but tried to answer her with the banal—it's a small town, not the big city, where exes can cohabit peacefully, meaning they never, ever have to see each other. What I later realized was that I didn't want to be reminded constantly of the callow girl that I was when I was with him. The one who didn't know herself well enough to know that this person wasn't right for her. Eleanore got that part.

But here's the good news: When I ran into him at the A&P, I realized at once that Cliff was infinitely better than he was, and not just better for me, but a finer human, a better man. Bruce's wife had wanted to live in a New Jersey town where she wouldn't have to use one of the tunnels to get into Manhattan. He'd told me that she had a phobia of tunnels. I figured then that because of that, they wouldn't move here. When I reminded him of that conversation, he shrugged and said, "She'll get over it."

24

Plantation Luggage

MONTCLAIR/UPPER MONTCLAIR is one town with two zip codes. It's a leafy suburb on six square miles, twelve miles west of Manhattan. There are about thirty-eight thousand people, three supermarkets, a Whole Foods, four parks, one high school, one private school, three parochial schools, and a country club (although it's technically just over the West Orange border). There are five public elementary and three middle schools, two movie theaters, three firehouses, eighteen public tennis courts, and forty-two houses of worship. Recently the non-millionaire residents have nicknamed it "the People's Republic of Montclair" because of its high property taxes. The taxes are so high that Cliff and I were looking forward to downsizing.

I cried during relaxation in yoga class when the teacher, in her spiritual reading to us, asked, "Who are you really?" And I thought, *I'm Clara's daughter.* After class, I hurriedly rolled up my mat, put on my shoes and coat, and cried all the way to the parking lot. I went to Ford's school, even though it was Friday, and I knew he had his standing playdate with his best friend, Ryan. I just wanted to see Ford. Ryan's mom, Pam, was there, waiting for them to finish wrestling around on the grass in front of their school—so happy, so simple. I watched Ford and Ryan and a few of their friends while I chatted with Pam and some other moms. After Pam took the boys to her house, I was left with the realization that I had no one to pick up. Baldwin was getting a ride home from lacrosse practice. I walked across the street to the playground to say hey to Carmen, who I knew would be there with her two young ones. I stood there chatting with her for at least forty-five minutes. When I got back to my car I realized that I had left the car running with the passenger-side window down and my purse on the passenger seat.

I went home, poured myself a glass of wine, and sat in the yard, trying to wrap my head around how I could've been so distracted as to leave the car running, with my purse on display. I was feeling slightly numb as I struggled to forgive myself.

The next day I felt okay, then good. I realized I was actually feeling a little bit happy. I thought—I allowed myself to hope—*maybe it's lifting,* but I wouldn't allow myself to dwell on it too much, I didn't want to jinx it.

Then I went on Facebook and saw a notification from a writer I used to be friends with. He had made a career in film and TV. His Facebook update: *Hanging at Sundance with Zoë Saldana.*

I got so jealous.

I was still thinking about my boring suburban life as I was getting dressed to go to my son's Saturday soccer game. I went downstairs, where my husband had made breakfast, and got Ford's uniform together for his game. Ford was putting on his cleats, and I knelt down in front of him and, for the umpteenth time, tried to teach him to tie his laces. As I always did, I took my time showing him how to tie and loop. I was feeling calm, resigned perhaps.

This time, for some reason, he moved his foot away from me and said, "Let me try it."

I stood up and watched him do as I had done. He tied it perfectly.

A feeling washed over me that was whole and beautiful. Seeing his face, the look of accomplishment, of happiness, filled me with something I've never experienced outside of mothering.

Later at the game, when Ford's laces came undone, Cliff, his coach, knelt down to tie them while not taking his eyes off the game. Ford swatted Cliff's hand away.

"I can do it," he said, and he did.

I was watching from my seat in the bleachers a few feet away. He looked over at me, and our eyes locked. I put up my thumb up and beamed him a smile. His eyes brightened while he gave me a grin. It was a moment I know I'll never forget.

I did forget my Sundance envy.

The next day, Sunday, was sunny with that first real springtime warmth where the air feels like cashmere on your face. My friend Hillary knew I'd been suffering—all my friends did. She and I took our little fluffy dogs out for a walk. We sat on a bench in Watchung Circle, and Hillary got us coffee and egg sandwiches. We'd been friends since her two boys and Baldwin were in nursery school at Montclair Cooperative School, a hippie little island of a school. We went through periods of not seeing each other much, but she was a constant, solid presence, someone I'd never had to pretend with, and she got the idea of deep sadness in the midst of a life that others envy. On this day—the third in a row—I actually felt good. Again I thought, hoped, maybe the depression had lifted. Maybe it was gone for good, and I'd be myself again.

Monday a hard, cool rain came down. Baldwin was late getting out of the house and forgot her lacrosse gear. Cliff was late coming downstairs to drive her to school. Ford had a hard time waking up and ate his breakfast slowly and complained about having a headache. I finally got him to school—late. Then I walked Charlie. I forgot to carry a bag to pick up his poop, so I scraped it up with a napkin and missed, and some of the poop got on my finger.

I was behind schedule and would be late to my gym class. I could have still tried to make it, but my stomach felt queasy. I hadn't eaten enough for breakfast, and I just didn't feel like going. I was supposed to meet Susie at the Starbucks near the gym, but it was on the other side of town. The blackness that had vanished for a few days was edging its way back. I called Susie and tried to cancel. I wanted, needed, to get to my bed and pull the covers over my head. I told her the truth.

She heard in my voice that this wasn't just a bad moment on a rainy day. She insisted on coming over.

"I won't stay. I'll bring you soup and a sandwich. You need to eat."

I was wrapped in a blanket, which I dragged to the door like Linus when Susie arrived. We went into the TV room and sat on the couch. She put the bag she was carrying on the coffee table and took out a container of butternut squash soup and a vegetable sandwich on focaccia from Raymond's, which had some of the best food in town.

"My sister suffers from severe depression," she said. "I know some of what it's like. I just wanted you to know that you're not alone, that I think you're great. You don't have to do anything, be anything." I was so grateful for her kindness and yet I wanted her to leave. I felt a great weight trying to hold a conversation. I just wanted to go to bed. In the days following, friends just kept appearing: Eleanore, Lynne, Andrea, Jeanine, Iqua. They would come over and just sit with me or take me out to the mall or on errands or out to lunch or for a low-key dinner. Lynne took me to the Metropolitan Museum of Art one afternoon just to walk around. They seemed to understand that I couldn't do places that were scenes, where I'd run into people who required small talk.

Cliff, realizing that I was underwater again, waited anxiously for me to come up for air. He tried to give me breathing room. When we were newly married, Jill, a writer friend, said to me, "You've got to give Cliff a lot of credit for marrying you." I wasn't offended, because I knew exactly what she meant—that I was a lot, layered and complicated and often tremendously oversensitive. Given his milieu, the world of finance, Cliff had dated lots of women who worked at careers like his. It would've been easier for him to marry one of them. "It says a lot about who he is, that he didn't," Jill had said. He wasn't another boring suit, was what she meant.

I'd been trying for a while now to get back into a writing routine but had to take a break to go to Ford's concert at school. "Please, I want you to come," he'd pleaded. I never say no when Ford asks me to come to his school. I just do it because I know it means a lot to him. Frankly, I'm so touched that he wants me—anywhere.

Cathy from Jack and Jill had also called to ask me to bring pie and flowers for tonight's meeting. Most people, especially nonartist types, think that if you work at home you're not really working. So they call, they want to stop by, they ask for a favor that requires tending to during the day. When I'm really immersed in the writing, I simply say no or don't answer the phone. But when I'm struggling, as I have been for six years now, I can let myself get dragged away. Initially, it's easy to allow yourself be distracted, but eventually all that distraction backs up on you and you feel worse.

As I cast around for a topic in which to immerse myself, it occurred to me that I'd probably written about social class as much as a sociologist. I think people who don't know me personally assume I've written so much about upper-middle-class Blacks because either it's my background or I endorse those social mores. The fact that my first novel was entitled *Good Hair* didn't help. For the record, my original title was *Good Hair and Other Plantation Luggage.* My publisher thought the title was too political, too scary, and wanted to shorten it. I, being a novice and thrilled at being published, went along with the new title. I don't regret it. The title was provocative. The concept of good hair versus bad hair is not something I subscribe to, but I know for sure that folks are going to have opinions and judgments, and it makes no sense to worry about them. I once heard someone say, "What you think about me is none of my business." I like that. Of course as an HSP—highly sensitive person—the truth is, I *do* care. I want to be seen as I think I am, but that is not always possible. Some people consider me as an extrovert, but I once took the test included in *The Highly Sensitive Person* by Elaine N. Aron, PhD, and scored slightly higher on the introvert side.

Some of the HSP traits are:

Easily overwhelmed by bright lights, strong smells
Rattled when asked to do a lot in a short amount of time
Startles easily
Avoids violent movies and TV shows
Needs to withdraw during busy days for relief
Parents/teachers have thought you shy

On the test, fourteen points qualify you as an HSP. I scored nineteen. So it's no surprise that the flack I got from some people about the title of my first book bothered me more than I liked to admit. Growing up, I had never actually heard the term "good hair." Not once. When I've told this to my friends, like Eleanore, who grew up in DC, they either don't believe me or think I'm delusional. At Howard, where I came face-to-face with judgments about skin color, hair texture, and social class for the first time, I realized that I'd been fortunate. Not knowing these distinctions existed provided me with a freedom I've come to value and have tried to pass on to my kids. In Newark, when I was coming of age, the zeitgeist was, the darker the better. Huge Afros were in vogue. Color was simply a description, at least in my house: light, medium, and dark. No values attached.

I never felt inferior or that something was wrong with being Black. I felt that being Black was normal, partly because everybody around me was, but also because all of them were working, taking care of their families, planning for a better life for the next generation. Back then there were places called Area Boards, which were community centers where I'd hang out during my adolescence. We'd play checkers, my brother Duane played chess, we'd make cobra-stitched key chains. We learned to knit while the counselors played recordings of speeches by Martin Luther King. His voice boomed from speakers that hung from upper walls and outside the building, giving his words even more power and importance than the snippets we heard on the evening news.

Postriots, Black-owned businesses began sprouting everywhere. There were many in my neighborhood, but two had a major impact: Tiffany's, a hamburger shop with a jukebox, where we'd go at lunchtime and dance to James Brown's "I'm Black and I'm Proud," and Kaboobie's Cool Spot (named by my brother Marc because he said the owner, James Sedgwick, looked like the camel from the TV show). Kaboob, as we called him, was a Hampton graduate and a race man. He first opened a record store, and then he opened an Italian ice/candy shop a few doors down. My brothers and their friends all used to hang out at the record store where Kaboob played mostly jazz, insurgent comedians like Dick Gregory, and the speeches of Malcolm X.

Years later, when I was first married and living in South Orange, a community organizer turned lawyer I knew from my *Star-Ledger* days asked me how it felt to have traveled so far from where I grew up. At first what he said stung. I told him that I realized Hunterdon Street, to him, was as far as the moon from my lovely street and pretty yellow, black-shuttered center-hall Colonial, but that I didn't see it the way he did. In addition to it having been my home, it used to be a lovely block in a beautiful neighborhood, too. What I didn't tell him was that I never looked at him the same after that. At the time, he worked with communities in Newark and considered himself a man of the people, not separate, not looking down on the kinds of housing they lived in. He saw himself as some kind of crusader for poor Black people. His comment made me wonder what he actually thought of the people he was supposed to be helping.

25

Blues People

"EVERYONE IS a moon, and has a dark side which he never shows to anybody," wrote Mark Twain, another depressive writer.

The thing about depression is it's invisible. And it's chemical. No amount of family support or pride in one's beginnings will make you immune. It could be that I am simply made this way, and my mother's death kicked me into a deeper crisis.

I scrolled back through memory, trying to find early clues to this dark pit of despair I'd fallen into. I suddenly remembered that when I was dating Bruce, we got on the road from his Boston apartment and took a spontaneous trip to Freeport and Kennebunkport. After we'd wandered around the towns, we found a cute motel, which had a fireplace in our room and pretty, albeit conservative, New England décor. I'd decided to take a bath and read a book I'd brought with me. It was William Styron's *Darkness Visible,* a memoir of his depression. I remember lying in the tub, reading all the names of writers who'd suffered from depression—

some who'd committed suicide, including Virginia Woolf and Primo Levi. For some unknown reason, I'd brought this book. It didn't occur to me that this was an unusual choice, given that I was with the guy that I loved, in sweet surroundings. I didn't know then that depression was different from sadness. At the time, Dr. Chisholm's diagnosis of dysthymia (mild depression) hadn't yet been given, even though I knew that something wasn't right, or more specifically, that right for me didn't seem like what it was for everyone else.

"Depression is a disorder of mood, so mysteriously painful and elusive in the way it becomes known to the self—the mediating intellect—as to verge close to being beyond description. Thus it remains incomprehensible to those who have not experienced it in its extreme mode . . ." Styron wrote.

Andrew Solomon, author of *Noonday Demon,* captured his illness this way: "Depression is not just a lot of pain; but too much pain can compost itself into depression. Grief is depression in proportion to circumstance; depression is grief out of proportion to circumstance."

For a year and a half after Mom's death, I dealt with my pain by assuring myself—and was assured by a hospice therapist and others—that it was grief over losing my mom. But the grip didn't let up as time passed. I tried everything I could think of. I went to a naturopath, thinking maybe it was my diet, to an allergist, an acupuncturist, my ob-gyn, my internist, a hormonal specialist, a psychiatrist, and a psychologist. I tried a parade of supplements to avoid the prescription meds:

SAMe
St. John's wort
L-tryptophan and 5-HTP

Chinese herbs

Megadoses of vitamins B and D

Pricey, pure fish oil

Testosterone and estrogen creams

Progesterone and progestin pills

Neurotransmitter supplements—Kavinace and Avipaxin

I also stopped eating sugar, dairy, and wheat. The not eating sugar worked, but that couldn't be sustained. I stopped drinking. I exercised like an athlete.

Nothing worked for long.

⁂

I sent this email to my brother Duane on March 9, 2010, a year after Mom's death:

> I'm sitting here now feeling so down I can't even describe it. I've been having a really rough time—it's been harder in the last two months than it was when Mommy first died. I can't stop crying, I sleep all the time, I'm seeing a therapist and have tried various mood-lifting drugs, but nothing seems to help; I exercise, I pray, I meditate, I read spiritual literature and none of those things lift me up for more than a few minutes or an hour or two. I try really hard to hold it together around Daddy because I don't want him to worry about me or to make him think about how much he misses her. It takes all that I have . . . I'm telling you I'm in this black hole. I don't want to talk to most people, don't want to go out. It's a gorgeous day and I'm inside in the bed. I did take Charlie to the park and walked and walked and sat on a bench in the sunshine. It did feel good.

And I sent this one to my friend Gabrielle:

I'm okay now—it's hour to hour. This morning, after I worked
out at the gym I came home, lay on the couch, and cried out
loud for probably a half an hour, begging for my mother; I
talked to my mother's picture, pressing it to my chest before
I napped a little, got cold, went upstairs and got in the bed,
prayed for this sadness, this heaviness to lift, went back to
sleep and woke up, read a little, picked my daughter up
from high school, and now I'm feeling a little better. I'm
at my computer trying to write a little. Just got the nicest
Facebook message from a reader who said she'd just
read *Who Does She Think She Is?* "for like the umpteenth
time" and is "dying to know what happens" with the main
characters' marriage.

Gabrielle Glaser was one of those people with whom you feel
an instant connection. When we initially met, she was visiting
the pool club where I was a member. We got to know each other
when our kids played an indoor soccer game. Gabrielle and I were
sitting in the stands and she asked how I was and I began crying.
She looked at me with a caring in her deep blue eyes that enveloped
me. After that, we began emailing each other. Our emails back and
forth were long letters. We got to know each other through them.
She was such a comfort: having dealt with her own depression, she
knew.

In an odd way, such emails were my attempt to do what Cliff
and Baldwin kept telling me to do, write my way out of the depression. And it did help when I was able to find words for what I was
feeling. I just hadn't been able to break through to writing again in
any regularly structured way.

But slowly, moment by moment, I was climbing up from the depths of my black hole. I remember an afternoon when I let Charlie out into the backyard. When I did look out to make sure he hadn't squeezed under the gate and gone walking up the block, I saw his little white fluffy body galloping across the gorgeous expanse of green. He was partially blind now, but he knew where everything was in his yard. He was happy, even though he was losing his sight, and I felt the same way as I peered at him through my living room window. I was learning to appreciate these exquisite moments: Baldwin and Ford holding hands as they walked up the driveway; Ford's tying his shoelaces, Charlie bounding free.

July 10, 1994, Journal Entry: *Just put Baldwin to bed. What a wonder she is. She's beautiful; she's got brown saucer eyes, curly, unruly light brown hair, golden skin, and a smile that makes my face ache. She's beyond precious. Even when I'm tired, brain dead, and all that goes along with being a new mom, she's a wonder. Tonight Cliff is out with a client and we're on our own. Usually he helps with her bath and puts her to sleep (he can get her to sleep, often I can't because she smells her food, my milk). Anyway, we played a little after her dinner. I watched* The Client *on HBO. She started fussing at about nine, which is bath time. I began nursing, but she wanted to play. She kicks her legs hard against the bed—it looks so cute I smile at her, which makes her smile her two-teeth smile at me. She is perfection. I kiss her constantly because she's just so irresistible. This is love like I've never come close to knowing. There's nothing that I wouldn't do for her, and all these feelings are terrifying because I know I'll always feel this way, and when she's older and asserting her independence I'll need Cliff to help me let her go. She'll have to, I know in my mind, but*

my heart will want to keep her the way I put her to sleep tonight,
close to my chest, my heart.

⚜

Fifteen years later, Baldwin and I entered the Princeton campus. I
stopped at the guard booth and the woman said, "You must be here
for the lacrosse camp."

"How'd you know?" I said, genuinely wanting to know.

"I just know. That's what everybody's here for today."

"How're you doing today? Is it driving you crazy?"

"They got y'all parking all the way down there. I'ma give you a
pass where you can park close to where you gotta go. Don't you tell
nobody where you got it."

She handed me the small piece of cardboard.

I thanked her and drove off.

Baldwin was amazed. "Go, Mom."

"Why do you think she did that?"

She hunched her shoulders, not really interested but knowing I
was going to tell her anyway.

"Because I treated her with respect. That's all people want, remember that, especially Black people, especially people who have
been disenfranchised."

We parked the car and walked a few yards to where the registration was; the line was out the door and down a walkway. We got in
the line and soon a familiar face walked up and said hello. It was a
dad from Jack and Jill. He told me that his wife and daughter were
inside.

We made small talk about where his daughter played, what
school she went to.

Then he said: "How about that parking lot? Could you believe
they had us park so far away?"

Even if I hadn't been sworn to secrecy, I wouldn't have told him that I'd been given the pass for the lot next door. I just looked at Baldwin and didn't have to say anything else.

After we registered, we had to get her duffel bag, bedding, gear, snacks, and fan to her dorm. There was no way to drive right up to the building. She was carrying some of her stuff, walking behind me complaining.

"It's so hot."

"How come there's no shuttle?"

"This is heavy."

I ignored her.

It must have been 95 degrees with almost that much humidity. My back hurt, and the duffel bag strap was digging into the skin on my shoulder. I muttered to myself: "I hate her, I hate her, I hate her." Strangely, the mantra made me feel better. I softened toward her. I turned around.

"Come on, you're an athlete. You can do this."

My words seemed to give her strength. She stopped complaining, and we hiked the hill to her dorm, which we weren't quite sure we knew how to find. We found it, went up a short flight of stairs, and I opened the lock. Her roommates greeted us: two blondes, one a very perky girl from Colorado, the other from Arizona. The room was a two-bedroom suite. Baldwin would have the small single to herself. Thankfully, they'd told us to bring a fan, since the rooms were not air-conditioned.

I was happy to be leaving Baldwin for three days. I loved her to pieces, but at fifteen she took up a lot of air. We hugged a full-on body hug, wrapping our arms around each other. No one else hugs me like she does. All the intensity of our feelings toward each other is in those hugs. She had to walk back to the car with me because she'd left her iPhone in the glove compartment. When we parted this time, there was no more affection. I was in the car, in the driver's seat, and she was walking away.

"Hey, do I get a kiss?"

She blew one to me. I drove away.

I was exhausted by the time I made it home. The back of my T-shirt remained soaked in sweat during the air-conditioned hour-and-fifteen-minute drive. I imagined a glass of wine, lounging on my sectional in my basement in front of the giant TV that Cliff had to have, but my neighbor was in the softball playoffs and I'd been promising that I'd come to see her play all summer. Ford and I walked up the street to see the game, and I got lucky because they shut the other team down in six innings. I could go home and exhale. Nope. Baldwin had texted me six times telling me that I'd somehow removed one of her cleats. I went out and looked in the back of the trunk, pretty sure that when I'd repacked her bag I'd put the shoe back. No shoe in the trunk.

"You sure you looked everywhere?"

"Mom, I emptied out everything. My roommates helped me look. It's not here."

I kept texting her to see if she'd found the shoe. I was thinking about how I could get a new pair to her—go to Sports Authority and then drive back to Princeton? "You would do that?" she asked. I could call a store in Princeton, pay for the shoes over the phone, and have her go pick them up. I told her these options to calm her down. One more phone call and I asked if she'd looked in all the pockets of the duffel bag. She said yes.

"Did you look in the side pocket?"

"Yes," with attitude.

"Did you look in the front pocket?"

"The front pocket?" She laughed. "I didn't know there was a front pocket."

She unzipped it and, voilà, the other shoe.

More laughing.

"Oh, God, I hate myself," she said. "I'm sorry, Mommy."

"It's okay."

I hung up, climbed onto the couch, and flicked on the TV. I watched Bill Maher's film *Religulous* until I fell asleep.

26

My Insides Don't Always Match My Outside

I HAD to admit that, with my eldest applying to colleges, I was having a problem aging. I hadn't thought I was the kind of person who would. I'd always had older friends, always wanted to be older, but now that there was a physical component to it, I didn't like it one bit.

It started out as groin pain. I was working out all the time back then, so I figured I'd pulled something. Not sure what to do about it, I waited and then went to a physical therapist, who suggested the Hospital for Special Surgery. The surgeon told me I didn't have much cartilage in my left hip and would need a replacement. I was only fifty-three. He said, "I've told thirty-three-year-olds this news." I was still not ready to hear it. I began seeing a chiropractor who was able to manage the pain, and I'd do the hip stretches he instructed me to do.

Two years later, after my good hip became so inflamed that I could barely walk, I went to a different surgeon at HSS. Same thing, no cartilage. This time I scheduled the surgery. Then I canceled. Months later, I scheduled it again, but my gut was not letting me relax with this decision, even though I was hearing all the great things about what happened afterward. When the surgeon's administrative assistant called to book the preoperation appointment, I was astonished that between the CAT scan, more X-rays, and the postsurgery hip class, I'd be there for more than eight hours. Postsurgery you're up and out right after, but the reality is you're not really healed for eight to twelve weeks. All I could see was the darkness coming back. Being forced to stay on one floor for a week would make me crazy. The surgery had been scheduled, my insurance had been cleared, but something inside me couldn't do it.

Then all of a sudden, my hip stopped hurting. After a week of no pain, I began to think about what I'd done differently, and the only thing I could point to was that I'd begun taking antioxidants. Reading up on them, I learned they help with inflammation. I decided to seriously start back with my hip stretches and to begin a meditation and chanting practice.

I slowly became conscious of the fact that I had turned against a current that was moving in a direction I didn't want to go. I had taken control and it felt really good.

However, my looks were now taking up too much headspace. On the one hand, I didn't believe in Botox and fillers and breast jobs, although looking at my formerly perky boobs that were now in tight with my upper ribs and my face that was getting jowly, I felt I could probably benefit from a little sculpt. I was sick to death of my dry hair that needed to be colored every six weeks, which made it even drier. My mother had cared about how she looked but didn't seem to stress about her appearance. She got her hair shampooed and hot-combed every other week by the same woman, Olivia, at the same salon, the same Friday appointment for twenty-five years. She wore sensible classic clothes, like shifts and shirtwaist dresses, pants, turtlenecks, with no big swings in trends (save for that damn green polyester jumpsuit).

Obsessing about my hair had been ongoing for as long as I could remember. I'd made peace with the fact that I liked to change my hair. I liked it natural, and sometimes I could wear it blown out straight. I could wear extensions or not, a wig or not. I used to beat myself up about it. Like how could a serious woman spend time on her looks? I wanted to appear as if I didn't spend any time at all putting myself together, like a Frenchwoman. I had real jewelry—diamonds and watches and high-end designer stuff—but I enjoyed wearing my fake jewelry, too. I wore them with the same "whatever" attitude, but I often questioned why I even needed all those accessories. What was I lacking? What was I trying to say? What void was I trying to fill?

Norman Mailer once said that Ronald Reagan was "as shallow as spit on a rock." That's what I thought of people who were obsessed with their appearance, and yet, if I were honest, I was overly concerned with how I appeared, too. It was an inner skirmish, one that I finally decided was okay. I'd read an interview with a conceptual and installation artist named Karen Kimmel. Her picture showed a woman with straight long hair, dressed in traditional-looking, Brooks Brothers–type clothes. The reporter said, "You don't look like a conceptual artist."

"I don't look eccentric enough?" she said. "That's funny, since I'm attracted to eccentric things, but my visual veneer doesn't reflect my internal attractions."

I often feel the same way.

I read that interview on the day after my birthday. I was sitting at my vanity, where my jewelry was, and found a ring that I hadn't worn in a while. It was a big dome shape, covered in shimmery pavé cubic zircona. I'd bought it during my mad-shopping-binge phase. It was way too much for daytime, way too much period, but I liked to wear it sometimes. When I did, though, I took myself through mental changes about what it meant—or looked like—when I wore it. Just as I was walking around my bedroom wearing it, Ford came up to get me to help him get online. His tutor was with him. I typed his password on her computer, forgetting I was wearing this big dome. I became self-conscious, imagining his tutor looking at it and judging me. She probably wasn't, but I realized that I was constantly monitoring my inner and outer self, hyperaware.

While I was waiting to get my hair done at Hair Rules, a natural hair-care place in the city, I ran across another quote that resonated. This one was in an article about the actress Naomi Watts. "I was so afraid of judgment that I had diluted myself into an intense ball of nothingness and neediness," Watts had said. "I was so desperate to please everyone: You want funny? I'll be really funny! You want sexy? I'd be sexier than you could ever imagine." Wow.

I liked clothes, I liked reading fashion magazines, liked to dress nice, and that meant quirky combinations. I tried to be age-appropriate hip, and right then that translated to skinny jeans, a fitted tee, and blazer, chunky-heeled boots, good jewelry, and a good leather bag. I had furs and some expensive handbags, but often I didn't want to wear them. Sometimes I felt like two people. My writer self thought that the person who thought too much about appearance was shallow. But there was the other side of me that sometimes wanted to look fly.

There were days when I looked like I just rolled out of bed, and there were days when I made an effort to look decent and like I took a shower. It depended on how I felt, and it was all me, and it was all fine. I was mostly free to wear what I wanted and appear how I wanted without worrying about what others were thinking about me—except when I had to meet with the kids' teachers; for them, I knew I had to pull it in a little. I admired the way Baldwin rocked whatever she wanted, whenever. She thought nothing of stomping around in high-heeled boots and what my mom would call a dressy dress.

I remember when I was on a book tour with my third novel, *Acting Out*, a reporter from the *Chicago Tribune* came to my hotel room at the Ritz-Carlton to interview me. After pictures were snapped by the photographer she'd brought along, we settled in for a talk. I had been excited to meet her because she had written a glowing review of my book for the *New York Times*. It was my first (and only) *New York Times* review, the publishing world's gold standard. The reporter was an aggressively unadorned White woman with a short haircut, dressed in a rock band T-shirt and cargo pants. I felt uncomfortable during our meeting, and at first I couldn't figure out why. After three books and five book tours, I was generally used to being interviewed. Finally, when she made a comment about my appearance being polished, I realized that she had expected someone different from me, perhaps that I would be a similarly unadorned woman.

In our interview I talked about materialism being rampant in our culture and particularly among the characters I wrote about. I observed that *things* are sometimes used to boost self-esteem (this was a year before Kanye West brilliantly wrote about this same subject in "All Falls Down"), but the point in the novel is that the characters struggle with this very thing. I was then and still am now interested in the navigation of presentation and selfhood. The reporter didn't get that. I felt as if she had judged me and decided I wasn't being honest, with my nice clothes and makeup.

I looked up the story she wrote and found this quote to be illuminating in terms of the problem she seemed to have with me: "Little's anti-consumer stance is hard to reconcile with the lip-lickingly plush world in which she has set all her novels . . . . Little describes a tight-knit group of black urban professionals who enjoy a level of affluence that's hard for most people, let alone most African-Americans, to imagine . . . Breitling watches and Kelly bags."

I still struggle almost daily with reconciling the inner sense of myself with my outward appearance, and the judgments others make of me because of it. Clara would have told me to get over it—or maybe she would have encouraged me to revel in their delusions about me. I remember when I came home from the hospital after having Baldwin, my mom came over to help for the first few days. She wore her white nurse's uniform and white nurse's shoes. A neighbor came over to see the baby and bring a gift. My mom answered the door wearing the uniform. She didn't introduce herself as my mother, just told the woman that I was napping. Later I asked my mother about the uniform, and she laughed and said she wanted the neighbors to think that I had a baby nurse. I guess she thought I wasn't presenting myself as fancy enough.

Of course, we all have opinions about how others present themselves, whether we voice them or not. Case in point: A writer whose book I had blurbed declared in a story online that she was looking for "White ambassadors" to help her publicize her novel. It was tongue-in-cheek, I think, but it made me feel queasy. "I love White people," she had written. "My husband is white (actually from Spain but to look at him one would think just a white guy)." She went on to say that in order for her book to "shine," she needed White people to "spread the word," both for reasons of numbers and to break out of the ghetto of African American lit in bookstores.

On one level, I understood where she was coming from. No one wanted to be relegated to the segregated section. However, I have to say, having blurbed her book with the idea of helping a fellow author, I was offended at what she posited as her editor's advice to "get a White author/friend to blurb the novel and we'll put in on the front."

So my blurb gets put on the back of the bus because I'm Black?

Not a good move. A successful Black novelist wrote a comment on the site and asked, "What are you saying to the thousands (millions?) of Black women who bought your last book, who spread the word, came out to your signings—that they're not enough? Thanks, but can you make some room in the front of the bus for my White friends?"

The writer talked about having to have the awkward conversation about race. I don't share the opinion or experience that it's awkward to talk with close friends who are White about race. My girlfriends, Black, White, Asian, are just my friends. They, without me even asking, will pass the word about my books. My pal Mary Anne (who's very posh and very British) keeps my books on the nightstand of her guest rooms. She's done so without me ever thinking to ask and has gotten me many international readers as a result. She also threw me a fabulous book party. All writers have a hard time getting attention. I've been fortunate to have been published and pushed to a general audience, but also to have a place in AA fiction. I think it's great to be in both. I've been on the gold coast (front tables) in major chain bookstores—front window displays, all of it—because my publisher believed in the book. We know we don't live in a country where meritocracy is always the way to success, and I'm not implying that the cream always rises to the top, but I am saying, do the work, push the work, establish real friendships, and then let it go. It demeans the process to do anything else.

Aware that I was silently judging a fellow writer in ways that had been painful for me to be judged, I went and found this writer's memoir on my bookshelf and read the opening pages. In the first paragraph, she wrote that she was in third grade in 1980. I graduated college in 1981. *My God, she's a child*, I thought. Well, thirty-eight isn't exactly a child, but it's fourteen years younger than me. It's a different generation—is it "X" or "Y"? Anyway, I began to soften toward her. She didn't grow up in the shadow of the Black Power era, when we freely discussed race and believed that there was something wonderful about being Black. She'd had her own unique experience, just as I'd had mine.

The other thing that had my head spinning on the same day was *Essence* magazine choosing a White woman as fashion editor. After lots of talk, TV and web attention, opinions were divided even among former staffers. Some said it was a good thing or that it shouldn't matter. To me it was just plain wrong. Imagine *Hadassah,* a magazine for Jewish women, hiring a Christian as their religion editor. What was up with us? Always extending our hand in "let's be color-blind." Yeah, I'm sure Anna Wintour is drinking her tea and saying to herself, yes, color doesn't matter, when there is not one Black woman editor at *Vogue.* One of the very few ways a Black woman is going to be near the front row at fashion week is if she represents *Essence.*

I began to grasp that my renewed engagement with what was going on in the world of publishing was a hopeful sign. It had been a year and a half now since my mother's death. Sometimes a day or two would go by and I'd realize that I hadn't cried. I was even starting to get back into an intermittent writing routine. But it was summer and my kids were home, along with our nephew Julien from Atlanta, who stayed with us for a few weeks each year. Summer was the worst time for writing because after the kids came back from camp, they were just hanging around the house. The good thing about Julien being here was that he would go for bike rides to the park and play basketball with Ford. But Baldwin was downstairs in front of the TV or the computer or both. Cliff kept calling me from work with suggestions for how to occupy them, but if I did any of what he suggested, then I wouldn't be writing and then I'd be pissed off and take it out on him.

I went downstairs to check on Baldwin. She was reading *People Style Watch* and watching *Two Can Play That Game,* which she'd seen at least three times before. I told her to read her book, going through her bookshelf and holding up *Rebecca* and *A Tree Grows in Brooklyn.* For some unknown reason the school hadn't given them a required reading list this year; so I made one up for her on the fly. She whined about my choices. We decided to compromise. She'd finish her Jodi Picoult.

27

Where I've Landed

BALDWIN HAD a big sweet sixteen party. There were about forty kids, more tried to crash—ten or so in one pack. There were all kinds of girls and boys, straight, gay, White, Black, biracial, Latin, Asian, jocks, arty types, all that makes our town so special. However. The majority were Black kids. Baldwin said she felt bad for her White friends, some of whom were visibly uncomfortable. I told her that she shouldn't ever take that on; sure, you want your guests to feel comfortable in your home, but when it comes to feeling out of sorts because most of the room doesn't look like them, that is not on you.

A woman I'm casual friends with is White and married to a Black man. They spent a weekend at a Boulé convention. Boulé is a fraternity of very successful Black men. My friend was one of maybe three or four Whites in a group of maybe three hundred Blacks. She said every White person should have that experience— to know what it feels like to be the only one. Many Black people encounter that situation almost daily, and we have to simply deal, act like we don't notice, and proceed with our business. I'm hoping that the kids who felt uncomfortable will get something out of having been here, even if it's just a little more sensitivity to what it's like to be a "minority."

My kids have never been deterred by being the only or one of a few Blacks; although Ford is much more of an introvert, it's his personality, I think, and not his race that oftentimes prevents him from seeking the spotlight. When Baldwin was in middle school, her acting class entered a countywide competition. (Ford would rather pull out his eyeballs than act.) She won second place in the monologue category. I had no idea she was interested in acting or even that she'd be participating. (Middle school is when they stop telling you anything, and the schools don't send much home in the way of information, either. It's the beginning of the parental lockout.) When I picked her up I was late, and she and her teacher Mr. Kitts were standing alone. He came up to the car and was bursting with excitement at how good Baldwin had been: "She had the judges crying! Whatever she does, acting has to be a part of her life."

Hmmm. I smiled and thanked him, apologized for being late, and we drove off. Baldwin held her trophy on her lap.

"So, I didn't know you were interested in acting? How come you never said anything about it?" She shrugged. She said she didn't know it either until she took the class. "Is it something you want to pursue?" I asked, praying that the answer would be no, already imagining the waitressing, the one-bedroom apartment in the city shared with three other people, the rejection and heartbreak.

"I don't know. Maybe."

She slumped down in her seat, indicating that this conversation was over.

That summer, at her beloved overnight camp, Baldwin insisted we fly back early from Chicago, where we'd gone because Cliff had a business trip and Ford and I had tagged along. Baldwin asked that we drive the two hours and forty-five minutes to Pennsylvania, where her camp was, to see what she'd learned. She wouldn't tell me why it was so important, just that we had to be there.

We arrived at the converted barn just as Baldwin walked onto the stage, barefoot, dressed in a simple white eyelet dress. "Winter's Song," by Sara Bareilles and Ingrid Michaelson, began to play, and Baldwin performed sign language to the song. She was transcendent. When she was done, she got a loud, standing, whooping (okay, I was whooping) ovation. People said they had goose bumps. A celebrity photographer sitting next to us, wanted to take head shots and promised he could get her an agent. He'd taken Tom Cruise and . . . *Yeah, yeah, yeah,* Cliff and I said.

"She has that thing, star quality."

After the performance, we walked the grounds to pick up her luggage from her cabin. I asked her again if acting was something she wanted to pursue. She was slightly more affirmative. "I don't know, I don't think so." So I let it drop.

As most parents do, I want Baldwin and Ford to be happy and fulfilled in their lives, in their work. I think of myself as someone who is outside of the suburban middle-class conventional thinking that either of them has to go to an Ivy League or Very Competitive College in order to have a happy life. Still, I know that I've tried to hedge the bets, giving them something of a backup plan; forcing Baldwin to be in the Civics and Government Institute at her high school, because rumor had it that this small learning community was where the smart kids were. Many of them did seem destined to argue their way through Harvard Law School, but Baldwin had absolutely no interest in that, and she was miserable the year she was in it. Now, of course, I kick myself for making her do it. Ford has extra work and a tutor four days a week after school.

What would happen if I just let them be, not do some of the things to ensure their place at the Black bourgeois table, a table from which I sometimes feast, but from which I get little sustenance? The people from whom I get sustenance are vast and varied: My best friends are women who never married; one who is married but has no children; one who is a lesbian with children; one from college; one who is married with two kids; writers of varying racial and socioeconomic backgrounds; Black women who are successful and are thinkers; a Jewish woman; an Italian American divorced psychologist; a WASP guy who used to be a banker. I don't limit my social interactions to just the Black intelligentsia. I'm both simpler and more complicated than that.

The other day I was shopping in Target. I needed a new can opener, Dove body wash, and plastic storage containers. I go to Target every chance I get. I love Target. I don't know why. I browse the entire store: pillows, picture frames, little gifts, clothes for Ford, cosmetics, books. On this trip, I discovered, at long last, that my Target has a full-on grocery section. Ah, Nirvana. Cliff called me on my cell right then. I answered.

"Hey, what you doin'?"

"I'm at Target. They have groceries now. I'm *sooo* happy."

Cliff was silent for a moment. Cliff is never silent for a moment.

"Do you realize you just said you're so happy because Target now sells food?"

"Yes, I know. Pathetic, huh?"

Is this what my life has become? I asked myself as I pushed my load of toilet paper and paper towels, the prices of which rivaled those at Costco; cheese and chicken and eggs and green peppers and bananas and Lactaid. I thought: *If this is what does it for me, I'm good with that.*

It's April 2011, three years and a month since my mom died. I'm doing the work—therapy, meditation, medication, acupuncture, sometimes a chiropractor and recently a woman who does amazing bodywork, which I can't even describe other than to say it's unwinding my body and my spirit. I spend time alone and time with friends. Cliff and I are together a lot more now that Baldwin is away at college. He and I spend a lot of time in fall, spring, and summer going to Ford's baseball games. I'm not my previous self, and I'm still trying to let go of her and welcome the new self that's struggling to emerge.

Cliff and I had just finished breakfast at the kitchen table. He was looking for a number on my cell phone and scrolled down and saw seven numbers for various doctors, some of whom are for the kids.

"You have a staff," he said. "Do you have them all on speed dial?"

He launched into a skit about me speaking to all these different doctors. We both laughed until I begged him to stop. Tears rolled down my face; my stomach hurt; I felt that great release from a good laugh.

Cliff can always make me laugh.

I still do yoga, which works to calm my mind and gives me an extreme sense of well-being, although my hip has limited mobility, so I can't do some of the poses. I stopped the running and other intense cardio exercise because of my hip and while my alternative treatments have eliminated most of the pain, I know that one day I will have the hip-replacement surgery.

Several years ago when Baldwin and I went on a third round of college tours which included Wesleyan, we stayed overnight in a motel in Middletown, Connecticut. We each lounged on our separate full-sized beds. We were quiet together, reading, napping. We talked like girlfriends, laughed till our bellies hurt, and I told her I heard her when she farted. We laughed at the same things, read each other's thoughts. and had the exact same take on each of the colleges we visited. The next day we looked at Marist. Afterward, in the car heading to see Bard, I reflected on a question about sorority life asked by one of the girls during our Marist tour.

"So, do you think you'll want to pledge a sorority?" I asked Baldwin.

I was driving but could feel her staring at me.

"Have we just met?" she said.

I laughed out loud.

"You are so my child."

We got turned around trying to find Bard, which was partly buried in the woods. We were late but caught up to the small tour composed of all mothers and their daughters, a few of whom had already been accepted. After a few minutes, as the guide said that coed roommates were acceptable, Baldwin whispered, "Let's get outta here."

Because it was such a small group, I didn't want to leave just yet, but I knew this wasn't Baldwin's place. Soon we peeled off, but not without the student guide looking at us with an incredulous "You're leaving?"

After we got back and spring break was midway over, I felt that I needed to do something with Ford, just the two of us. Thinking of something to do with an eleven-year-old who is a classic boy can be a challenge. His best friend's mom suggested go-kart driving. I drove about a half hour to a huge place called the Funplex. It looked kind of deserted and not particularly clean, but I was determined to have fun. The game area was dark and depressing, and the teens who worked there were disaffected at best. We found the go-kart track and settled into our cars, anxiously waiting for the people already driving the track to finish. We took off. I passed him and was speeding around, hip cramped in the car but thrilled. He was trailing behind and I knew his competitiveness had kicked in and he was trying hard to pass me. I wanted to see his face; I wanted to see the joy in it. I let him pass me, grinning that satisfied smile that comes from winning. My spirit and my face were so joyful; my cheeks ached from smiling.

One of the things I've questioned as a mother raising children in a privileged environment is how much cushion to provide. I know that too much produces disaster; children need the skinned knees, the disappointments, and to be told no. I sometimes tell my kids no, and when they press for a reason—which they always do—I say, because I'm the parent and my job is to raise you to be the best person you can be and getting everything you want is ultimately unhealthy. That answer usually shuts it down.

My mother was my biggest fan, tied with Cliff. She wanted always to give me things. She also desperately wanted for me to get back to my writing, to finish another book. "Hector wanna know when you gone write another one," she'd say. She often called her friends by their last names. Or she'd say, "I ran into Bethea, she said she just can't wait for the next one." Or: "Davis said she gone keep reading your books till you come out with a new one."

Mom never came right out and asked me why I wasn't writing. The most she would say is, "When you gone write another one?"

Now that she's not here urging me on, cheering for me, I have to do it for myself. After dealing with her death and the death of Cliff's dad, my father's dementia, the loss of income, Cliff's cancer, and all the other stuff life can throw at you, I took a hard look around, stopped shopping, and quit a lot of the drinking. I got a job teaching writing at a college. It was part-time and left time for me to get back to my own writing.

I've had to figure out who I am. How many times was I going to have to do this? Didn't I do this in my twenties, my thirties, and forties? Didn't I prove myself to myself—as a writer, daughter, mother, woman? The answer, I now know, is I'm going to have to do this as many times as it takes.

The good news is I'm still standing. I found Diana, the psychologist and nurse practitioner who helped me get back my life. We found a medication that worked for me after coming to grips with the fact that talk therapy alone would not work. I now own my diagnosis of major depressive affective disorder—clinical depression. Five years later, I have settled into good place. Are things perfect? Of course not. But, as Baldwin pointed out so elegantly to me, I'm a "grown-ass woman."

I've incorporated what Clara taught me with my own view, my very own take on life. I no longer expect that happiness is some kind of birthright. I know in my soul that there is danger in pursuing perfection, that life is messy, and growth requires that we get dirty. There will be highs and lows: your kid gets a countywide acting award; your mother dies; your other kid is named player of year; your father-in-law dies; your husband gets prostate cancer; your dog goes blind; your best friend's mother dies. I had to learn to recognize moments of grace in the midst of all that—seeing my kids walk together across the street in front of my car to the bookstore, the same long and taut bodies, same butterscotch skin, simply gorgeous, inside and out.

As much as I want to be like my mother, there are things that I've done, and that I'm proud of, that she couldn't do. I'm not talking about going to college or having an artistic career; circumstances beyond her doing made those things impossible. But in other ways, I am more like Clara than I like to admit. My mother couldn't tell my father that he was a good man, even though he was and she'd sometimes admit it to other people. I, too, often want to tell Cliff that he is a good man, and sometimes I do. When Ford was ten, after one of his baseball games and after we'd had dinner, it was time for him to shower and go to bed, but Baldwin came downstairs to the basement where we all were, whispered something to him, and off they went. I was distracted, thinking about the papers I needed to grade. I'd needed to make up for a lost day's work because I wanted to see my boy play shortstop. He also pitches, but Cliff, his coach at the time, hasn't been using Ford on the mound. "You're not firing the ball hard enough, and these kids are much bigger," Cliff would tell him. "They can hit you too easily." Ford was slightly taller than average and quite thin.

That night, I was lost in my head, trying to figure out which task I should attend to first: grading papers or signing Baldwin up for a summer program at the Fashion Institute of Technology. It gets filled quickly. A lot of kids want to go into fashion. I was on my way upstairs to my office when Cliff motioned to me and told me the kids were outside jumping on the trampoline.

"Come here, look out the window. Let's go watch them."

I joined him at the window that looked out into our backyard, where the trampoline was set up behind a swing set and some hedges.

"They love that thing," Cliff said, as he put his arm around me.

"See, it was a good thing," I said, reminding him that it was my idea to get it, although I didn't have to convince him. I never do when it comes to something for the kids. We watched them, holding hands, bouncing up and down in unison, squealing. Baldwin was almost seventeen, and too often now that she was a teenager, her brother got relegated to the "annoying" corner of her life. At that moment, standing at the window next to Cliff, seeing our kids happy together, was a feeling so delicious, like eating a perfectly sweet, ripe peach. I looked at Cliff's face, and he beamed back at me what I felt but couldn't say.

"I gotta get some work done," I said to him. He nodded and continued to look out of the window, mesmerized by these miracles we'd created.

"We have a happy family."

I heard this simple statement and knew that it came from me. I surprised myself by uttering it. I'd thought it over our years as parents but never said it aloud. Now that it was out, it felt good to acknowledge this accomplishment, even though Cliff didn't respond. I don't think he heard what I'd said; perhaps he was too enraptured with what was going on in the yard. *I did it,* I thought as I walked up the stairs to my office. I wasn't so angry anymore. I had broken the family cycle.

28

I Hope You Know

IN THE days after Mom's death I was in high-productivity mode, planning the funeral: I was at the printer's for two days while they typeset the program, which I filled with pictures of her. I selected a casket with Daddy, spent hours selecting flower arrangements with Joni and the florist. The task was made easier by my mom, who had listened to my suggestion and written down everything she wanted for her funeral. She'd done this a decade earlier, when she was still healthy but had entered that phase of life when her main social outlet was going to funerals. It had seemed like my parents attended a wake or funeral once a week. She'd call me and tell me how Evelyn's hair just wasn't done the way she would have liked, or that Charles wouldn't have wanted Cora to sing—everybody knew Cora couldn't sing. The ultimate was when the service for my godmother, Grandma Ida, was held at a funeral parlor. Grandma was a member of Mt. Zion A.M.E. for many years, but for some reason her family decided to have the service at Cotton Funeral Home. My mother cried her heart out at losing her good friend. She told me again and again that having the service at the funeral parlor instead of her church was just sacrilegious for a churchgoing woman like Ida.

After hearing this for years, I told her to write down exactly what she envisioned for her own service. And she did. My brother Duane took on the chore of writing the obituary and picking up her underwear and her mint-green silk dress with the lace jacket; it was the dress she'd worn to my wedding. Even during that desolate time, I remember laughing to myself as I tried, over the phone, to help him find the falsies Mom always wore to fill out her bra. Years of breast-feeding had left her flat.

Joni was with me the whole time, and one day on our way back home from the printers we decided to stop at the Short Hills Mall to have a drink. In the mall I saw a woman who was probably in her late forties arguing with her elderly blue-haired mother. The mother wanted to go to some store that wasn't near where they stood. She had a walker. They argued and the daughter became more and more impatient with her mother. Eventually the mother said, "Fine, I'll go by myself." She began walking away, on her own, and the daughter watched her, clearly irritated.

Without even thinking about it, I went to the woman and said, "Excuse me, I don't want to interfere, but I just lost my mother, and it is the most painful thing I've ever felt. I just wanted to say to you, don't let little things get in the way of this time you have together."

The woman was silent for a moment and I, in my altered state, didn't consider that she might curse me out. But she listened and then she said thank you and walked away to catch up to her mother who, while tenaciously slamming the walker on the granite floor with each step, hadn't gotten very far. The daughter gently touched her mother's elbow and walked with her, presumably to wherever she had wanted to go.

A year later, I was driving in my town when I noticed an elderly woman dressed in a flower print housedress like the kind my mom used to wear. She was walking arm in arm with a late-middle-aged woman. I figured that they were mother and daughter and something struck me about the patience with which the younger one was walking slowly with the other; the elderly woman looked to be well into her eighties, maybe even her nineties. I thought of my mother, of how she didn't reach a very late age. I'd always assumed she would have. But she died a month after her eighty-fourth birthday, her fist balled up, her lips open in a silent howl. She didn't go softly into the good night. She went out fighting. I thought she'd live until she literally couldn't anymore, and I guess that's what she did. I wanted so much more of her. Like so many daughters of indomitable mothers, I thought that she'd live forever.

As I watched the mother and daughter on the street that day, I felt myself welling up. I thought I'd have to pull my car over to sob. Instead, I was able to admire the way the two women walked arm in arm, and I smiled at the memory of doing that with my mom. I now knew that I would always miss her. And while I also knew that I'd never see her again—a thought so powerfully sad I sometimes have to just sit and weep—I could hold on to my fortune at having had her at all.

※

It's now been a long five years since my mom died. I've struggled with the idea that I'd have to be my own fierce wind. I'd have to figure out how to be as proud of myself as Clara was of me, as a woman, a Black woman, a mother, writer, wife, as someone productive, capable of floating a lot of balls. I still struggle to embrace all of myself, be my own warrior, while also taking my mother's place as the family matriarch.

I look forward and backward at the same time, grateful for the ferocious love my mother gave me, and confident that in loving my kids the same way, I am giving them what they need in order to live full lives. I know now that I'm strong enough to handle whatever life throws my way, and that I am worthy of a great life and don't need to apologize for it. Although she'd read some James Baldwin, I doubt that my mom knew this quote he was credited with—"Your crown has been bought and paid for. All you must do is put it on"—but I'm sure she believed it. She had a vision for me, a belief in me that she didn't have for herself. I've done the same with my daughter, Baldwin, pushing her, knowing that she had the ability not only to go to a great college like Sarah Lawrence, but also to succeed there, even though she wasn't sure that she was able to do it. My son, Ford, now an adolescent, sometimes struggles with certain subjects in school. When that happens, I put my hands on his shoulders, look deep into his eyes, and tell him that I'm running his race right beside him, and that sometimes he'll win, sometimes he won't, but he'll always pick himself up and try again. More than my words, I know that he feels the intensity with which I say it. He can't help but know that I got knocked down for a while, but I got back up. I can finally say I'm better.

It's not that life has stopped throwing curveballs. Cliff and I hit a terrible patch recently where I actually called a lawyer and seriously considered separating from him. I'd found a text message from a woman that was more than a red flag. I intercepted something about to happen physically with a woman he'd met at a bar. He admitted to an emotional connection and that it was an indiscretion. I was furious and hurt and put him out of our bedroom for several months. I went away to my friend Linda's vacation house in the Hudson Valley. I continued my meditation practice, I went back to weekly therapy, and I got still. While I listened and talked with friends, I knew that the most important person to listen to was myself, and through that I came to the decision that I wanted to work on our marriage, which would also mean working on myself.

We are still working it through. Cliff has had individual sessions with McCurtis, and we see a couples' therapist together. I had to own that I'd pulled away from Cliff years earlier, consumed by my grief and midlife malaise. I had nothing for him, and the more he asked of me, the more I resented him, and the more I moved away. I understand that finding that text was a gift. He promised to stop the flirting that led to the texting and what we've agreed to refer to as his "indiscretion." He asked for my forgiveness, and I'm working on giving it to him. Together, we're turning the tide, riding the rough currents sometimes, and sometimes turning against them.

Either way, I've taken control of my ship.

I'm remembering that the night before she died, my mother stopped talking. We didn't know that would be the night, but in retrospect I should have known. Before Sonia left that evening, she'd looked at me and said, "Don't leave her alone." Sonia never said more than "Good-bye, Miss." She must have sensed the end coming. Cliff and I stayed with my mother till late into the night. She was sitting in the chair we'd equipped with blankets and pillows and a plastic cover over the cushion in case her diaper leaked. I was on the floor, at her feet. "Mom," I said, feeling like her silence meant she was angry. "I'm doing the best I can."

She had put her hands up, almost as if to arm-wrestle. Her hands were covered in cotton gloves; she was always cold. I took one hand in each of mine, and we sat that way in silence for a long time.

I felt everything she could no longer say.

It's okay now. I'm not mad. I'm happy. I'm going home.

Every day when I open my eyes, I see her face in the photograph that I keep next to my bed. It's a picture that I took at the seventieth surprise birthday party that I gave for her. She was beaming. As I held the camera, I called her name. She turned around and I snapped the photo.

Every morning now, I say to the face in the picture, or sometimes I just think it:

I hope you're still proud of me.
I hope you know I tried to do the right thing.
I did my best.

Family picture, spring 2013, at high school graduation awards program for Baldwin. (Photo by Mikel Colson)

Goofing-off Christmas picture, 2013.
(Photo by Chester Toye@Toye Photography)

Family photo with our dog Charlie, Christmas 2013.
(Photo by Chester Toye@Toye Photography)

Acknowledgments

There are so many people I would like to thank: my girlfriends, my dog friends, my family, who have provided me with various forms of sustenance and who have walked this journey with me, but if I were to include all my people, both those who have cried with me and for me, and those who, in passing, may have said one thing that kept me together for another hour or a day, and those who looked after my son or walked my dog or invited me over for a cup of coffee or a glass of wine, the list would be enormous. There are just too many of you kind souls to name. However, I know, I hope, that you know who you are and that you are etched in my heart.

There are a few friends who provided me with a crucial writing retreat, to whom I am forever grateful: Eleanore Wells, Linda Villarosa, and Monique Greenwood.

Like the path to writing this, the road to getting it into the public sphere has been fairly circuitous. For buying, editing, shaping, ushering—thank you to Carolyn Reidy, Judith Curr, Malaika Adero, Rosemarie Robotham, Greer Hendricks, and Leslie Meredith.

Thank you to my amazing agent and friend, Faith Hampton Childs.

Thank you to my sublime Baldwin and sweet-tempered Ford. It's an honor to be your mother.

To my funny, supportive husband, Cliff Virgin, my partner and biggest champion; and to Mom, for giving me everything I need.